HEIDEGGER'S
TRANSCENDENTAL AESTHETIC

Presenting an original and thought provoking interpretation of Heidegger's philosophical anthropology, this book offers a comprehensive interpretation of the conception of human sensibility in early and later Heidegger. Beginning by isolating Heidegger's understanding of the Kantian idea of pure intuition, Moyle suggests that the early and later work present radically different answers to the underlying problem that this idea generates.

This book offers an original perspective on the relation between early and later Heidegger and a distinctively different approach to later Heidegger's ontology of language. Moyle acknowledges Heidegger's significant debt to the Romantic tradition and takes seriously his later philosophical claim that thinking is the highest affirmation of life. On the other hand, Moyle challenges the assumption that Heidegger's later work falls back from philosophy into a poetic form of mysticism and argues that the work on language can be used constructively in contemporary philosophy, especially in relation to the recent work of John McDowell.

ASHGATE NEW CRITICAL THINKING IN PHILOSOPHY

The *Ashgate New Critical Thinking in Philosophy* series aims to bring high quality research monograph publishing back into focus for authors, the international library market, and student, academic and research readers. Headed by an international editorial advisory board of acclaimed scholars from across the philosophical spectrum, this monograph series presents cutting-edge research from established as well as exciting new authors in the field; spans the breadth of philosophy and related disciplinary and interdisciplinary perspectives; and takes contemporary philosophical research into new directions and debate.

Heidegger's
Transcendental Aesthetic

An Interpretaton of the *Ereignis*

TRISTAN MOYLE
University of Essex, UK

ASHGATE

Published by
Ashgate Publishing Limited
Gower House
Croft Road
Aldershot
Hampshire GU11 3HR
England

Ashgate Publishing Company
Suite 420
101 Cherry Street
Burlington, VT 05401-4405
USA

Ashgate website: http://www.ashgate.com

British Library Cataloguing in Publication Data
Moyle, Tristan
  Heidegger's transcendental aesthetic : an interpretation of the Ereignis. – (Ashgate new critical thinking in philosophy)
  1. Heidegger, Martin, 1889-1976 2. Ontology
  I. Title
  193

Library of Congress Cataloging-in-Publication Data
Moyle, Tristan, 1976-
  Heidegger's transcendental aesthetic : an interpretation of the Ereignis / Tristan Moyle.
    p. cm. — (Ashgate new critical thinking in philosophy)
  Includes bibliographical references and index.
  ISBN 0-7546-5119-3 (hardcover : alk. paper)
  1. Heidegger, Martin, 1889-1976. 2. Philosophical anthropology. I. Title. II. Series.

  B3279.H49M69 2005
  193—dc22
                                                                              2005004112
ISBN-10: 0 7546 5119 3

Printed and bound in Great Britain by MPG Books Ltd, Bodmin, Cornwall

Contents

Acknowledgments

I would like to thank the Philosophy Department at Essex University and especially my doctoral supervisor Simon Critchley, and Béatrice Han-Pile for providing the friendly and encouraging atmosphere within which the research for this book could flourish.

Most of all, I would like to thank my parents Margaret and Terry, my sister Vicky and my grandparents Thomas and Joan Shaw, and Billy and Miriam Moyle for the unfailing love and unwavering support they have always given to me. I would also like to thank, in the same breath, Maria for her love and patience over the many years it has taken to complete this work. Without them it would never have been written.

List of Abbreviations

KPM   Heidegger, M. *Kant and the Problem of Metaphysics*, trans. Taft (Indiana University Press, Indianapolis; 1997)

BT   Heidegger, M. *Being and Time*, trans. Macquarrie and Robinson (Blackwell, Oxford; 1995)

PI   Heidegger, M. *Phenomenological Interpretation of Kant's Critique of Pure Reason*, trans. Emad and Maly (Indiana University Press; Indianapolis, 1997)

OWL   Heidegger, M. *On the Way to Language*, (Harper and Row, New York; 1971)

ID   Heidegger, M. 'Onto-theological Constitution of Metaphysics', in *Identity and Difference*, trans. Stambaugh (Harper and Row, New York; 1969)

OWA   Heidegger, M. 'Origin of the Work of Art', in *Poetry, Language, Thought*, trans. Hofstadter (Harper and Row, New York; 1975)

CPR   Kant, I. *Critique of Pure Reason*, trans. Kemp Smith (Macmillan, London; 1929)

CJ   Kant, I. *Critique of Judgement*, trans. Pluhar (Hackett, Indianapolis; 1987)

MW   McDowell, J. *Mind and World*, (Harvard University Press; Cambridge, 1998)

Introduction

*All is Rhythm, the entire destiny of man is
a single celestial Rhythm, just as the work
of art is one unique Rhythm*

Hölderlin

The history of metaphysics is characterised by Heidegger as the history of onto-theology. What he means by this is that the subject matter of metaphysics is, in the tradition of Western thought, either universal Being, the object of the science of ontology, or a perfect, supreme being, the object of theology. Metaphysics is onto-theological because in the unfolding of the history of thought either one or the other of these objects has constituted the matter of philosophical thinking. The content of these metaphysical objects are, Heidegger argues, fatally entwined. Ontology investigates the nature of Being as such, on the basis of which we are able to say that and what beings are. In other words, ontology determines Being as the ground for the essence and existence of beings. However, Heidegger points out, although Being is the ground for the coming to-be of beings, nonetheless beings *are* most of all: beings appear to be that which pre-eminently exist. Thus Being is gradually conceived within the philosophical tradition as an indeterminate and abstract object without any real content. Metaphysics sways at this moment from ontology to theology: the grounding of beings by Being, understood as something that *is*, is accounted for in terms of the activity of the all-highest and supreme being.[1] Thus, determined as the power of divine causation, the grounding of Being is itself grounded by that for which 'it gives' ground. This oscillation to-and-fro from the metaphysical concept of God, *Zeus*, to the science of Being, *ousia*, and back again to *prima causa*, *causa sui*, and so on, constitutes the essential dynamism at the heart of onto-theology.[2]

This oscillation reaches its pitch, according to Heidegger, in Hegelian metaphysics, where an ontology of Being is elevated into a theology of the Absolute. Hegel, Heidegger remarks, unveils the ontological truth of indeterminate, immediate Being as the self-knowing Absolute will, willing itself in the self-present *parousia* of the will to will.[3] In the modern epoch of the will to will disclosed by Hegel and brought to fruition by Nietzsche, beings, including the human being, are experienced simply as materials or resources for the unconditional production and regulation of everything that exists. The production, calculation and ordering of things is a process that has no goal or purpose other than itself. Beings are ordered for the sheer sake of this ordering process.[4] The nihilism of the present age of technology thus fulfils a metaphysical tendency that is rooted in the entire tradition of Western thought. Ontology and theology are consummated in an unconstrained will to will that has no other object than itself.

However, though the history of metaphysics appears to be constituted by the difference between beings and Being, in which each circles round the other in an endless *danse macabre*, in reality one side of the difference is dominant. We remain riveted by the sight and pressure of beings; Being is experienced by us either as the ground for beings or as given by a unique and perfect being. Being in-itself, however, is *not* seen. Hegelian metaphysics completes the oblivion into which Being falls by identifying thinking and Being, an identification that ultimately secures the present tyranny of ontic existence. On the other hand, the matter for thinking *after* onto-theology, Heidegger writes, is the *difference* between thinking and Being.[5] In the *Ereignis*, as Heidegger puts it, we think the truth of Being, i.e. Being as it is in itself – as 'it gives' itself.

This essay offers an interpretation of the *Ereignis*, i.e. of the way the truth of Being-in-itself gives. The interpretation takes shape by addressing the following problem. How is it possible to experience Being in-itself without determining Being either as the universal condition for the possibility of beings or as a transcendent, divine being? The kind of thinking experience that resolves this problem must remain within the immanence of finite existence, without recourse to theology and the matter of faith. Yet, such a conception of experience must also preserve the irreducible difference or relation between thinking and Being within this immanent determination of finitude. If it is possible to disclose the ontological ground for this kind of experience then it becomes conceivable how the human being might be released from the breathless crush of beings and how, in turn, beings might be released from our relentless drive to order. After metaphysics, beings are not disclosed as material to be ordered, but as they give themselves from out of a living depth that both elevates and animates them. In the *Ereignis* our understanding of Being is no longer a screen for the calculation of things, but a gift that we receive. In the intuition of this gift, which bestows life and living things upon us, thinking receives the intimate bond of a relation to its own outside. This outside is the exterior difference of Being itself. The problem is how to determine concretely the relation of thought to the exteriority of Being without lapsing back into a theology of the transcendent or a nihilistic form of ontology. To restate the problem in more Heideggerian terms: the aim of the following essay is to make phenomenological concrete the nature of the 'it' of the 'it gives' without determining the 'it' as a divine creator or as a given ontological horizon grounded in the manifestation of the beings that the horizon itself discloses. Such a conception of the 'it' intends to capture and clarify the unique way in which Being gives.

The following interpretation thus attempts to elucidate the gift-exchange between Being and the thinking of the human being that lies at the heart of later Heidegger's ontology. This work, therefore, makes central Heidegger's repeated claims that there is a relation of need and belonging between Being and man, of giving and returning of gift, of mutual favouring, of calling and thanking and of 'speaking' and what is spoken.[6] Thus, rather than assuming a straightforward transition in Heidegger from an earlier analytic of the human being to a later conception of the unilateral giving of Being, i.e. a move from a focus on 'what man is' to a form of quasi-structuralist antihumanism, the following interpretation argues that there is an analytic of the human being in the later work as well as the earlier. To put the point another way: this essay represents an interpretation of later

Heidegger's philosophical anthropology. However, the question of what man is, according to Heidegger, can only be addressed from the perspective of the *relation* between the human being and Being. To interpret the *Ereignis* is to determine this relation. Indeed, the early *and* later work of Heidegger should be understood as interrogating both the relation between Being and man and the nature of the 'it gives' with which this relation is intimately connected. Against orthodox Heidegger interpretation, just as an analytic of man is implicitly present in the later work, so too a notion of the 'it gives' is rooted in the early work. Heidegger does not turn from Dasein to Being, but rather from an early analytic of the relation between Being and man to a later, radically different analytic in which the relation itself comes to the fore. Heidegger, in this sense, offers two philosophical anthropologies, two determinations of the human being's finite experience. The task of the following interpretation is to make the later philosophical anthropology of man phenomenologically concrete and to contrast it with the earlier analytic of Dasein, i.e. to compare and contrast the early and later determinations of the relation between the human being and the 'it gives'. Broadly speaking, the division between these two determinations of man in Heidegger, it is argued, are centred on a different use that Heidegger makes of Kantian philosophy. Whereas *Kant and the Problem of Metaphysics*, interpreting the *Critique of Pure* and *Practical Reason*, discloses the essential nature of human subjectivity for early Heidegger, later Heidegger's philosophical anthropology, on the other hand, is grounded in an analogous existential-ontological analytic of the *Critique of Judgement*.

The core of the following essay takes its shape from a question initially raised by early Heidegger, in his reading of Kant's Transcendental Aesthetic, regarding the nature and possibility of *a priori* sensibility. The argument is that this question appears to generate an antinomy: Being must both be given and not given by the ontological subject. Early Heidegger attempts to resolve the antinomy by making use of the Kantian notion of pure, temporal self-affection, whereby Dasein is understood to give Being to itself. This attempt, however, fails. The content of *a priori* ontological sensibility regresses to ontic, factical existence. Later Heidegger, on the other hand, the argument goes, successfully resolves the antinomy by introducing an ontological distinction within an immanent conception of subjectivity between Being in itself and the human being. In his early and later work, therefore, Heidegger is addressing the same problem, though in each period he comes up with a radically different answer.

Therefore, the following is an ontological analytic of *a priori*, human sensibility as conceived, through a glass darkly, by later Heidegger. The goal of the analytic is to offer a sketch for an idea of experience that avoids onto-theology. It elucidates the giving of the 'it gives' from the immanent perspective of the human being's finite reception of the difference of Being. As Heidegger remarks, 'analytic' in this context does not mean the dissection of a complex entity into atomic parts but rather an unknotting or disentangling that frees the elements of human sensibility into the affinity of an articulated form.[7] Each part of the work takes up and explores a particular element of our finite sensibility, sinking its roots into and taking nourishment from the preceding stage. However, the ground of the *Ereignis* in later Heidegger does not float on the surface of the corpus, waiting to be seized in the rush to overcome metaphysics. Heidegger's early determination of man is deeply mired within the onto-theological tradition from which it attempts to extract itself. Consequently, in order for each element of later Heidegger's conception of human sensibility to be retrieved from the depths, the flotsam must also be cleared. Retrieval is always partly critique. There is then in the following interpretation of Heidegger an element of violence. However, the aim is neither critical rejection nor uncritical acquiescence but rather to fulfil the animating spirit of the Heideggerian corpus. In a Heideggerian register – to extract Heidegger's unthought, i.e. to complete Heidegger's turn from the metaphysical tradition. As Heidegger himself puts it, such an extraction must entrust itself to the concealed inner passion of a work in order to be able, through this, to place itself within the unsaid and force it into speech.[8] To paraphrase a comment by Kant regarding the relation of his work to Leibniz, the following may well be the proper *apologia* for Heidegger, even in opposition to those who elevate him with dishonourable words of praise and who cannot see, beyond the etymology of what Heidegger says, what he had wanted to say.[9] The guiding idea driving this extraction is articulated concisely in the opening quotation taken from Hölderlin: all is rhythm. Focusing on the idea of rhythm, the interpretation takes shape as a translation of the *Ereignis*. The act of translation is here intended not simply as the translation of a focal concept from one language to another but also as cultural rapacity, the plundering of a holy relic. The ultimate aim of the following interpretation is to translate the *Ereignis* into the alien fields of the English tradition.

As such, if this essay succeeds in making intelligible a form of immanent gift-exchange that avoids both theology and ontological nihilism and yet bears a family resemblance to the essential tendencies of Heideggerian philosophy, then it has fulfilled its goal. On the other hand, if either the conception of immanent gift-exchange is not intelligible or if the work bears no resemblance to Heideggerian ontology, then it has not fulfilled its task. Genuine translation can never be annihilation. The methodological principles driving this interpretation and translation, however, cannot prejudge and predetermine in an external fashion the substantive content of the work. On the contrary, in the unfolding of the content itself the nature of the form and method that gathers and orders this content should become manifest. It remains merely to assert at this stage that if, as Heidegger claims, a thinker's unsaid is the determining ground and origin of the sayable, then all genuine commentary on Heideggerian ontology, if it is faithful to the letter, must also attempt to repeat and renew its underlying, inner spirit.

PART I
ONTOLOGICAL RECEPTION AND THE SPATIALITY OF BEING

Chapter 1

The Question of Man

Fundamental ontology, Heidegger writes in *Being and Time*, is the interrogation of the nature of Being as such. Being as such is the *transcendens* pure and simple.[1] Following Aristotle's determination of the unity of this transcendental 'universal' as a unity of analogy, Heidegger insists that, although Being is said in many ways there is nonetheless an underlying meaning of Being to which its manifold ontological determinations belong. This underlying, unified meaning is the 'as such' of Being; the task of fundamental ontology is to determine and clarify what Being as such means. However, fundamental ontology is realised, as Heidegger famously points out in the introduction to *Being and Time*, in an existential analytic of that entity which, in its being, is already in relation to Being. This *a priori* relation is phenomenologically elucidated in *Being and Time* on the basis of an analytic of Dasein as Being-in-the-World. After *Being and Time* the metaphysical or ontological structure that underpins and sustains this *a priori* relation is developed and clarified by Heidegger in a series of works written between 1927-30, which concentrate on an analytic of what Heidegger calls finite transcendence. The connection Heidegger draws in *Being and Time* between fundamental ontology and the analytic of human finitude already marks a significant shift in his work away from Aristotle and medieval ontology. However, in the work produced immediately after *Being and Time* on finite transcendence, the philosopher with whom Heidegger is increasingly preoccupied becomes explicit: Kant.

Heidegger's interpretation of Kant's *Critique of Pure Reason*, published as *Kant and the Problem of Metaphysics* (1929), consolidates a series of lectures Heidegger gave on Kant in the winter semester 1927-8, eventually published as *Phenomenological Interpretation of Kant's 'Critique of Pure Reason'*.[2] The proximity of these lectures to the publication of *Being and Time* (1927) is not coincidental. Indeed, Heidegger remarks that the book on Kant is a historical introduction to the earlier work.[3] The reason why *Kant and the Problem of Metaphysics* serves as a guide and introduction to *Being and Time* is because in Heidegger's reading of Kant the true character and nature of a metaphysics of human transcendence, i.e. an analytic of Dasein, comes explicitly to the fore. Indeed, the overall purpose of such an analytic of Dasein, as described in *Being and Time*, retains a strong resemblance to the ambitions of Kant's own work. Just as for Heidegger the object of metaphysics has fallen into the torpor of unquestioned self-evidence, so too for Kant the terrain of metaphysical inquiry is no longer a battlefield but a site of weary indifference.[4] Like Kant, Heidegger proposes the restoration and renewal of metaphysics through a critique of the possibility of metaphysical knowledge. Such a critique, according to Heidegger, determines and clarifies the sources, scope and limits of the understanding of Being of that being, which, in its being, is in relation to Being. The aim of Heidegger's interpretation of Kant is to demonstrate that Kant's attempted renewal of metaphysics ultimately tends in the same direction.

In contrast to the predominant Marburg School reading of Kant, Heidegger's *Kant and the Problem of Metaphysics* emphasises Kant's scholastic inheritance. Heidegger interprets the *Critique of Pure Reason* not as a theory of scientific knowledge or epistemology, but rather as an attempt to determine anew the philosophical foundations of traditional ontology. Scholasticism, according to Heidegger, arose from the Christian division of the totality of beings into God, nature and humankind, with each sphere assigned its correlative scientific discipline, respectively theology, cosmology and psychology. These separate disciplines constitute the branch of study named special metaphysics. The subject matter of general metaphysics, on the other hand, is not a particular region of Being, but rather Being in itself, i.e. general Being. However, the scholastic division of first philosophy into the separate branches of general and special metaphysics is not arbitrary, Heidegger argues, but in fact represents scholasticism's inheritance of an aporia contained within the earlier metaphysics of Aristotle. This aporia presents ontology as, paradoxically, both a science of Being as Being and of a primary, pre-eminent kind of being. The aporia is generated in Aristotelian metaphysics because of a justified concern that if Being is conceived as common or general, then this generality cannot be that of a genus that contains under it specific, differentiable species. This is because the independent, species-specific differentia, as a determinate thing that exists, already contains within itself the content of the genus from which the species must be differentiated. But, as Heidegger puts it, for a genus to be able to be a genus, it may include nothing of the content of the species forming differentiae.[5] Whereas the species plant, animal and human each possess a determinate content separable from the genus living being, the content of the categories of being cannot be separated from the content of Being itself, in the manner of species and genus, because devoid of this content they possess neither unity nor existence *as* specific differentiae.[6] In this case, the unity of Being cannot be an instance of one over many, nor can the categories of Being, the different ways in which being 'is', be classified according to natural kinds or species. Rather, the unity of general Being is determined as the primary, essential mode of Being – substance – to which the manifold categories of Being are fundamentally and diversely related. Aristotle determines substance in the *Categories* as a particular 'this', as that which *is* most of all, whilst in the middle books of the later *Metaphysics* substance is determined not as a particular 'this' but as the universal essence that makes a thing *what* it is. Propelled by this onto-theological oscillation, book twelve of the *Metaphysics* further determines primary being as divine substance. Aristotle's ontology of universal Being at this point sways back into a theology of the unique and supreme being.

Scholasticism formalises this distinction between the *ens commune*, the object of general metaphysics, and the *summum ens*, the object of the branch of special metaphysics called theology. The divine *esse*, on the other hand, is the object of the highest science of sacred doctrine whose principles are only revealed in and for faith. The tradition of Christian thought furthers the movement of ontology to theology, though by the late scholastic period theology has swayed once again back to ontology. Not only is the object of general metaphysics, the *ens commune*, increasingly independent of any possible divine *esse* or *summum ens* that might give or create it, but the concept of being taken from created things is, after Duns Scotus, univocally applied to the way in which God 'is'. Being once again becomes the highest object of metaphysics (reason), whilst God is solely the revealed object of *sacra doctrina* (faith). The fallout from this Scotist turn is that the idea of common being, inherited from late medieval scholasticism, is increasingly conceived as the most universal and indeterminate of all concepts. It is, according to Heidegger, against this sedimented indifference to the meaning of common Being that Kant writes his first critique.

Kant excludes the branches of special metaphysics – theology, rational psychology and cosmology – from the science of metaphysics. *A priori* metaphysical knowledge is grounded entirely within the autonomous and independent discipline of general metaphysics. This is why Heidegger remarks that transcendental philosophy, which is determined as epistemology, is actually the modern form of ontology.[7] According to Heidegger's interpretation, Kant reinvigorates and renews his scholastic inheritance by posing the question of the nature and possibility of a general making manifest of Being as such. Consequently, the *Critique of Pure Reason* is to be conceived as a treatise that elucidates and delimits the origin and bounds of the manner of universalisation of the *ens commune*. As Heidegger puts it, the indeterminacy and obviousness with which general metaphysics treated hitherto the 'commonality' of the *ens commune* disappears.[8] Kant's re-posing of the question of Being thus represents a genuine re-awakening of the science of ontology for the first time since the Greeks. Kant lays the ground for metaphysics, like Plato and Aristotle, by asking again about the inner possibility of ontology. From this perspective, Kant's question 'How are *a priori* synthetic judgements possible?', on Heidegger's interpretation, asks how the transcendental content of Being, i.e. ontological knowledge, is brought forth *a priori* by the finite subject, as the condition for the possibility of ontic knowledge. The grounds of these *a priori* judgements concerning the Being of beings cannot lie in experience but are principles supplied by pure reason. Given that the faculty of knowing *a priori* according to principles is named pure reason, the unveiling of the possibility of ontological knowledge is therefore a critical delimitation of the essence and scope of pure reason. Thus, laying the ground for metaphysics, unveiling the inner possibility of ontology, is essentially a critique of pure reason.[9] As such, transcendental philosophy investigates the way in which a determinate understanding of Being is brought forth; this determinate understanding constitutes the ontological horizon of objectivity within which a being can be experienced as an object. Ontology in Kant, Heidegger suggests, is not an abstract science of general Being but a questioning of the human being's understanding of Being. The subject matter of ontology is the systematic body of *a priori* judgements or principles that are presupposed as the metaphysical foundation for both the appearance of beings and the finite subject's comportment toward these beings. As Heidegger writes:

> ...transcendental knowledge does not investigate the being itself, but rather the possibility of the preliminary understanding of Being, i.e. at one and the same time: the constitution of the Being of the being. It concerns the stepping over (transcendence) of pure reason to the being, so that it can first and foremost be adequate to its possible object... . This is why Kant uses the designation "Transcendental Philosophy" for *Metaphysica Generalis (Ontologia)* in order to make the problematic of traditional ontology discernable.[10]

However, according to Heidegger, Kant's laying of the ground for metaphysics is only partially successful. Although the Copernican Turn marks a decisive methodological shift from ancient ontology, nonetheless Kant fails to follow through his own insight. Specifically, Kant fails to offer a subjective deduction correlative to the objective deduction contained in the second edition of the Critique.[11] This allegedly missing side of the deduction, the possibility of which Kant tentatively posits in the preface to the first edition, consists in a metaphysical analytic of the Being of the finite subject for which the understanding of Being is objective. The reason, Heidegger argues, that Kant recoils before this analytic of subjective transcendence is due to a confusion of the method of transcendental phenomenology with empirical psychology.[12] If Kant had access to this method he would not, according to Heidegger, have shrunk back from the deduction of the subjectivity of the subject towards which the entirety of the Critique tends. On the other hand, the task of fundamental ontology and of the interpretation of the *Critique of Pure Reason* is to follow through and complete this 'missing', unthematised ontological analytic of the being of the subject. A critique of ontological knowledge, upon which the possibility of a renewed metaphysics depends, must take shape, therefore, as an analytic of the mode of existence of the human being:

> Fundamental Ontology means that ontological analytic of the finite essence of human beings which is to prepare the foundation of the metaphysics which 'belongs to human nature'. Fundamental Ontology is the metaphysics of human Dasein, which is required for metaphysics to be made possible.... fundamental ontology means.... to make clear for what purpose and in what way, within which boundaries and with which presuppositions it puts the concrete question: what is the human being?[13]

For Heidegger, demonstrating the possibility of *a priori* ontological knowledge requires a determination of the way the finite human being *a priori*, that is, independently of all experience, is in relation to Being. As with Kant, the price of renewing the science of metaphysics is the relegation of its object to the *a priori* conditions of finite experience: 'Being "is" only in the understanding of those entities to whose Being something like an understanding of Being belongs'.[14] The possibility of ontology is grounded in the being that *is* ontological in its very nature. Following Kant, metaphysics is not an abstract science of general Being but a critique of itself as a 'natural disposition of man'.

The laying of the ground for metaphysics is grounded in a metaphysics of Dasein. Thus, Heidegger argues, the science of metaphysics takes over the question of 'what man is' from philosophical anthropology. This ontological analytic of man is not anthropology if the being of man is simply differentiated from the being of plants and animals and is then determined in its specific regional composition. As Heidegger argues, the goal of this methodological differentiation and determination is the working out of a worldview in which, using the results of the regional ontology, man is the first given and most certain in the order of grounding.[15] The result of such a science would be to cover over and neglect the fundamental relation of the human being to Being itself, conceiving instead this relation as between diverse regions of living organisms and human beings. However, despite the caveat, if an analytic of man is a questioning of the way Being is in relation to the human being, then, as long as the meaning of Being itself is understood to fulfil the essence of 'what man is', it remains a *kind of* philosophical anthropology. Indeed, if the question of man and of Being belong together in an ontologically adequate philosophical anthropology then this would be nothing other than a completion, Heidegger concludes, of Kant's ultimate predilection for special metaphysics. Though, as we have seen, Kant's immediate inheritance and concern is with general metaphysics, nonetheless, Heidegger, suggests, the interests of reason aligned to the separate disciplines of cosmology, psychology and theology – What can I know? What should I do? What can I hope for? – are unified and grounded in the underlying question, What is the human being? The fourth discipline correlative to this unifying interest of reason is philosophical anthropology. Philosophical anthropology determines the final purpose of metaphysics.[16] Early Heidegger makes central what he regards as this essentially Kantian thought: to renew and restore metaphysics requires a critique of man, a philosophical anthropology of the subject.

If Heidegger's reading of Kant uncovers the metaphysical structure and purpose underlying the earlier analytic of Dasein in *Being and Time*, it also determines with more precision the question – 'What is the human being?' – that propels and grounds this analytic of finite existence. *Kant and the Problem of Metaphysics* is therefore of much more than merely historical interest in understanding the ontology of early Heidegger. The human being, Heidegger remarks, is finite in that it possesses an *a priori* sensible reason.[17] The sensibility of reason refers to the fact that the human being has a capacity for non-creative intuition; i.e. intuition that is dependent upon what is intuited as something that exists in its own right. Hence, this peculiarly human form of intuition cannot give the object from out of itself. Sensibility is a capacity for receiving that which gives or offers itself; it is a capacity for being-affected by that which is already there. Empirical sensibility yields sensation or matter, which is received from beings through the empirical, corporeal sense-organs. The human being is affected by sensation; it cannot produce the matter of beings in ontic experience, as can infinite intuition. The experience of sensation, writes Heidegger, citing Kant, '...presupposes the actual presence of the object'[18] and '...stands for what is material (real) in them (that through which something existent is given)'.[19] The Real is the matter of beings received through the senses, i.e. empirically intuited matter or sensation. As Heidegger writes: '...Being (not entities) is dependent upon the understanding of Being; that is to say Reality (not the Real) is dependent upon care'.[20] The Real manifests the presence of an independent, already-given existence upon which the experience of a finite creature depends. However, ontic sensibility does not, according to Heidegger, exclusively constitute the sensibility of human existence:

> Human intuition… is not 'sensible' because its affections take place through 'sense-organs' but rather the reverse… . The essence of sensibility exists in the finitude of intuition. The organs that serve affection are thus sense-organs because they belong to finite intuition, i.e. sensibility. With this Kant for the first time attains a concept of sensibility which is ontological rather than sensualistic. Accordingly, if empirically affective intuition of beings does not need to coincide with 'sensibility' then the possibility of a nonempirical sensibility remains essentially open.[21]

> For Kant, sensibility means finite intuition. Pure Sensibility must be the sort of intuition that takes what is intuitable in stride in advance – prior to all empirical receiving.[22]

Heidegger's point is clear: the corporeal, ontic sensibility of the human being is grounded in a capacity for pure, ontological sensibility. This *a priori* sensibility of reason constitutes, according to Heidegger, the innermost finitude of man. Kant's Transcendental Aesthetic, Heidegger suggests, offers the first provisional analytic of nonempirical sensibility: space and time are pure forms of *a priori* intuition, devoid of empirical sensation. The spatial and temporal relations ordering the material manifold of beings are generated by the transcendental subject and lie ready for the sensations *a priori* in the mind. These Kantian pure forms, Heidegger argues, constitute the preliminary groundwork for an ontological idea of sensibility. This question of the nature and possibility of this pure, ontological sensibility drives early Heidegger's analytic of the subject.

However, Kant, according to Heidegger, fails to ground fully the idea of ontological sensibility because he neglects to thematise or make explicit the pure content or *a priori* manifold that this idea presupposes. Indeed Kant, on occasion, appears to suggest that *a priori* intuition consists only in the pure form of sensibility whilst the content of all intuition remains a posteriori.[23] This, nonetheless, as Heidegger and more recently Allison point out,[24] conflicts with the conception of pure space as an infinite, given magnitude. It also conflicts with Kant's statements, at other times, in which the pure forms of sensibility are said to 'give' a manifold of their own.[25] Elsewhere, Kant mentions the manifold of *a priori* sensibility[26] and suggests that time contains an *a priori* manifold in pure intuition.[27] The notion of an *a priori* intuitable content is vital, for Heidegger, because without it the idea of the originary sensibility of reason is lost. Not only must the finite subject 'give' form but it must be able to intuit or let be given to itself in advance the content of this *a priori* ontological framework. This is why Heidegger remarks that the content of Being is always 'caught sight of' or discerned, i.e. intuited, in advance prior to the experience of Being. Being is the primordial intuition.

Hence the human being is *a priori* sensible in that it gives, following Kant, the forms of intuition from out of itself, ordering in advance the empirical manifold of beings. On the other hand, the human being is ontologically sensible in that it is constituted by a capacity for receiving the intuited content of Being, independently of all ontic, empirical experience. Without this element the receptivity of human sensibility is reduced to the a posteriori intuition of the content of ontic sensation. The idea of ontological sensibility, if this were to happen, would then fall back into the opposition of an *a priori* giving and an a posteriori receiving. Given that a capacity for receptivity constitutes the ontological essence of human finitude, this collapse is fatal for any system that, like Heidegger's, purports to offer a critique of the *a priori* sensibility of reason.

However, if the distinction between a form of intuiting and an intuited content remains within the *a priori* ontological, then equally fatally, an antinomy appears to be generated within the idea of ontological sensibility. The a priority of sensibility entails that the subject gives the form of Being to the manifold of beings, independently of and prior to experience, for that experience to be possible. As Kant puts it, 'we can know *a priori* of things only what we ourselves put into them'.[28] If the forms of ontological intuition are not 'in' the transcendental subject prior to experience, the origin and nature of their a priority becomes inconceivable. Hence, pure sensibility is an *a priori* giving of form; it necessarily arises from out of the Self. However, the idea of ontological sensibility is constituted internally both by the idea of a form of intuition or giving and by the idea of the receiving of an intuited content. As Heidegger rightly points out, the receptivity of the human being means that it has a capacity for intuiting an external existence, which is already there and upon which the finite subject depends. Empirical sensibility is receptive in that the Real of entities manifests itself independently of the Reality of the understanding of Being disclosed by the human being. The human being cannot produce the matter of things from out of itself. Ontological sensibility is, however, devoid of sensation; the content which it receives as an external existence already there is *a priori* ontological. Sense experience cannot yield this ontological intuited content. As *a priori* sensibility, the finite self gives from out of itself the form of ontological content or pure manifold: man gives Being. Yet ontological reception entails that the finite self intuits Being as already there, an exterior existence upon which it depends. In the move from ontic to ontological sensibility the ontological correlate of the Real in ontic experience seems to have been lost. However, without this ontological Real, the possibility of *receiving* Being as an external existence becomes inconceivable. The antinomy is thus: the idea of ontological sensibility entails the *a priori* giving of the form of Being to beings; therefore Being must necessarily arise from the finite self. On the other hand, the idea of ontological sensibility entails the intuition of an already-given content upon which the ontologically receptive subject depends; therefore Being must necessarily not arise from the finite self. If the intuited content does not arise from the form-giving subject it would appear to be no longer *a priori*. If it does arise from the subject it would appear to be no longer genuinely intuitable. The idea of an *a priori* ontological sensibility appears to demand, impossibly, that the human being both gives and receives Being.

Thus, the question 'What is the human being?' that Heidegger poses at the beginning of *Kant and the Problem of Metaphysics* acquires greater precision in the unfolding of his interpretation of Kantian finitude. To ask 'what man is', i.e. to pursue an analytic of Dasein, is to question the nature of the finite relation between Being and the human being. This relation is, paradoxically, both *a priori* and receptive. As such, given the antinomy of *a priori* ontological sensibility, the question 'what is man?' might be determined more precisely in the following way. What is the nature of the relation between the human being and Being, if this ontological relation necessarily involves both a giving and receiving of Being within the *a priori* immanence of finite, sensible experience?

Chapter 2

Time and the Will

Heidegger does not explicitly formulate the question that drives his early analytic of the human being because he thinks the answer appears already at hand in Kant's *Critique of Pure Reason*: pure self-affection. This Kantian idea, according to Heidegger, determines the innermost essence of transcendence;[1] it lies at the core of Heidegger's deduction of the subjectivity of the subject before which Kant recoiled. Kant, as Heidegger puts it, shrank back before the unknown root of the faculties of the understanding and intuition. The subjective deduction reveals this root to be the temporal power of *a priori* transcendental imagination, determined by Heidegger as the ground of both the understanding's 'I think' and the mode of intuiting belonging to the faculty of sensibility. A consequence, Heidegger writes, of the introduction of temporality into the innermost core of subjectivity is that it manifests the way in which the transcendental imagination of the human being is 'ecstatic' in its ontological constitution.[2] It is through the Kantian idea of pure temporal self-affection that the ecstatic character of the transcendental imagination, the root of the understanding and sensibility, takes concrete shape.

Imagination, as the common root of the temporality of intuition and transcendental apperception, is – so the argument in *Kant and the Problem of Metaphysics* goes – the power of *a priori* synthesis, the fruit of which are the transcendental schemata. These schemata comprise the ontological predicates that state something about the Being of beings: they constitute the human being's understanding of Being.[3] The transcendental schemata ground, therefore, the possibility of *a priori* ontological knowledge. Hence, the ontological synthesising of the imagination, the primordial root of subjectivity, unifies concept and intuition into the system of transcendental schemata, which allows Being to be intuited. Being is a horizon that is discernible in advance prior to ontic experience because the temporalised categories, the schemata, form a 'pure look', a 'perceivable offer'.[4] Without this schematic image the pure categories could not be perceived or intuited in advance of experience as the objective horizon within which beings appear. Proximally and for the most part, the human being does not thematically reflect upon the already-given horizon of Being. Man comports himself toward beings. Phenomenological ontology, on the other hand, makes explicit the understanding of Being on the basis of which experience of beings is possible by laying out the ontological schemata that form the totality of ontological knowledge. Ontology brings the implicitly perceived horizon of Being to light; this horizon is the true, though for the most part hidden, object of phenomenology:

> ...that which shows itself in the appearance as prior to the "phenomenon" as ordinarily understood and as accompanying it in every case, can, even though it shows itself unthematically, be brought thematically to show itself; and what thus shows itself in itself (the 'forms of intuition') will be the "phenomena" of phenomenology.[5]

The schema of the category of substance is particularly important. The *a priori* concept of substance is schematised in the pure image of time as a 'persistence of the real in time'.[6] This pure image of persistence allows the objectivity of the horizon of Being to become distinct and discernable.[7] Heidegger's temporal schematism of the concept of substance follows Kant's first analogy of experience in the A edition of the *Critique of Pure Reason*. A Kantian analogy of experience is a regulative rule of the synthetic unity in time-relations of all empirical perceptions. The premise of the first analogy is that there is change in perceptual experience; objects either change their state or come to be and cease to be. However, change can be experienced only if appearances are determined in time-relations of past, present and future and these relations of time must belong to a single underlying time if there is to be unity in our perceptual experience of change. Therefore, the experience of the change of appearances presupposes the perception of something permanent which does not change, of which the changing temporal relations of past, present and future are alterations or modifications. Hence Kant's conclusion 'in all change of appearances substance is permanent':

> All appearances are in time; and in it alone, as substratum (as permanent form of inner intuition) can either coexistence or succession be represented. Thus the time in which all change of appearances has to be thought remains and does not change. For it is that in which, and as determinations of which, succession or coexistence can alone be represented. Now time by itself cannot be perceived. Consequently, there must be found in the objects of perception, that is, in the appearances, the substratum which represents time in general and all change or coexistence must... be perceived in this substratum and through relation of the appearances to it.[8]

> ... the permanent is the substratum of the empirical representation of time itself...permanence, as the abiding correlate of all existence of appearances... expresses time in general. For change does not affect time itself, but only appearances in time (co-existence is not a mode of time itself; for none of the parts of time co-exist; they are all in succession to one another). If we ascribe succession to time itself, we must think yet another time, in which the sequence would be possible... in all appearances the permanent is the object itself, that is substance as phenomenon.[9]

In the first edition of the *Critique of Pure Reason*, consequently, the permanent substratum of empirical time-determined representations is given in the abiding permanence of what Kant calls time in general. The underlying co-existence of matter merely represents or expresses time in general. This 'other' time is the permanent form of inner intuition that is expressed or represented as the abiding correlate of the existence of all temporal, changing appearances, both in inner and outer experience.

In his discussion of the Kantian schematism of substance, Heidegger connects the principle of permanence in the first analogy of experience with Kant's notion of the transcendental object. For Kant, the necessary and original consciousness of the identity of the self requires a consciousness of the unity and identity of its act, whereby its object-related representational activity is synthetically united in one objective knowledge. The pure concept of the transcendental object unifies the sensible manifold, conferring upon it objective reality, and thus allows for the identification of the acts of the conscious self in relation to the manifold of knowledge that it represents. The object-related acts of the mind, hence, belong to the same object in general; the transcendental object, a 'Something = X', is, in this sense the objective correlate of the persisting and unchanging synthetic unity of apperception. The transcendental object is therefore identified by Heidegger with the substantial presence of time in general; the abiding of the co-existent horizon of time in itself is correlative to the unity of the transcendental 'I'.

On Heidegger's reading of Kant, therefore, the fixed and abiding I of pure apperception brings before itself in advance fixedness and persisting in general – it lets the horizon of objectivity 'stand against'.[10] The pure concept of substance – the transcendental object – is schematised, accordingly, as an abiding and persisting horizon of objectivity correlative to the temporal persisting of the self. This 'standing against' the subject of the temporally schematised transcendental object cannot itself be ontically intuited – as Kant remarks in the first analogy, time in itself cannot be perceived. In this sense it is nothing. Yet this non-empirical non-being is still 'Something = X'. For the most part, though it is regularly in view, the pure horizon is not thematically discerned: it is a mere 'X'. Phenomenology, however, articulates the transcendental determinations of time that constitute the transcendental object:

> The X is a "Something" of which in general we can know nothing at all. But it is not therefore not knowable because as a being this X lies hidden "behind" a layer of appearances. Rather, it is not knowable because it simply cannot become a possible object of knowledge, i.e. the possession of a knowledge of beings. It can never become such because it is a Nothing. Nothing means: not a being, but nevertheless "Something". It "serves only as correlatum", i.e. according to its essence it is pure horizon. Kant calls this X the "transcendental object", i.e. the Being-in-opposition which is discernable in and through transcendence as its horizon... this horizon must be unthematic but must nevertheless be regularly in view. ...[11]

The transcendental object is the objective and persisting correlate of the 'I'; it forms the futural horizon of recognition, reflected out of the horizon of having been, within which the self encounters beings. It is, as such, what early Heidegger names 'Being'. This ecstatic temporal relation enabled by the transcendental imagination, of projecting the future back upon the past, releasing from this exchange the present, constitutes the fundamental relation between the human being and Being. The transcendence of Dasein means essentially that Dasein transcends or leaps over beings toward Being, disclosing thereby in advance, from out of the exchange of future and past, the ontological horizon within which a being can appear. This transcendence constitutes the metaphysical nature of the human being. Hence the possibility of ontology is ultimately rooted in the originary, temporal transcendence of man – the subjective side of the deduction before which Kant recoiled.

A principal failure of Kant's transcendental aesthetic, according to Heidegger, is that it fails to instate the idea of movement next to the forms of intuition in the faculty of pure sensibility.[12] Although Kant notes that the concept of motion unifies the forms of time and space he argues, notwithstanding this, that the idea of movement presupposes something moving, i.e. something empirical, and therefore it cannot belong to the faculty of pure sensibility. Heidegger in both the early and later work criticises Kant's apparently unnecessary exclusion of the concept of motion from the idea of *a priori* ontological sensibility. In the early work, movement is articulated in the following way:

> Play distinguishes itself by the absence of constraint; it is free. And yet play is not without direction and rhythm. Space and time as pure viewing are play, i.e. they are not tied to the extant but are a free enacting of the pure manifold of what is intuited in them.[13]

The forms of time and space are essentially play, i.e. the free enacting of ontological content. This playing movement gives pure intuition. Play is the motion or act of the finite subject.[14] Hence, Dasein gives the forms of temporality: ontological movement is rooted in the spontaneous activity of the transcendental imagination. On the other hand, Heidegger's determination of the nature and origin of ontological movement after the 'turn' is radically different: objective rhythm, not subjective play comes to the fore. Early Heidegger, however, elucidates further the idea of the act or motion of the subject by tying it to the Kantian conception of pure self-affection. Kant describes pure self-affection in the following way:

> … we intuit ourselves only as we are inwardly *affected*, and this would seem to be contradictory, since we would then have to be in a passive relation to ourselves. …

> The understanding… in respect of the manifold, which may be given to it in accordance with the form of sensible intuition, is able to determine sensibility inwardly. Thus the understanding, under the title *transcendental synthesis of imagination*, performs this act upon the *passive* subject, whose faculty it is.

> The understanding does not, therefore, find in inner sense such a combination of the manifold, but *produces* it, in that it *affects* that sense.[15]

Without the act or figurative synthesis performed by the understanding there is no combination of the manifold in intuition. It is for this reason that Kant argues in the transcendental aesthetic that inner sense is pure self-affection. Inner sense intuits the synthetic act of the understanding which, combining the given manifold, produces determinate intuition. Hence the mind is affected through its own activity.[16] This motion or action of the subject produces, according to Kant, the concept of succession; it is the act 'through which we determine the inner sense according to its form'.[17] As the Marburg School reading of Kant points out, the power of synthesis, in this case, even in relation to the manifold of sensible intuition, is grounded in the faculty of the understanding: it determines sense *a priori* in accordance with the unity of apperception.[18] Heidegger is close to the Marburg interpretation at this point: the transcending Self is affected by the horizon of objectivity or temporally schematised transcendental object that 'it gives' from out of itself. Dasein produces the objective horizon of substantiality that it intuits in order for ordinary empirical experience to be possible: as transcendence, the human being is in a passive relation to its own activity. This spontaneous activity is the movement that constitutes the temporal, ecstatic essence of man: as pure self-affection, 'it gives' to itself.

Heidegger proceeds to elaborate further the imaginative transcendence of the human being through an analysis of the idea of freedom.[19] The imagination is free because it is a productive power that brings forth from out of the subject the schematised horizon of Being. The essence or substance of the subject resides in this free activity. The feeling of existence is not merely an 'I am' but an 'I can' or 'I am able'.[20] The activity of the 'I' gives the unity of the futural horizon of objectivity in general, allowing the 'I' to identify its object-related acts as the same, and thus to identity itself in this activity as an abiding and persisting self. The subject possesses and grasps itself in its own free activity.[21] Being, the transcendental object correlative to the activity of the I, is the 'primal concept'; it is the 'transcendental affinity'[22] of *a priori* determinations that constitute the idea of world. Hence the human being's transcendence is characterised with the expression Being-in-the-World:[23]

> … the world described primarily by the for-the-sake-of is the primordial totality of that which Dasein, as free, gives to itself to understand. Freedom gives itself to understand; freedom is the primal understanding, i.e. the primal projection of that which freedom itself makes possible. … Being-in-the-world is accordingly, nothing other than freedom. …[24]

To be free is for the human being to give to itself the totality of world. Freedom is primal understanding. However, the freedom of Dasein is not an arbitrary and contingent phenomenon, it is bound up intimately with the experience of necessity. Dasein is free insofar as it places itself under a self-given law; it is a 'free creature which determines itself'.[25] The submission of Dasein to the law that 'it gives' to itself constitutes the pure sensibility, i.e. *a priori* reception, of the free subject. This law or necessity that Dasein receives is the resistance of Being, i.e. of the horizon of objectivity, which Dasein freely gives from out of itself.[26] Hence, the transcendental object, as an *a priori* rule-governed horizon of objectness in general, though it is the correlate of the free activity of the 'I', nonetheless, according to Heidegger, resists and binds this activity. Hence, the transcendence of Dasein involves, essentially, both a free, spontaneous giving of Being and a receiving of, a being affected by, the resistance of this self-given horizon of objectivity.

The freedom of Dasein as Being-in-the-world (transcendence) is primarily constituted by the self-giving of an understanding of Being because it is temporally ecstatic. This notion of the ecstatic temporality of the self lies at the heart of early Heidegger's analytic of subjectivity. As ecstatic, i.e. structured by the ecstatic horizons of past, present and future, time is the primordial 'outside of itself in and for itself'.[27] The ecstatic nature of time is constituted by an 'outside of itself' in that the individual horizons are external to each other within the immanent relationality of the whole 'in and for itself'. The whole is not a singular totality in relation to its own outside qua totality. Unlike Augustinian Trinitarian temporality, time, and the idea of experience grounded in this Heideggerian conception of time, is closed in upon itself. Hence, free Dasein gives to itself the understanding of Being that comprises the primordial totality of its world:

> Temporality temporalises itself primarily out of the future. This means that the ecstatic whole of temporality and hence the unity of horizon, is determined primarily out of the future. That is the metaphysical way of saying that the world, which is grounded in nothing else than the ecstatic totality of the time horizon, temporalises itself primarily out of the for-the-sake-of. This for-the-sake-of is, in each case, the for-the-sake-of willing, of freedom, i.e. of the transcending being-towards-oneself.[28]

The power of Dasein's imagination forms the futural horizon of Being, projects this back upon the past horizon of 'having-been' and releases from this exchange the present. The transcendence of man is described by Heidegger as a nihilating because, to offer a concrete phenomenological description of this ecstatic relation, it involves the giving of the Nothing of World, disclosed in the mood of anxiety, to the null basis of thrown existence. From out of the exchange of future and past possibility, the actuality of ontic, present existence is given. This ontological nihilation or transcendence grounds, according to Heidegger, the freedom of the human being.[29] Man is free in that he resolutely wills, from out of the spontaneous activity of subjective life, the ontological horizon within which beings appear. Free Dasein gives to itself the ontological *a priori* grounds of its own ontic existence.

However, this self-giving activity that underlies everyday existence is for the most part concealed. It would appear that Being is not given by the human being, but rather that, in order for perceptual, empirical experience to be possible, man must intuit or receive the understanding of Being that he has inherited. On the basis of this intuition of an already-articulated significance, we do not *infer* the existence of objects on the basis of a sensory manifold to which we have immediate access: we *see* things. We see the wagon, hear the crackling fire. As Heidegger points out, it takes a complicated and derivative frame of mind to perceive unadulterated sensory content. Rather, perceptual data is intuited as already organised into articulated units of meaning or facts. These units or facts comprise the horizon of intelligibility in which we live and into which we are thrown. However, Heidegger remarks, this everyday understanding elides the way in which an inherited tradition has significance in ordinary experience only insofar as it is given from out of a horizon of the future, which incessantly anticipates and regulates the criteria on the basis of which the beings we experience can be articulated as this or that. The meaningfulness of the past horizon requires the active formation and animation of this articulated significance in its exchange with the future. In its full ontological breadth, the true significance of an inherited world, according to Heidegger, is given from out of the exchange of future with past, from out of which is disclosed what Heidegger calls Dasein's current factical Situation. An analytic of authentic experience uncovers the metaphysical structure that pervades the significance of our everyday, inauthentic world. Heidegger's account of authenticity not only makes explicit the active spontaneity underlying the human being's everyday relation to the world but also demonstrates how the idea of pure self-affection is central to early Heidegger's attempted resolution of the problem of ontological sensibility:

> Only as the Present in the sense of making present can resoluteness be what it is: namely letting itself be encountered undisguisedly by that which it seizes upon in taking action. Coming back to itself futurally, resoluteness brings itself into the Situation by making present. The character of the 'having been' arises from the future and in such a way that the future which 'has been'... releases from itself the Present.[30]

> The primordial truth of existence demands an equiprimordial Being-certain in which one maintains oneself in what resoluteness discloses. It *gives* itself the current factical Situation, and brings itself into that Situation.[31]

The Situation is the 'there' of the current factical circumstances upon which the authentic Self resolves. It comprises the factical possibilities of existence into which the human being is thrown and which it can either pass over or it can resolutely face. This Situation before which the human being brings itself is manifest in the Present of what Heidegger calls the 'moment of vision'. The authentic present discloses the actuality of the human being's ontic, factical existence; factical life is, in this moment, not just unthinkingly inherited from the articulated significance of a tradition. In authentic resoluteness the 'having-been' of the past is repeated and disclosed anew from out of a futural projection of the Nothing of Existence. Hence the character of having-been arises from the future in such a way that the exchange of each with the other releases the Present. Authentic Dasein receives the present necessity of its actual factical existence; it gives itself this current factical Situation, it affects itself, in the sense that present necessity is disclosed from out of the prior spontaneous activity or giving of past and future.

Heidegger's use of the Kantian idea of pure self-affection is clear. Dasein receives or is affected by the present, factical Situation that 'it gives' to itself. The necessity of ontic actuality is therefore the law or resistance that constrains the freedom of Dasein's ontological transcendence:

> But this for-the-sake-of has the intrinsic possibility of such a coming-toward-oneself in the mode of binding only in the ecstatic temporalisation of the primordial making-present. ...[32]

> ...Dasein is, in each case, beyond beings, as we say, but it is beyond in such a way that it, first of all, experiences beings in their resistance, against which Dasein is powerless. This powerless is metaphysical, i.e. to be understood as essential.[33]

The free possibility of Dasein's for-the-sake-of-itself is bound to the actual, present Situation that 'it gives' from out of future and past. Ontological resistance is manifest concretely as a resistance of the ontic. The horizon of objectivity is therefore phenomenologically manifest as a resisting of the human being *by beings*. Against the resistance and refusal of actual beings, Dasein is powerless. Yet this factical constraint is disclosed and thereby received as a constraint only from out of the human being's free, active giving of Being. Man both grounds and is grounded by ontic life. The ontological exchange of future and past possibility is cancelled by the given actuality of the ontic Real, which man's understanding of Being (Reality), at the same time, ceaselessly gives. From out of the spontaneous activity of futural exchange with past, Dasein lets be given to itself the necessity of its ontic, factical present; submitting to the resistance of the beings that are nonetheless released from out of the horizon of its own immanent activity.

This constitutes early Heidegger's response to the problem of how the *a priori* relation between man and Being can involve both a giving and receiving of Being.[34] Man intuits or is affected by the present necessity that it gives to itself. Fatally, therefore, the intuited content that the human being *a priori* receives, in early Heidegger, regresses to the ontic. In authentic experience the human being intuits the content of factical life that 'it gives' to itself: minimally this means – man experiences the fact *that* beings *are*. This represents a partial collapse to the Kantian position; although the nature of the content received reverts to the ontic, this ontic content is nonetheless experienced as already there. In Kant, the content of empirical sensation is intrinsically a posteriori: matter is brought into form by intuition and the categories of the understanding before it can appear in objective human experience. For Heidegger, conversely, the a posteriority of ontic sensation, reveals itself in the horizon of Being, within which it is manifest, *as* prior to this *a priori* horizon. In authentic experience, the matter or Real of beings is paradoxically experienced *from out of* the resolute human being's understanding of Being *as* prior to the a priority of Being. Beings are already *there* in the face of the human being's *a priori* understanding of Being:

> Entities *are*, quite independently of the experience by which they are disclosed, the acquaintance in which they are discovered and the grasping in which their nature is ascertained. But Being 'is' only in the understanding of those entities to whose Being something like an understanding of Being belongs.[35]

> ...Being (not entities) is dependent upon the understanding of Being; that is to say, Reality (not the Real) is dependent upon care.[36]

In Heideggerian ontology, the realm of objects is not divided into appearance (phenomena) and thing in-itself (noumena). Being 'is' the understanding of Being that constitutes the Reality of the human being's world: it is the phenomenon *par excellence*. For Kant, objects are in-themselves, aside from the particular way the human being experiences them; as such the independence of the empirical Real is guaranteed by Kant's transcendental distinction. According to Heidegger, on the other hand, there is no such guarantee: though entities exist in themselves, this being-in-itself of a thing can only be manifest *in* Reality. The weight of ontic independence, given Heidegger's phenomenological critique of the dualism of transcendental idealism, therefore rests entirely on the real or matter of the things themselves. The existential independence of ontic matter is therefore manifest in the *refusal* of ontological Reality. The Real of entities refuse or resist Reality, but this refusal, as something that *is*, must nonetheless appear *within* the horizon of existence disclosed by man. In this sense the Real of entities in Heidegger takes upon itself the role of thing-in-itself. The thing in itself is here not, as in Kant, an unintuitable noumenon but rather *appears* in finite experience *as* the ontic Real.[37] This Real in-itself of things is manifest, consummately, in the sheer Fact that they are.

Heidegger, in *Origin of the Work of Art*, offers a decisive account of the nature of the 'a posteriori priority' of the ontic Real. The sheer Fact that an artwork *is* becomes phenomenologically manifest, according to Heidegger, in the sensuously perceived matter of that work. The createdness of a work, referring not to who made it or when or for what reason but merely to the fact 'that such a work *is* at all rather than is not',[38] is experienced when the work's material is not used up in equipmentality but rather subsists in its own self-contained presence. This thing-like presence is the earthy element of the work. Wood is hard. Metal shines. Sound rings. Colour simply shines – and nothing more. This sensuously perceived matter of the work is the phenomenologically appropriate consummation of the kind of content yielded by early Heidegger's conception of *a priori* self-affection. The human being *a priori* experiences the ontic priority of a sheer, sensory Given presence. This ontic content is not a posteriori ordered and arranged into units of significance as it is in Kant's conception of empirical experience and in Heidegger's conception of inauthentic experience. It is an unintelligible sensory weight that refuses and cancels the field of ontological meaning within which it *a priori* subsists and from out of which it is given. This peculiar ontic Real shows itself as already-there prior to ontological disclosure only *after* and *in the face of* this same *a priori* disclosure, an intuited content manifest as prior to the a priority of Being. The idea of pure ontological sensibility has regressed, fatally, to the intuition of an already-given ontic content: our finite sensibility sensuously perceives the sheer, unintelligible givenness of matter. Matter simply *is*: before this Fact, Dasein is powerless. This content is the mute, sensory presence of the Real in-itself of things. The poetic preservers of the artwork, repeating the structure of finite transcendence, receive and submit to this ontic presence in the actuality of a self-given authentic present.[39] In the authentic present of the Situation, likewise, the sheer Fact that Dasein *is* remains enigmatic.[40] Facticity *refuses* comprehension.

A constitutive element of the regression, in early Heidegger, of the reception of ontological content to the sensuously manifest Fact of ontic existence, is the determination of the *a priori* relation of the human being to Being as one of spontaneous giving. In the idea of the transcendence or pure self-affection of Dasein there is no ontological receptivity: on the contrary, in relation to Being the human being is productive. Heidegger admits that this is the case; pure intuition is 'creative'; the power of imagination is 'ontologically creative'.[41] Man gives the Nothing of existence and releases from this disclosive self-giving the Given fact 'that beings are'. However, Heidegger's stated aim in *Kant and the Problem of Metaphysics* is to demonstrate the co-originality of pure sensibility and pure spontaneity in the being of man.[42] The transcendental faculty that purports to fulfil the role of unifying ground is the transcendental *a priori* imagination, a faculty that is, consequently, determined as both receptive and spontaneous in its innermost essence. Whereas, according to Heidegger, Kant neglected the proper ground of the Transcendental Aesthetic, especially in the second edition of the *Critique of Pure Reason*, the ontological analytic, on the other hand, understands itself as deducing the original and unified 'receptive spontaneity' that constitutes human finitude.[43] Nonetheless, the ontological analytic of Dasein conceives the pure receptivity of the subject as a being-affected by what the subject has *a priori* spontaneously given to itself. Transcendence, as pure self-affection, is the 'pure taking in stride of that which gives itself, i.e. the taking in stride which gives to itself (spontaneously)'.[44] There is reception only on the basis of the originary giving or activity of Dasein; the spontaneity of ontological gift-exchange releases the Given ontic to which the factical human being must submit. As Heidegger points out, the faculty of the understanding is spontaneous because it gives from out of itself whilst the faculty of sensibility is characterised as a capacity for receptivity. Yet, although Heidegger criticises the Marburg School of Neo-Kantianism for attempting to dissolve the Transcendental Aesthetic into the Logic,[45] the concrete outcome of the analytic of Dasein is perhaps not so far from the Marburg interpretation of Kant as Heidegger suggests. The receptive, aesthetic nature of the human being that comprises the idea of ontological sensibility is given from within, and on the basis of, the temporal, immanent activity of the *a priori* imagination. The result is a failure to ground, within an ontological analytic of finite essence, a true and originary unity between spontaneity and receptivity.

Chapter 3

Receptivity and Spatiality

Early Heidegger's determination of the human being's capacity for receptivity results therefore in a phenomenological distortion of finitude; rather than intuiting Being, authentic existence grasps the sheer manifestness of beings. Minimally this means: that beings, including the human being, are. The content disclosing this Fact reverts, especially in *Origin of the Work of Art*, to an ontic, sensuously perceived materiality. The ontological essence of finitude is thus covered over. However, the nature of human receptivity, and the conception of finite experience associated with it, also preoccupied Kant in the period between the first and second edition of the *Critique of Pure Reason*. In the B edition, Kant inserts a Refutation of Idealism and General Note on the System of Principles into the First Critique.[1] The proof of the refutation attempts to show that we have experience, and not merely imagination, of outer things. *Contra* Descartes, we do not infer the existence of outer things but presuppose the immediacy of outer experience as the condition for the possibility of inner experience. Even the Cartesian sceptic, Kant argues, is unable to doubt that I am conscious of my own existence as determined in time. However, if this premise is accepted then: all determinations of time presuppose something permanent in perception. This is because the time relations of past, present and future, in order to be determinations of a single time, presuppose something permanent of which they are alterations. This permanent cannot be something in me (in my inner experience). As the condition for the possibility of inner representational activity, permanence cannot simply be another inner representation. Therefore perception of permanence must depend upon the existence and intuition of actual things outside of me. The crucial part of the refutation is Kant's following remark:

> Not only are we unable to perceive any determination of time save through change in outer relations (motion) relatively to the permanent in space (for instance the motion of the sun relatively to objects on earth), we have nothing permanent on which, as intuition, we can base the concept of a substance, save only *matter*; and even this permanence is not obtained from outer experience but is presupposed a priori as a necessary condition of determination of time and therefore also as a determination of inner sense in respect of our own existence through the existence of outer things.[2]

In a footnote to the preface to the second edition, Kant further determines the idea of permanence that is presupposed *a priori* for inner experience to be possible:

> ... *empirical consciousness of my existence...* is determinable only through relation to something which, while bound up with my existence, is outside me. [This 'something permanent' is] an external thing distinct from all my representations and its existence must be included in the determination of my own existence.[3]

'Something permanent' is understood to be outside us in the sense that the human being is in relation to it. The relation is such that this permanence is understood to be an external thing distinct from the subject's representations; the existence of the external thing must be included in the determination of inner experience. Hence, the possibility of finite experience is grounded in *a priori* relation to an external existence outside us, upon which we depend and to whose existence we are bound. This experience of an external, distinct existence to which the 'I' is *a priori* related involves outer sense because spatial intuition is, according to Kant, uniquely, a 'relation of intuition to something actual outside me'.[4] Hence, Kant argues:

> ...we must... immediately distinguish the mere receptivity of an outer intuition from the spontaneity which characterises every act of the imagination.[5]

In empirical intuition the mere receptivity of outer sense is manifest in the fact that perception represents the real or actual in space. The real of sensation or matter is given to the subject. Hence the externality of spatially intuited objects is constituted by their material, sensory givenness. However, the intuition of space is supposed to contain within it *a priori* the relations of externality of objects to the self and to each other. The *a priori* externality that the form of spatiality gives, cannot depend upon empirically intuited matter. Hence Kant refers to an *a priori* or transcendental conception of matter:

> But it is an even more noteworthy fact, that in order to understand the possibility of things in conformity with the categories, and so to determine the objective reality of the latter, we need, not merely intuitions, but intuitions that are in all cases outer intuitions. When, for instance we take the pure concepts of relation, we find, firstly, that in order to obtain something permanent in intuition corresponding to the concept of substance, and so to demonstrate the objective reality of this concept, we require an intuition in space (of matter).[6]

As Heidegger notes, here space returns in Kant's pure schematism of the categories: the transcendental function of space comes to the fore.[7] However, the question arises as to why Kant felt the need to instate spatial intuition as a key element of the schematism in the second edition. Whilst in the first analogy of experience in the A edition spatially schematised substance (matter) expresses the abiding of time in general, in the B edition, Kant writes:

> ...space alone is determined as permanent, while time, and therefore everything that is in inner sense, is in constant flux.[8]

By the time of the second edition, time is conceived a pure flux and permanence is evident in the spatial schematism of substance as matter. The concept of time in general and the idea that matter merely expresses this temporal permanence have been discarded: time is now pure flux. However, Kant neither acknowledges nor addresses this modification and tension in his analytic of the schematism of the pure concept of substance. Nonetheless, a clue for explaining Kant's modification of his position on the schematic form of the concept of substance can be found in the Transcendental Dialectic, in the chapter on the paralogisms of pure reason. A transcendental paralogism is a formally invalid conclusion inferred from a transcendental concept. The concept Kant is concerned with is the judgement 'I think'. Rational psychology commits a paralogism by identifying the formal unity of apperception (the transcendental ground and unity of self conscious experience) with an intuitable object or soul that is substantial, simple and unified and which we can therefore both experience and know *a priori*. On the contrary, Kant argues that the 'I think' can be determined no further than as a transcendental subject of the thoughts = X:[9]

> The appearance to outer sense has something fixed and abiding which supplies a substratum as the basis of its transitory determinations and therefore a synthetic concept, namely, that of space and of an appearance in space; whereas time, which is the sole form of our inner intuition, has nothing abiding and therefore only yields knowledge of the change of determinations, not of any object that can thereby be determined. For in what we entitle 'soul', everything is in continual flux and therefore there is nothing abiding except... the 'I'. ... This 'I' is however as little an intuition as it is a concept of any object; it is the mere form of consciousness. ...[10]

Kant's problem is that if permanence, as in the first analogy of experience, expresses time in general, then, given his commitment to transcendental idealism and the consequent determination of temporal relations as 'in us', the underlying 'I' of apperception would have to be identified with the intuitively schematised concept of substance. However, this is what Kant must avoid – the transcendental concept 'I think' is not an object that can be experienced. Hence the schema of permanence cannot belong to the subject as an abiding substratum amidst the constant flux of nows. The concept of time in general consequently drops from view in the second edition and space comes to the fore. This argument is put to use in the refutation of idealism, as has been shown. The anxiety generated by the first analogy, therefore, is the danger of repeating the kind of paralogism of the transcendental subject found in Descartes. Kant's response to this anxiety is to determine the schema of substance as the abiding of external matter intuited in outer sense. The possibility of finite experience, hence, presupposes both the transcendental concept of matter and the transcendental concept of the 'I think'. The difference between the objects of these two concepts is that whereas synthetic *a priori* judgements can be made regarding the nature of matter or impenetrable extension, there cannot be a correlative *a priori* physiology of the object of inner sense. The reason for this is that nothing can be *a priori* synthetically known from the concept of a thinking being.[11]

Heidegger, however, contrary to the insight into spatial intuition opened up in the second edition, prioritises and develops Kant's analysis of time in general in the first analogy of experience in the A edition. As such, the content of the spatial schema of matter, according to Heidegger, is grounded in underlying temporal relations of succession and co-existence. It is from the conception of time in this analogy that the analytic of Dasein flows. According to Heidegger, if time is conceived as a series of now-points, then it will always be understood as equiprimordial with space: the spatial line would be, in this case, the underlying continuum on the basis of which a unified succession of temporal moments (past-present-future) is possible.[12] However, Heidegger argues, concentrating solely on the intuited content of time ignores the specific way in which the pure intuition of time gives or supplies this content, i.e. it ignores the form of intuiting itself:

... it is not in this form but rather as pure self-affection that time is the more original ground of transcendence. As such, it is also the condition for the possibility of the representing-forming, i.e. making apparent, of pure space. The rejection of the priority of time in no way follows from the insight into the transcendental function of pure space.[13]

In other words, if the spatial intuition of matter is granted, nonetheless the perception of permanence that this involves is still further grounded in pure time. Heidegger dismisses the anxiety that led Kant to fear a paralogism of the subject – the persisting of the ecstatic subject does not involve ontic assertions about the unchangeability of the 'I'.[14] In other words, the human being is not conceived as a given being or object that might be interrogated by a science like rational psychology. Rather, the abiding of the 'I' and the objective horizon = X that 'it gives', are transcendental determinations of the subject that, in the system of *a priori* schemata, yield ontological knowledge. Kant's difficulty is that he does not have access to the phenomenological account of the ecstatic essence of the human being. Thus, on Heidegger's interpretation, Kant cannot conceive, in an explicit way, how the externality of matter, determined as the horizon of the future, might still be internal to the temporal, relational nature of finite existence.

A consequence of Heidegger's adherence to the first edition of the *Critique* is that time retains a priority over space in the analytic of the human being. Heidegger, hence, preserves the Kantian idea that space is subordinate to time because the latter is the universal *a priori* condition of all appearances whatsoever, whilst the appearances of the former are limited to outer intuition. Time is, for Kant, the immediate condition of inner appearances and the mediate condition of outer appearances: 'all objects of the senses are in time and necessarily stand in time relations'.[15] Heidegger develops this general thesis by showing that the intuited content of space as an infinite, given magnitude on the basis of which matter is *a priori* intuited, is itself grounded in the form of intuiting or giving of time. There is perception of permanence qua matter only because there is an abiding horizon of objectivity formed by pure time within which this spatial intuition is possible. Time gives or supplies the content of space: authentic temporality allows spatial intuition to 'spring forth'. Hence 'only on the grounds of original time is the self "spatial"'.[16] Therefore, although Heidegger refers to the transcendental function of space in the second edition as a new insight, he closes down the possibility of interpreting this insight in a radical way. Temporality immediately reasserts ontological priority over space.

Indeed, Heidegger repeatedly raises the question as to the status of space throughout the corpus and invariably answers the question by re-asserting the primordiality of time. In an early marginal note in his Kantbook he writes 'How was the question of space included here?', next to the comment that the understanding of Being must be projected upon time.[17] This same question regarding the essence of spatiality in relation to time is raised even more pointedly at the very end of his philosophical life, when, in the late lecture *Time and Being*, he declares that the argument in his early work which founds space upon time is untenable.[18] Indeed, Heidegger writes elsewhere that 'one day' he may not 'shun' the problem of the relation between the 'open' and pure space and ecstatic time.[19] If the concept of the Open *is* elucidated in terms of the clearing of ecstatic time nonetheless, as Heidegger here explicitly admits, in shunning the question of the relation between the Open and the phenomenon of space there is a recoil, as in Kant, before the intensity of an unthought and yet animating knot in the semantic web of his text.

Despite this, Heidegger writes incisively on the significance of the question of space, as early as 1925:

> It is incumbent on us to see... primary spatiality... only then are we in a position to avoid a course which is always and above all adopted, even by Kant, for the definition of... spiritual being. This course involves defining spirit negatively against the spatial... conceiving spirit as always non-space. By contrast... Dasein itself is spatial. There is absolutely no reason to oppose this and to think... that... the authentic being of man is some sort of aura, which... can have nothing to do with space, because we associate space primarily with corporeality and so move in constant fear of materialising the spirit.[20]

The primary spatiality mentioned here in *History of the Concept of Time* is also mentioned in *Kant and the Problem of Metaphysics* as the spatiality of the self, as has been mentioned. However, *Kant and the Problem of Metaphysics* founds the intuited content of space in the 'representing-forming' of ecstatic time and thereby follows Kant's derivation, in the A edition, of the representations formed in outer sense from inner sense as the *a priori* condition of all representations. Given that Dasein's primary spatiality is so grounded, then, at the very moment when Heidegger attempts to extract himself from the tradition, he falls back into it, almost as a reflex, by grounding his analysis of existential spatiality upon the non-spatial essence of pure, finite temporality.

However, the way in which the early work repeats the traditional definition of spirit as non-space attains its fullest elaboration and transparency, not in *History of the Concept of Time* or *Kant and the Problem of Metaphysics*, but in

Being and Time. Dasein *is* Being-in-the-World and exists as a factical being 'alongside-entities-within-the-world', 'in' the world. This constitutes the structural element of Being-in-the-World that Heidegger names 'Being-in'. *Contra* Descartes, the worldhood of the world Dasein is 'in' does not consist in a uniform, indefinite extendedness within which extended bodies are placed. Nor do the extended boundaries of these present-at-hand entities subsist in the externality of a mutual indifference. For Heidegger, the ontologically primary mode of being of entities in the world is ready-to-handiness. Entities are ready-to-hand in the sense that they appear to Dasein as items of equipment to be used in Dasein's everyday concerns and dealings. Each ready-to-hand entity is related to others from out of an equipmental whole or totality of involvements in terms of which the entities signify assignments of an 'in order to', 'with which' and 'towards this'. Thus, the primordial worldhood of the world of factical Dasein's 'Being-in' is comprised of a totality of reference relations on the basis of which beings appear in the web of a mutual involvement. Heidegger proceeds to determine further this mode of being of entities in the world through an account of Dasein's existential spatiality. This spatiality is 'de-severant', 'directional' and 'oriented', consisting primarily of a movement of nearing and distancing. Dasein 'makes room' for a region or equipmental whole and from out of the distance of the region 'brings an entity close', nears it in the signification of its assignment relation. Nonetheless, there is distance in Dasein's existential spatiality only insofar as Dasein understands the whole it has made room for. Only insofar as Dasein has a pre-ontological understanding of the region, and thus is *near* to it as a horizon of intelligibility, can it form the distance required in order to bring an entity close. Consequently, the essential element of de-severance is the nearing of things such that the Being of Dasein is pervaded by a 'frenzy for nearness',[21] a tendency reinforced by the nature of modern technology.

However, Dasein's existential spatiality, as the distancing of the region from out of which entities can be brought close, is articulated within the purview of Dasein's everyday, concernful dealings, in which, as factical, Dasein forgets itself and falls into the world. Falling is the mode of being of the inauthentic existence of Dasein in which it is fascinated by, and absorbed in, its dealings with ready-to-hand entities whose being is not of the nature of Dasein's own Being. In this case, as Heidegger writes, 'Dasein can be spatial only... in the sense of existing as factically falling'.[22] This constitutes the spatiality of 'spiritual being' of man demanded by Heidegger in *History of the Concept of Time*. In addition, as Heidegger suggests, if temporality is the meaning of the Being of care, then Dasein's specific spatiality must be grounded in time.[23] Hence the self-directive discovery of a region is the whither of an 'ecstatically retentive awaiting', from out of which 'bringing close' manifests itself as a 'making-present' enabling the 'here' of the place of an item of equipment to be disclosed. The nearing of inauthentic spatiality is founded in the present of a mode of temporality that makes de-severance and directionality possible. Heidegger concludes, in a phenomenologically concrete elucidation of the position of the Kantbook, that given the temporal essence of Being-in-the-World 'only on the basis of its ecstatic-horizonal temporality is it possible for Dasein to break into space'.[24]

Nevertheless, if the spatiality of inauthentic Dasein is founded in originary time, the question arises as to the nature of a possible authentic correlate of inauthentic spatiality. Authentic Dasein comes face-to-face with its factical possibilities of existence in the Situation. Nonetheless, according to Heidegger, even if the here of the Situation has an 'overtone' that is spatial, nonetheless it is not spatial because it is disclosed in resoluteness, the meaning of which is essentially temporal.[25] The temporality of the act of authentic resoluteness is that of the futural projection of the horizon of Dasein's ownmost nullity upon its thrown, factical ground. Finite, resolute Dasein, as has been shown, receives the present necessity released from the spontaneity of its temporal willing. Dasein thereby encounters in the Present of the authentic 'now' the explicit array of factical possibilities of existence (Situation) that are available to it as a historical, thrown being. The Present of the Situation, disclosed in the resoluteness of authentic Dasein's moment of vision, is the truth of its existence. By the time of *Origin of the Work of Art* the concept of site or place – as earth – has more than merely spatial overtones; yet it remains founded in the present of an authentic, temporal 'now'.[26]

Nevertheless, given the concession in the late lecture *Time and Being* that the argument according to which Dasein's spatiality is founded in ecstatic time is untenable, Heidegger's subsequent discussion of space would be expected to explore the possibility of an authentic spatiality released from temporal foundation. This expectation is heightened with the introduction of the notion of 'time-space' as an originary phenomenon. However:

> Time-space now is the name for the openness which opens up in the mutual self-extending of futural approach, past and present. This openness exclusively and primarily provides the space in which space as we usually know it can unfold. The self-extending, the opening up of future, past and present is itself prespatial; only thus can it make room, that is, provide space.[27]

The spatiality of time-space is an openness or clearing which opens up in the mutual self-extending of 'true time'. This self-extending of time is clarified as follows:

> Approaching, being not yet present, at the same time gives and brings about what is no longer present, the past, and conversely what has been offers future to itself. The reciprocal relation of both at the same time gives and brings about the present.[28]

The form of this temporality, as the giving of the future to the past from out of which exchange or extending, the present is given or released, is in no way different in content or structure from the nature of ecstatic temporality analysed in *Being and Time* and *Origin of the Work of Art*.[29] The stretch between future and past opens up an open region – this constitutes the dimensionality or Open of time-space, which 'belongs to true time and to it alone'.[30] If, as Heidegger argues, the untenability of the argument in *Being and Time* must lead to 'an insight into the origin of space as site',[31] as has been shown, the concept of site repeats the foundation by reducing the place of the site to the happening of an authentic present. Hence, Heidegger, concluding that true time is 'pre-spatial',[32] despite recognition of the problems that this conclusion generates, stays faithful until the very end to the traditional predilection for a temporal interpretation of spirit.

Nevertheless, despite this, Heidegger adds enigmatically that once insight into the origin of space as site has been gained:

> Since time as well as Being can only be thought from Appropriation as the gifts of Appropriation, the relation of space to Appropriation must also be considered in an analogous way.[33]

Heidegger at no time elucidates the nature of space that is here intimated as a gift from the 'it gives' of Being. Yet the possibility of such an elucidation is raised, even if there is hardly any elaboration. Nonetheless, a concrete step in this direction is made in Heidegger's subsequent description of true time as four-dimensional. The fourth dimension is the 'giving that determines all',[34] the unity of the interplay between the three dimensions, the 'playing' in the heart of time:

> ...giving brings about to each its own presencing, holds them apart thus opened and so holds them toward one another in the nearness by which the three dimensions remain near to one another.[35]

The fourth, unifying dimension of time is a 'nearing nearness', the giving of which gives the movement of temporal exchange. Nearness gives the circular giving of temporality; it constitutes the presencing of the ecstatic relations that Heidegger many years previously determined as the movement or play of Dasein. Nearness is thus the giving that gives the play or act of the Self. What then is distance? How might distance determine the giving or nearing that animates the movement of human sensibility? In the giving of Being itself, a glimmer of the outside of the temporal relations appears to have been partially revealed. Time, rather than being conceived as a primal phenomenon, seems to depend upon a giving which does not originate from out of its own spontaneous activity. However, Heidegger recoils before this possibility:

> ... 'nearing nearness'... brings future, past and present near to one another by distancing them... true time... is the nearness of presencing out of present, past and future...[36]

The nearness of the unity of the giving of temporality is a presencing which gives distance from out of itself in holding apart the horizonal ecstasies, the nearing of the self-present fourfold exchange of world. Distance is simply a mode of primal nearness, by which it maintains the unity of a closed exchange in and for itself. Nearness, the presencing of the fourth dimension, is not itself explicitly given from out of distance, although this is implicitly raised as a possibility. If this were the case, then the gift of distance would not be stretched open in the temporal relations that constitute Dasein's understanding of the world. Distance would rather give the totality of the fourfold world itself. Distance would then be the form of intuition through which we receive the world as a gift. Thus, if, as in *Being and Time*, the human being must understand world or Being in the sense of being near to it, then consequently distance must be that form of intuition whereby world itself and man's understanding of it are themselves given. Spatial distance, in this case, grounds the giving or play of temporal activity. Space, rather than being restricted to the human being's factical existence 'in' the world, constitutes the underlying relation between Being and the human being.

Indeed, as Kant realises when writing the second edition of the *Critique of Pure Reason*, the pure intuiting of space involves a distinctive capacity for receptivity that cannot be given by, and grounded in, the spontaneous activity of the temporal form of intuiting. Spatial intuition involves the *a priori* reception of an external, distinct existence to which finite, human existence is bound and upon which it is dependent. If the externality of this existence – the transcendental conception of matter – is given by the temporal act of the ecstatic subject as a transcendental object correlative to the abiding 'I', then this externality remains internal to the transcendence of man. In Heideggerian ontology, however, the weight of real existence separate from the Being of the human being, without Kant's transcendental idealism, falls entirely upon ontic matter (real). On the other hand, if the intuition of distance is conceived as giving the *a priori* relation of an external existence to the human being, then a path is provisionally opened toward a genuine form of ontological receptivity. In this conception of ontological sensibility, space is both 'in us' and yet 'it gives' to the human being. The act that gives distance, i.e. the 'it' of the 'it gives', is on this conception of experience something Other to the human being. Through the experience and intuition of distance, the otherness of Being is revealed.

If the spatial form of intuiting is a giving or 'it gives' then the underlying relation between the 'problem of space' and the turn in Heidegger also becomes more evident.[37] In early Heidegger, the 'it' of the 'it gives' is determined as the temporal act of the pure, *a priori* imagination; Heidegger turns in the later work, in the sense that the 'it gives' is inverted. Rather than the human being giving Being to itself, Being gives to the human being and man receives the gift of Being. Both the early and later interpretation of the 'it gives' involve a direct inheritance of the Kantian idea of the pure, *a priori* giving of the forms of intuition. Nonetheless, after the turn, Heidegger departs in a more radical way from Kant's Transcendental Aesthetic. In later Heidegger, the subject is not conceived as giving the forms of sensibility from out of itself: through distance the Self *receives* ontological movement. The 'problem of space' in Heidegger in fact refers to this essential change in the conception of the Kantian forms of intuition, the primal phenomena, that supply the intuited content. This is a change not only in the conception of the content of these forms of intuition but, more importantly, a change in the conception of the *origin* and *movement* of the giving of form within finite, immanent experience. Early Heidegger errs becomes he focuses on the intuited content of spatial intuition without grounding this content in the unique and originary act, the mode of intuiting, whereby this content is given. Instead

Heidegger founds the derivative content of space in the temporal mode of intuiting of Dasein's transcendence. However, contrary to early Heidegger, the unique form of intuiting of spatiality, the finite receptivity of the human being is grounded in the gift of an originary distance. Being – 'it' – gives the form of sensibility *to* man. Man does not simply receive the intuited content of distance; the act or form of intuiting offering the gift of distance is itself *a priori* received. Being opens up distance within the 'soul' of the human being.

PART II
ONTOLOGICAL DIFFERENCE AND
THE CONCEALING OF BEING

Chapter 4

Distance and Concealment

Early Heidegger addresses the problem of how the human being is able *a priori* both to give and to receive Being by making use of the Kantian idea of pure self-affection. However, the content intuited by the human being regresses from the ontological to the ontic; the reception of factical existence is subordinate to ontological spontaneity in the analytic of transcendence. The basis of the subordination of finite reception is the temporal essence of finitude. Time founds space. Yet the foundation of the intuited content of spatial intuition in the form of temporal intuiting neglects the unique way in which space *gives*. After Heidegger's turn, to which the return of space in the corpus is internally related, the temporal subject does not give the form of intuiting from out of itself. Rather, Being gives the forms of intuition *to* the subject. Pursuing hints in Heidegger's late lecture *Time and Being*, the gift of Being is intuited in the reception of distance. Distance gives Being as an external existence to which the Self is bound and upon which it depends. However, in order for these provisional points to be consolidated, the following questions must be addressed: What is distance? What is the nature of the 'it' that gives distance? How does Being give distance?

It is not uncommon in ordinary language to make use of the concept of distance in describing a variety of psychological states. As Wittgenstein points out, we are inclined to say that words spoken with feeling have not only a surface but also a dimension of depth.[1] We also are inclined to say in the same context that the words have an atmosphere, that 'something goes on in me' – however, not in the sense of a hypostatised 'process' accompanying the meaning. Rather, Wittgenstein suggests, the atmosphere or depth of words can be compared to the special feeling a musical phrase gives us when played with expression.[2] A description can only *hint* at the feeling: the experience is fully manifest only in its actual performance, when the phrase is played 'like *this*'.[3] Bergson asks, in a similar vein, why we describe states of inner experience, for example the emotion of joy, as *deep*. We do this, Bergson argues, not only in relation to certain forms of linguistic behaviour and word-usage, but also in diverse modes of aesthetic, intellectual and religious experience.[4] Unlike Wittgenstein, however, Bergson takes the tendency toward these kinds of description as revelatory of a more general philosophical problem: how can an inner psychological state be assimilated to a magnitude? To put the problem in another way, how can an interior feeling or intensity be experienced to a greater or a lesser degree when the magnitude required for measuring the more or less cannot be determined using the intuition of outer, spatial extension? We describe our feelings as deep, as more or less intense, yet it is unclear whether the conception of intensive magnitude that these descriptions involve is in fact possible. Bergson concludes that the possibility of intensive magnitude depends upon our differentiating qualitative from quantitative multiplicity. The experience of the former Bergson entitles duration. Although Bergson determines duration as a pure flux, merely defining it negatively (and dualistically) against consciousness, nonetheless he is right to point out that the phenomenological experience of depth within the subject cannot be explained in terms of spatial extension. Distance is not a quantifiable, homogeneous medium, an infinite, given magnitude; it is, on the contrary, a form of intensive magnitude, a felt intensity. The feeling of intensity, however, as with the feeling of pleasure in the experience of art, is not an empirical sensation conveyed by the corporeal sense-organs. The idea of the intuited content of distance is *a priori* ontological. As Deleuze suggests in a profoundly Heideggerian remark: depth is the intensity of Being.[5] Consequently, as a constituent element of the principle of *a priori* ontological sensibility, the intuition of distance is the depth of an intensive magnitude that yields within it an *a priori* relation of the human being to the exteriority of Being. Distance is not an empty or formal infinite: 'it gives' the intensity of transcendental content. In later Heidegger's transcendental aesthetic the concepts of movement and intensity are therefore determined as constitutive elements of the form and content of pure intuition. The external existence manifest in the pure reception of an interior intensity is Being itself. In the finitude of human experience, Being is the depth of intensity. How Being gives intensity and how correlatively intensity is the gift of Being remains however as yet undetermined.

In order to elucidate further the nature of distance, the relation between distance and the 'it gives' of the *Ereignis* must be addressed in more concrete terms. Nonetheless, prior to the analytic of this relation, the criticism of Heidegger by the French theologian Jean-Luc Marion, who specifically argues that there is no distance in Heideggerian ontology,[6] offers a useful foil for clarifying the issues involved. Distance, for Marion, is a gap that both separates and unifies; it preserves the gap between giver and gift.[7] As such, distance allows giver and gift to play through it their sending and return, their gift-exchange. However, according to Marion, there is no distance in the *Ereignis*. Beings are appropriated and exhausted in the idolatrous gaze of the human being. The ontological both gives and is annihilated by the actuality of ontic existence. Being fixes and is transfixed by beings. On the other hand, Marion suggests that the idolatry of the ontic-ontological difference is transformed, in the iconic experience of Christian love, into the non-appropriative distance between God and creature. God beyond Being – following Pseudo-Dionysus – saturates the visible idol with the invisible intention of the radically other, thereby releasing or disappropriating beings from the finite gaze of Being. Hence, Marion offers a stark alternative: the nihilistic ontology of the *Ereignis* or the infinite depths of Christian theology. Of course, if the *Ereignis* is exhaustively fulfilled in the giving of Dasein's transcendence then the alternative offered by Marion holds. However, though Marion's remarks offer an incisive refutation of early Heidegger's notion of the 'it gives', the later conception of the *Ereignis* remains untouched.

In order to develop his critique, Marion argues that Heidegger leaves the giver in suspension in the 'it gives' of the *Ereignis*, so that the 'it' is interrogated.

'solely in the light of the kind of giving that belongs to it'.[8] As has been shown, the giving of the 'it gives' is the self-extending reaching of the four-dimensional temporal fourfold, the presencing of which is determined by Marion as the originary appearing of Being.[9] Hence, for Marion, the ceaseless presencing of temporality incessantly appropriates the ontic. Beings, the gift of the giving, *are* only as they are denied in the nullity of the circular exchange between future and past, an exchange that is likewise sacrificed in the ontic present that the ontological nonetheless ceaselessly gives. As a reading of early Heidegger's interpretation of the 'it gives', Marion is, of course, entirely correct. However, as a reading of later Heidegger's interpretation of the 'it gives', Marion errs. The specific error is his identification of the meaning of 'it gives' with 'it appears'. It is on the basis of this identification that Marion determines Being as a conceptual idol. However, when Heidegger writes that the 'it' must be interrogated in the light of the giving that belongs to it, the point of this interrogation is to abandon the attempt to determine the 'It by itself in isolation'.[10] Such determination, as Heidegger rightly points out, would end up positing the 'it' as an 'indeterminate power'.[11] In other words, if the 'it' is isolated from the 'it gives' the 'it' is transformed into a transcendent source of the giving and the danger of a repetition of onto-theology arises. Because of this danger, the nature of the 'it' is to be elucidated on the basis of the determinations of the giving of time and of Being.

The giving of time, as Heidegger writes, is the ecstatic interplay of the four dimensions in which the reciprocal relation of the future and past gives and brings about the present. Nearness, the giving of this relationality, brings future, past and present near to one another by distancing them:

> …it keeps what has been open by denying its advent as present. This nearing of nearness keeps open the approach coming from the future by withholding the present in the approach. Nearing nearness has the character of denial and withholding… it grants the openness of time-space and preserves what remains denied in what has-been, what is withheld in approach. We call the giving which gives true time an extending, which opens and conceals.[12]

The giving of temporality is a concealing which withholds the future in its advent as present, holds apart what has-been and denies the present in the presencing of the exchange. The ecstatic nature of the relation is rooted in the withholding, holding apart and denying – concealing – of nearness. On the other hand, according to Heidegger, from the beginning of Western metaphysics, Being is 'seen' but not the 'it gives' as such. The 'it gives' withdraws in favour of the gift which 'it gives' and this gift is conceptualised and explained, from then on, in the characteristic manner of onto-theology, as the ontological ground *for* beings. Hence, the giving of the 'it gives' is a sending in that the giving holds itself back and withdraws:[13]

> The history of Being means destiny of Being in whose sendings both the sending and the It which send forth hold back with their self-manifestation. To hold back is, in Greek, *epoche*. Hence we speak of the epochs of the destiny of Being. Epoch -

[means]... the actual holding back of itself in favour of the discernability of the gift, that is, of Being with regard to the grounding of beings.[14]

The giving of Being, as with time, is a holding-back or withdrawing, as well as a self-manifesting. The giving of each belong together in the 'it gives' of the *Ereignis*.[15] From out of the 'it gives' of the *Ereignis* – the event of appropriation – *there is*, 'it gives Being' and 'it gives time':

> ... in as much as the modes of giving that are determined by withdrawal – sending and extending – lie in Appropriation, *withdrawal* must belong to what is peculiar to the *Ereignis*.[16]

Only as withdrawal belongs to the 'it gives' of the *Ereignis* can there be withholding in sending and holding-back in temporalising: the withdrawing in the 'it gives', as the originary giving by which they are determined qua giving, allows the singular giving of sending and temporal extending into their ownmost essence. The 'it gives' of the *Ereignis* withdraws because of the nature of the 'it' in the giving of the *Ereignis*. The 'it', Heidegger writes, names a 'presence of absence'[17] and hence is 'enigmatic'.[18] The 'it' belongs to the giving of time and of Being because it is the *ground* of their giving:

> Denial and withholding exhibit the same trait as self-withholding in sending: namely self-withdrawal... Insofar as the destiny of Being lies in the extending of time and time, together with Being, lies in Appropriation, Appropriating makes manifest its peculiar property, that Appropriation withdraws what is most fully its own from boundless unconcealment... it expropriates itself of itself. *Expropriation* belongs to Appropriation as such. By this expropriation, Appropriation does not abandon itself – rather it preserves what is its own.[19]

The *expropriating* of the event of appropriation, the *Ereignis*, is the withdrawal of the enigmatic 'it' from unconcealment in the originary giving. The 'it' giving therefore in the 'it gives' conceals itself; on the basis of this originary withdrawal there is concealing in the giving of time and holding-back in the epochal sending of Being. Marion's assertion that the 'it' in the 'it gives' 'does not provide... any privileged support'[20] to the giving and is absorbed within its presencing, neglects not only the modes of concealing evident in the 'it gives time' and 'it gives Being' but, more significantly, the fact that the entirety of this giving, on the contrary, is grounded in the withdrawing, expropriating 'it' in the giving of the *Ereignis*. Marion's error is to understand the belonging of the 'it' to the giving as an assimilation in which the 'it' evaporates. The 'it' is, indeed, immanent to the giving but only as the ground of this immanent activity. According to Marion, a giving that does not give through a giver cannot admit transgression outside the fourfold. However, the 'it' determines the nearing of temporality by withdrawing in the gift of the fourfold world. Consequently, with the concealing of the exterior 'it', the *outside* of the fourfold world and the distance from out of which there is 'nearing nearness', are revealed as the innermost elements of the *Ereignis*. Heidegger's provisional hint of an originary distance giving the nearness of world is thus further consolidated: distance is stretched open in the ontological act of self-concealing gift-giving.

Phenomenologically, the internal relation between distance and concealing is manifest concretely in a specific and well-known form of aesthetic experience: the feeling of the sublime. As Kant writes: in the aesthetic experience of sublimity, a 'depth' is revealed in the human being.[21] This depth is also described as, for the experience of human sensibility, an 'abyss'.[22] According to Kant, we feel in the experience of the sublime that we possess an inner purposefulness or power, which exceeds the conditions of empirical experience. Hence the depth is *in us*. However, Kant proceeds, the basis or ground for this inner purposefulness is 'concealed';[23] the distance is 'unfathomable'.[24] Within the domain of aesthetic immanence, the feeling of the sublime opens up an inner depth in the human being, revealing a power whose ground or reason nonetheless withdraws itself. Phenomenologically at least, there consequently appears to be a subterranean connection between the reception of Being and the feeling of sublimity. Distance would then be the intuitive schema that provides a perceivable and concrete image for the free purposefulness of human nature. In the unfathomable upsurge of an inner intensity we perceive the terror and sublime appropriation of Being.

Thus, if Being is determined by Heidegger as a 'giver', it nonetheless remains within immanent experience because the source of the giving of distance is concealed. The reasons why Being gives distance withdraw from our understanding: the sublime depth of intensity is unfathomable. The 'it' is enigmatic because it appears in the giving *as* that for which no exhaustive account can be given, manifesting itself in and through self-withdrawal. Heidegger writes in a note to the editors of a collection of his essays:

> ...can anything more be said about the relation a) the epochal transformations of Being b) Appropriation and c) Expropriation?... Appropriation and Expropriation can never be separated from each other but rather constitute a relation which is most original of all... . Between the epochal transformations of Being and Appropriation reigns the relation of giving ('it gives') but not even this can be said of the relation Appropriation-Expropriation.[25]

Contra Marion, the originary relation in the *Ereignis* – the ground for a determination of the nature of the relation between Being and man – is the self-withdrawing expropriating of the 'it' in the 'it gives'. Being withdraws in giving the gift that 'it gives'. This is the difference that sustains the gap between Being and thinking, a difference manifest in the pure intuition of distance through which *there is* gift-giving in the *Ereignis*. The translation of the *Ereignis* as 'Event of Appropriation', covering over the crucial expropriative movement at the core of the relation between Being and man is thus deeply problematic and wholly misleading.

Marion's conflation of Being with appearing, though it fails as an interpretation of the lecture *Time and Being*, nonetheless is no doubt influenced by Heidegger's general and pervasive subordination of the concept of concealing to the concept of revealing within the corpus. This subordination should not be surprising if we accept the underlying affinity between distance and concealing, given Heidegger's founding of spatiality in the nearness of ecstatic temporality. Indeed, Heidegger's definitive determination of the status of the concept of concealing in relation to the discursive whole of this philosophical work is marked out at the beginning of *Being and Time*. According to Heidegger, semblance, appearance and mere appearance are all derived from the prior showing itself of the phenomenon.[26] The concept of phenomenon means that which shows itself in itself, i.e., the manifest. The seeming of an entity that shows itself as something which in itself it is not dissembles only insofar as it makes a pretension of showing itself, i.e. of being a phenomenon. Thus, semblance is, Heidegger writes, a privative modification of a prior phenomenon. Likewise an appearance, which indicates something that does not show itself, is able to announce the appearing only as it shows itself in appearance; it therefore also presupposes the concept of phenomenon. Finally, appearing can be taken as that which emerges in what is itself non-manifest, in such a way that the non-manifest is something that is *never* manifest in its mere appearance. As a reference-relation mere appearance, too, is founded in the pure showing of phenomenon. If the Kantian objects of empirical intuition show themselves, Heidegger writes, nonetheless they are also an appearing or announcing of something, which *hides* itself in that appearance. That which shows itself in the appearance as prior to the phenomenon as ordinarily understood are, as has been shown, the primal phenomena of phenomenology, behind which there is nothing else. These primal phenomena are space and time, the forms of pure intuition. Although the forms of intuition are perceived unthematically in advance for experience of beings to be possible, ordinarily in themselves they remain hidden. Phenomenological ontology, described by Heidegger as a species of exhibiting, explicitly brings the forms to light and so thematises, from out of hiddenness, the Being of entities.[27] Being, however, can be hidden for empirical intuition only insofar as the phenomenon is primordially revealed

According to Heidegger, authentic Dasein comes face-to-face with the originary, phenomenal manifestness of Being. Anxiety in the face of death is anxiety in the face of that potentiality-for-Being which is Dasein's ownmost, non-relational and not to be outstripped. This is the possibility of death as the possibility of the absolute impossibility of Dasein. Anxious Dasein comes face-to-face with Being-in-the-World, as the indefinite Nothing of the world as such, in the certain, resolute anticipation of this possibility *qua* possibility, on the basis of which it is Being-a-whole. As fundamentally anticipatory, anxiety, springing from the future of resoluteness,[28] discloses the toward oneself as the meaning of existing in the face of the possibility of one's ownmost nullity. As the thrown, null basis of the projective nullity of Being-the-basis in which the not or Nothing is revealed as the ground of care, Dasein is a Being-guilty. The 'voice of conscience' summons Dasein, as authentic potentiality-for-Being, to its ownmost Being-guilty, in the 'It calls'. This call, Heidegger writes, comes *from* Dasein and yet from *beyond* Dasein.[29] Has Heidegger anticipated the concealing 'it gives' elucidated in *Time and Being* in guise of the 'it calls' calling from in as well as from outside Dasein in

Being and Time? No. The call of conscience comes from beyond Dasein in that it calls to the Dasein that is absorbed in the rules and standards of the They. Yet it comes *from* Dasein insofar as the 'it' *is* Dasein face-to-face with the Nothing of world. Dasein is summoned by the calling of the 'It calls' in that Dasein calls *itself* to its ownmost potentiality-for-Being:[30]

> In understanding the call, Dasein lets its ownmost Self *take action in itself* in terms of that potentiality for Being which it has chosen... letting one's ownmost Self take action in itself of its own accord is its Being guilty.[31]

Dasein receives and hears the call only as it is given from out of the activity of its authentic Being-towards-death. This activity is the nihilating of the Nothing, disclosed in anxiety. In other words, it is the futural projecting of the nullity of Dasein's ownmost potentiality-for-Being-a-whole back upon the null basis of having-been and the subsequent disclosive release of self-given factical possibilities of existence. 'Taking action in itself' is therefore another description of the pure self-affection of transcendence. Dasein receives the call from out of the active spontaneity of its *own* calling. Hence, Heidegger rightly concludes that the voice of the 'It' in the 'it calls', unlike the concealing-withdrawing it in the *Ereignis*, is *not* mysterious or secret.[32] *What* is disclosed in the voice is unequivocal, the content of the call is appropriated unconcealedly and the call is *not* returned.[33] In the call of conscience Dasein summons itself from out of the concern of inauthentic involvement into the already perceived and understood, but not appropriatively grasped, potentiality-for-Being of its authentic possibilities of factical existence. The 'it calls' brings Dasein face-to-face undisguisedly with the temporally grounded phenomenon of the Nothing of world as such:

> Anticipatory resoluteness... is... that understanding which follows the call of conscience and which frees for death the possibility of acquiring power over Dasein's existence and of basically dispersing all fugitive Self-concealments.[34]

In the mastery of authentic existence all self-concealments appear dispersed. In the transparency of the moment of vision disclosing the truth of existence, the self-concealments of inauthentic, factical life, are banished from beings, from Being, and from the relation between man and Being. Hence, the concept of concealing, far from grounding immanence in early Heidegger, is derived from the prior manifestness of the self-showing Being of authentic Dasein. This derivation is the ground for the possibility of the banishment and dispersal of self-concealment in authentic resoluteness. As Heidegger writes: 'to be closed off and covered up belongs to Dasein's facticity. ... But only insofar as Dasein has been disclosed has it also been closed off'.[35] The dominating stance of the early work unfortunately colours Marion's interpretation of Heidegger and the translation of the *Ereignis*: Being as appearing or coming-to-presence.

In sum, the intuited content of distance is an *a priori* intensive magnitude. Ontological receptivity is constituted in the pure intuition of the depth of intensity. The 'it' that gives intensity withdraws in the giving. No exhaustive explanation determines why Being gives this gift. In the intuition of a felt intensity, man is dependent upon an exterior, self-concealing existence to which he is internally bound. This relation constitutes the ontological difference between the Being of man and Being itself. Being does not conceal itself in the sense of keeping an already given content hidden. Being does not have 'something' to which it denies the human being access; it does not 'keep a secret'. Rather Being withdraws in the act or form from out of which 'it gives' distance. Distance is not intended as a particular mode of existential comportment in the sense of the human being's factical existence. Distance, on the contrary, is the form of intuition on the basis of which *there is* world for the existential subject. World, contra *Being and Time*, is not the comprehended nearness of a ready-to-hand region but a unified, transcendental field of experience received from out of the hidden depths of Being.

Chapter 5

Art and Difference

Heidegger, therefore, in the late lecture *Time and Being*, intimates an originary self-withdrawal of Being in the *Ereignis*. This withdrawing is neither a mode of temporal presencing nor of epochal sending but rather gives the possibility of both as their ground. Here, the concept of concealing asserts its priority in the analytic of man: it is no longer subordinated to revealing, as space is no longer subordinated to time. If we accept the underlying affinity between distance and concealing then, of course, this twofold insurgency no longer appears coincidental. However, if the ontological priority of the concept of phenomenal manifestness over its counter-concept of concealment pervades Heidegger's analytic of authentic existence, the question arises as to whether this prioritisation of the self-showing presencing of Being continues through the middle and later period of the corpus. According to many commentators, there is a shift in Heidegger's writing in the mid-thirties, epitomised most of all in the essay *Origin of the Work of Art*.[1] Whether this is an accurate interpretation of Heidegger might be gauged by assessing the use that he makes of the concepts of revealing and concealing in this work.

Because, according to Heidegger, art, as the origin of the artist and the artwork, exists only in the actual work, the question of the nature of art becomes the question of the work-being of the work. The workly character of the artwork displays a 'pure self-subsistence'[2] and 'self-sufficient presence'.[3] This self-subsistence is the 'thingly' aspect of the work,[4] and all works, for Heidegger, have this thingly character.[5] Heidegger elucidates the thingly nature of the artwork by clarifying the Being of the thing. The thingly element of the thing is, accordingly, its independent and self-contained character – a thing is 'strange and uncommunicative' and 'refuses itself'.[6] A thing, for example a block of granite, is 'hard, heavy, extended, bulky, shapeless, rough, coloured, partly dull, partly shiny'.[7] The source of these modes of 'sensuous pressure' – being coloured, resonant, hard, massive – is the 'matter' in things.[8] This 'matter' of the thing is something in a 'definite, if unshapely, form' and this form in the thing 'appears to have taken shape by itself'.[9] In equipment, on the other hand, material is formed for the purposes of the serviceability and use of the entity and thus the arrangement of matter is controlled and determined beforehand. Equipmentality uses up the material of the being as the product of a process of 'making for…'. The work of art differs from equipment in that although it has been produced by human hand it, like the mere thing, is self-contained and in its form appears to have taken shape by itself.[10] Heidegger elucidates further the thingly character of the artwork:

> There is something stony in a work of architecture, wooden in carving, coloured in a painting... sonorous in a musical composition. The thingly element is so irremovably present in the artwork that we are compelled rather to say conversely that the architectural work is in stone, the carving is in wood, the painting in colour... the musical composition in sound.[11]

Nonetheless, the thingly matter of the artwork which appears to have taken shape by itself must be conceived, according to Heidegger, by way of the work-being of the work:

> When a work is created, brought forth out of this or that work-material – stone, wood, metal, colour... tone – ...it is made, set forth out of it. ... What is the nature of that in the work which is usually called the work material? Because it is determined by usefulness and serviceability, equipment takes into service that of which it consists: the matter....It disappears in usefulness. ... By contrast the temple work... does not cause the material to disappear, but rather causes it to come forth for the very first time. ... The rock comes to bear and rest and so first becomes rock; metals come to glitter and shimmer, colours to glow, tones to sing. ... All this comes forth as the work sets itself back into the massiveness and hardness of stone.[12]

The thingly element of the artwork exists as the glittering of metal, the shining of colour, the heaviness of stone. That is to say, it is through the sensuous perception of the matter that the distinctive thingly element of the work-being of the work comes forth. In *this* sense, the thingly aspect of the thing is *aistheton* – that which is perceptible by the senses belonging to empirical sensibility, i.e., what the senses of sight, hearing and touch convey in the sensations of colour, sound, roughness and hardness.[13] However, as Heidegger rightly points out, this notion of the sheer sensuous presence of the thing has degenerated into a conception of the thing as the 'unity of a perceptual manifold',[14] just as the notion of the thing as 'formed matter' is distorted in terms of equipmental production. Heidegger's self-appointed task – a point often neglected in the readings of the artwork essay – is to recover the 'defining power'[15] of the concepts of form and matter and to do this through an analysis of the thingly element of the work. The concepts form and matter are not therefore simply rejected: the intention is to reformulate and ground them in their proper domain. If the thingly element of the work is the sensuous presence of its materiality, a sensuousness that the work in a yet obscure way brings forth, Heidegger proceeds to give a further elucidation of this sensuousness, which connects it still further to the idea of a thing:

> A stone presses downward and manifests its heaviness... it denies us any penetration into it. If we attempt such a penetration by breaking open the rock.... the stone has instantly withdrawn again into the same dull pressure and bulk. If we try to lay hold of the stone's heaviness... by placing the stone on a balance... the weight's burden has escaped us. Colour shines and wants only to shine...It shows itself only when is remains undisclosed and unexplained. Earth thus shatters every attempt to penetrate into it.[16]

If the artwork, like the mere thing, is manifest in the sensuousness of the material form that appears to have taken shape by itself, its pure self-subsistence is grounded in the nature of the sensuousness of matter. Colour simply shines – and nothing more; the dull pressure of stone is heavy and massive – and nothing more. The work-being's materiality is experienced in this sheerly sensuous element. It cannot be explained, disclosed or penetrated any further. The sensuousness of the artwork discloses merely that it *is*. Like the thing, the artwork, showing itself only in the palpability of its sensuous existence, thereby *refuses* itself. Heidegger names the constitutive withdrawing, sensuous materiality of the work, *earth*. The earthy character of the artwork is its sensuous existence in matter:

> What looks like the thingly element... is, seen from the perspective of the work, its earthy character.[17]

As the shining of colour, the hardness of wood, the heaviness of stone, earth 'shatters every attempt to penetrate and understand it'. If earth 'shrinks from every disclosure and constantly keeps itself closed up'[18] and is 'continually self-secluding and to that extent sheltering and concealing',[19] this seclusion and self-withdrawal is grounded in the sheer, unintelligible sensuousness of its materiality.

Relatedly, another crucial aspect of the work-being of an artwork is that the work has been created: it is something worked out, brought about and effected. The thingly element – earth – enters into the work because it is, as matter, the medium out of which the work is created.[20] The making of equipment is also a bringing forth but equipment remains inconspicuous as something that has been explicitly created. On the other hand, in the artwork:

> Createdness is expressly created into the created being, so that it stands out from it, from the being thus brought forth... we must... experience the createdness explicitly in the work.[21]

Createdness is an essential part of the created artwork. The concept of createdness does not, however, mean the processes and circumstances of the genesis of the work or the activity of the artist. On the contrary, only when the ontic circumstances are unknown can the createdness of the work emerge into view. Createdness is experienced rather as the 'simple "*factum est*"': namely, 'that such a work *is* at all rather than is not'.[22] This is the '*that* it *is*' of createdness, the 'uniqueness of the fact that it *is* rather than is not'.[23] The 'that it is' of equipment disappears in usefulness because equipment uses up the material from which it is made. On the other hand, colour in a painting, for example, is not used up in the artwork but shines forth in the palpable opacity of its self-refusal. Colour simply shines: to perceive the shining of colour is merely to experience this shining or glowing in the sensuousness of its sheer material presence. If createdness stands forth from the artwork, the 'that it is' is perceived *in* and *through* the tangible ontic content of its thingly, earthy element. On the basis of an experience of the earth, the work is able to subsist in the unique, independent, self-contained and opaque Fact of its sheer existence.

Heidegger takes the analysis of the relation between the concepts of createdness and earth still further:

> The earth juts up within the work because the work exists as something in which truth is at work and because truth occurs only by installing itself within a particular being. In the earth, however, as essentially self-closing, the openness of the Open finds the greatest resistance (to the Open) and thereby the site of the Open's constant stand, where the figure must be fixed in place.[24]

The earth juts up within the work because truth occurs only by installing itself within *a particular being*. As the limit of a particular being, earth resists or refuses the Open of world: it is a site or place for truth to happen. The ontic Real returns at this point: the sensuous pressure of matter (earth) is the ontic resistance or actuality that refuses the ontological. As Heidegger puts it, creation is the bringing forth of 'a being such as never was before and never will come to be again', in such a way that the place of this unique being clears the openness of the Open:[25]

> Truth establishes itself in a being in such a way... that this being itself occupies the Open of truth. This occupying... can happen only if what is to be brought forth... entrusts itself to the self-secluding factor that juts up in the Open. The rift must set itself back into the heavy weight of stone, the dumb hardness of wood, the dark glow of colours. As the earth takes back the rift into itself, the rift *is* first set forth into the Open and thus placed, that is, set, within that which towers up into the Open as self-closing and sheltering. ... Createdness of the work means: truth's being fixed in place in the figure. Figure is the structure in whose shape the rift composes and submits itself... figure is to be thought in terms of the particular placing... as which the work occurs when its sets itself up and sets itself forth... artistic creation... is at all times a use of the earth in the fixing in place of truth in the figure.[26]

Earth is the place or site that clears the openness of the Open. The createdness of the 'that it is' of the artwork fixes truth in place insofar as its being-created rests in the already formed matter of the earthy sensuousness of the work. This thingly, sensuous element of the artwork comprises the work-being of the work insofar as the artwork is *a* particular being. As a unique, particular being the truth of the artwork is always singular; hence the open of Truth can only be *this* openness. Truth, as Heidegger remarks, does not subsist in itself only to descend among beings on occasion – it is essentially historical. This does not mean that art is simply an empirical happening within history, rather art originates and grounds history. In its historical manifestations art offers an understanding of what history actually *is*. In relation to the happening of truth in a being, Heidegger writes:

> Beings refuse themselves to us down to that one... feature which we touch upon most readily when we can say no more of beings than that they are. Concealment as refusal is... the beginning of the clearing of what is lighted.[27]

The concealing denial in truth – its un-truth as Heidegger puts it – is the self-refusal of a being, which conceals itself in the ontic resistance of the 'that it is' of its factical createdness. The sheer Fact of a created being, manifest in the palpable presence of a uniquely formed sensuous materiality, is, therefore, the untruth that fixes truth in place. Earth is the untruth upon which world (truth) depends. This opposition in truth is, according to Heidegger, the primal conflict. Indeed, as truth occurs *in* the artwork, the artwork *is* this primal conflict. The conflict is manifest in the artwork *as* the 'strife' between earth and world. World is the Open or Truth – the clearing of the decisions in the destiny of a historical people, the relations of birth, death, disaster and blessing that comprise the world, the possibilities of existence, of an authentic community. As the unconcealedness or truth of beings, world is, therefore, Being, i.e. the Nothing.[28] Being, i.e. the truth of existence, happens, Heidegger writes, only by establishing itself in a being. In the artwork this happening is described in terms of the strife between world (Being) and earth (a being). The artwork does not merely house this strife as a third party, somehow attached to, or containing, the strife. The work-being of the artwork is disclosive because, in its existence, it is both a being and Being, i.e. it *is* both ontic and ontological. The ontological truth of the artwork is in strife with its ontic un-truth. The untruth of the artwork is the sensuous pressure of its ontic materiality, which refuses to be penetrated by truth and which discloses the Fact that the work is, rather than is Nothing. As the element of a unique, already-formed sensuous existence, earth in the artwork is self-concealing ontic refusal. World is the presencing of the ontological. In the critical literature on *Origin of the Work of Art*, there is too little attention drawn to this simple yet crucial point: truth occurs in the artwork because the work-being of the work is a happening of the ontic-ontological difference.[29] The artwork *is* the ontic-ontological difference in the structure of its finite, truth-bearing existence. Indeed, this point is not explicitly drawn out even by Heidegger, except for a very brief but decisive remark in the 1956 Addendum to the essay, in which he admits that this is the case.[30]

Nevertheless, Heidegger argues, truth happens in the difference of the artwork insofar as there is a double concealment, denial or untruth in truth. Concealment of untruth prevails in the midst of beings in a twofold way. Beings dissemble; one being places itself in front of another being and presents itself as other than it is. As in *Being and Time*, the semblance of beings, for Heidegger, occurs *within* the clearing of the Open and is able to be a concealing only on the basis of the self-showing or unconcealing of Being. However, in *Origin of the Work of Art* there is yet another mode of concealing – refusal – in which a being is disclosed only to the extent that the Fact of its existence shines forth from it. On the one hand, the concealing untruth in truth follows *Being and Time,* in that both forms of denial are a concealing of beings; hence, untruth is restricted to ontic factical existence. Yet, on the other hand, the concealing-refusal of the earthy element of the artwork, as a uniquely formed ontic materiality, does not disappear in the happening of Truth but rather 'rises up as self-closing'.[31] The concealing of earth intensifies in the conflict with world and only thus can truth occur as a happening of the ontic-ontological difference. In regard to this refusal of earth, the decision projecting the unconcealedness of beings, i.e. world, Heidegger writes, 'bases itself on something not mastered, something concealed, confusing'.[32] It would appear that with the concept of earth in the artwork essay, an originary concealing in the advent of truth has been uncovered. With the notion of earth, the mastery of resolute Dasein, disclosing the transparent and explicitly appropriated truth of authentic existence, must therefore collapse and wither in the face of the unmasterable refusal of a self-closing, material sensuousness. Commentaries on *Origin of the Work of Art* often give this impression.[33]

However, contrary to these interpretations, the truth of the artwork in no significant sense goes beyond the elucidation of the nature of the truth of authentic existence in *Being and Time*. Dasein is disclosive in that it *is* existingly a happening of the ontic-ontological difference. Dasein is ontic in that it is a being which occurs in a world not of its own making, amidst beings whose Being is other than its own. Dasein is thrown into a world, inheriting and growing into certain factical possibilities of existence:

> ... every Dasein always exists factically. It is not a free floating self-projection; but its character is determined by thrownness as a Fact of the entity which it is; and, as so determined, it has in each case already been delivered over to existence.[34]

Nonetheless, Dasein is ontically distinguished in that it is a being for which, in its very Being, that Being is an issue for it. Dasein understands Being as the world into which it, as a factical being, has been thrown and to which it has been delivered over. Dasein, existing as Being-in-the-World, hence, is ontically distinctive in that it *is* ontological. Dasein has a pre-ontological or ontological understanding of the finite existentiality of the world that, as a thrown Fact, it is in. As existent, however, Dasein never comes back behind its thrownness:

> The Self, which as such has to lay the basis for itself can never get that basis into its power and yet, as existing, it must take over Being-a-basis.... Thus "Being-a-basis" means never to have power over one's ownmost Being from the ground up. This "not" belongs to the existential meaning of thrownness.[35]

Authentic Being-a-basis, projecting from the future back upon having-been, disclosing it as having-been in its ecstatic relation to the existentiality of primordially futural Being, nonetheless can never fully master, or have power over, the thrown basis. Thus finite, authentic Dasein, according to Heidegger, is not the basis of its Being. The meaning of the concept of authenticity, in *Being and Time*, thus contains within it an acknowledgment that the mastery of resoluteness has limits. The resistance of beings is metaphysically essential. For the most part, the Fact that Dasein is a factical thrown being is not experienced; it gets closed off.[36] On the other hand, in the transparency of authentic disclosure, Dasein comes face to face with itself *as* a thrown Fact whereby:

> ... the *"that it is"* has itself been disclosed to Dasein.[37]

In authentic state-of-mind Dasein comes 'face to face' with the *Fact* 'that it is' and that it has to be something with a potentiality for Being as the entity which it is.

Resolute Dasein does not banish the Fact of its thrown, factical existence. On the contrary, in coming face-to-face with the sheer Fact 'that-it-is', and so the *limits* of its disclosive power – the "not" of the thrown basis refusing Being-a-basis – Dasein encounters the explicit array of its ownmost possibilities of existence as a being 'in' the world. Thus 'as long as Dasein is, Dasein, as care, is constantly its 'that-it-is'.[38] Heidegger elucidates the authentic 'experience' of the 'that it is' in the following way:

> … mood brings Dasein before the 'that-it-is' of its "there" which, as such, stares it in the face with the inexorability of an enigma.[39]

Coming face to face with the Fact of its thrown existence is, for Dasein, to experience the enigma *'that* it *is'*. The 'that it is' is enigmatic because, Heidegger remarks, the 'why' of it is 'obscure and hidden'.[40] The 'that it is', manifest in the truth of authentic existence, hides from disclosure, concealing why it is, showing merely that Dasein is a factical, thrown being. The more transparent and intense the disclosive will, the more enigmatically the sheer Fact 'that-it-is' stares back. Enigmaticity is not only present in the truth of authentic existence but there is no truth without the factical untruth that Dasein is a being, already-there, thrown in the world. The already-there of Dasein, over which it can have no mastery, shows itself in the enigma *why* it *is* – and is not rather Nothing.

The concept of self-refusing earth in *Origin of the Work of Art*, which discloses *that* the artwork *is* and which *withdraws* from further explanation is, hence, a re-description rather than transformation of the enigmaticity of the 'that it is' of authentic Dasein in *Being and Time*. The same ontological concept of createdness is in operation. Just as the nature of sensuous existence withdraws from further explanation in the palpability of its self-closing presence, so too the 'why' of the *that* of Dasein is obscure and hidden. Similarly, just as the processes and circumstances of the ontic genesis of the artwork are *not* experienced in its created-being,[41] so too, when Dasein is brought authentically face-to-face with its thrownness, this thrownness, Heidegger writes, 'remains closed off from Dasein as regards the ontical whence and how of it'.[42] In the disclosive truth of both authentic Dasein and the artwork the ontic circumstances of their specific factical creation are irrelevant. Nonetheless, truth *is* only as it is established in a being – either Dasein or a work; in both cases the ontic untruth of the Fact of facticity appears as the self-concealing refusal in the face of which *there is* truth, i.e. an understanding of Being. Hence, the concept of earth develops the phenomenological experience of the 'that it is' in terms of the ontic sensuousness of the artwork. Createdness of the work is disclosed in the use made of the earth. The artwork essay therefore discloses the explicit and paradigmatic nature of the content received in the early analytic of finite transcendence: a sheer, unintelligible sensory presence.

Consequently, the already formed nature of the sensuous materiality, insofar as its has taken shape by itself, elucidates the phenomenological content of the already-there of the enigmatic Fact of authentic existence. Dasein is thrown *into* a world. Man is already-formed into the shape of certain possibilities of existence; this thrown form is the factical, finite boundary from which the Being of Dasein can begin its presencing. Earth as formed matter – the thingly aspect of the artwork – elucidates, therefore, the characteristic finitude of thrown, factical existence. Heidegger explicitly admits that this is the case in a note inserted into his personal copy of the Kantbook.[43] Both the truth of authentic existence and the truth of the artwork occur in a happening of the ontic-ontological difference in which Being encounters the self-concealing enigmaticity of the factical 'that it is' of a being. The price of displaying these underlying affinities between *Being and Time* and *Origin of the Work of Art*, however, appears to be an undermining of the previous claim that concealing is subordinated to revealing in Heidegger's early work.

In *Being and Time*, however, resolute Dasein comes face to face with the enigmaticity of its 'that-it-is' only from out of perceiving the Nothing of world. The "there" of thrown Dasein retreats and withdraws in the face of the temporal nihilating of the now of the moment of vision. If an explanation of the Fact of existence conceals itself, this concealment is a concealing *from* the disclosive existentiality of Dasein. The resistance of ontic actuality appears *as* refusal only in the authentic present of the Situation released from the exchange of future and past possibility. The facticity of Dasein is enigmatic *for* its understanding of Being. The resistance of earth in the artwork is determined in exactly the same way. The createdness of an artwork requires preservers in order to be experienced as created:

> ...it is only for such preserving that the work yields itself in its createdness as actual, i.e. now: present in the manner of a work.[44]

The createdness of the "that it is" of an artwork is actual, as a site that fixes truth in place, only as it is present in the manner of a work in the authentic 'now' of preserving. Thus Heidegger concludes that what is created cannot itself come into being without those who preserve it.[45] Yet preserving or 'knowing', for Heidegger, is essentially a 'willing' and this willing itself a 'being-resolved'[46] – the resolute 'poetic' projection of the preservers of the artwork freely bestows world. The authentic poets disclose from out of a futural anticipation of historical destiny, the thrown ground into which human being as historical is already cast.[47] The 'now' of the created artwork is thereby released and the factical necessity of the withheld vocation of the historical being of man, the truth of existence, is revealed:

> Genuinely poetic projection is the opening up or disclosure of that into which human being as historical is already cast. This is the earth and, for a historical people, its earth, the self-closing ground on which it rests together with everything that already is, though still hidden from itself. It is, however, its world which prevails in virtue of the relation of human being to the unconcealedness of Being... everything with which man is endowed must, in projection, be drawn up from the closed ground and expressly set upon this ground. In this way the ground is first grounded as the bearing ground.[48]

The site of the artwork whereby truth happens, as a now or authentic Present released from the exchange between future and having-been, manifests exactly the same structural being as the now of the present Situation in *Being and Time*. It is released from the spontaneity of a resolute, temporal acting and received as factically necessary. The earth is the factical Situation into which Dasein, as a thrown being, is already cast. Nonetheless, world or Being prevails in relation to facticity because the thrown ground is grounded as ground only from out of world, as a definite array of possibilities of existence explicitly disclosed by the Saying of the preservers. The preservers of the work are *not* dependent upon the artwork and neither is the allegedly autonomous artwork in *Origin of the Work of Art* 'community-creating'.[49] On the contrary, the being of the work is dependent upon the Saying of the preservers: the world 'worlds' in strife with factical earth, according to Heidegger, only on the basis of their resolute willing. This poetic Saying discloses the historical paths of factical existence in a communal world, just as resolute Dasein projects the destiny of a historical people in the fateful appropriation of the factical possibilities of the truth of existence. Heidegger declares intention to dismantle the modern subjectivism of philosophy of art and aesthetics. This prejudice is allegedly manifest in the idea of the creativity of the 'self-sovereign subject's performance of genius'.[50] However, contrary to Heidegger's explicit intention, the concept of the preservers merely re-locates this subjectivism in the community-creating resolute willing of the authentic poets. The truth of the artwork, as with the earlier conception of authentic existence, does not originate from beyond humanity, i.e. from the ontological exteriority of Being. Unlike the 'it' giving Being in the *Ereignis*, the concealing in *Origin of the Work of Art* is a self-concealing manifest only as the ontic, factical refusal of the thrown being of the work. This self-concealing present actuality can only be disclosed *as* enigmatic in the face of our nihilating possibility, i.e. the self-showing poetic understanding of Being.

However, although, in order to let truth happen, the work-being of the work establishes a site for the ontic-ontological difference, i.e. for the strife between world (Being) and earth (being) and *is* that site existingly, Heidegger extends, still further, the scope of the meaning of the concept of earth:

> The earth is the spontaneous forthcoming of that which is continually self-secluding and to that extent sheltering and concealing.... The opposition of world and earth is a striving.... . In essential striving... the opponents raise each other into the self-assertion of their natures.... . In the struggle each opponent carries the other beyond itself.[51]

Earth thus is here a spontaneous forthcoming that strives with world from out of the originality of its own self-concealing nature. Yet to describe earth as spontaneous is to determine it as a form of transcendental or ontological activity. However, earth in *Origin of the Work of Art* also means the sensuous materiality of a factical, thrown work. Clearly, the brute, factical being of a work cannot be the source of a spontaneous or active giving. How can a *gift* be received from the simple shining of sensuously perceived matter? The 'that it is' of facticity discloses Dasein or the work as thrown, but the enigmaticity of ontic refusal is not the self-refusal of ontological gift-giving. *There is* the sensuousness of materiality in the face of the Nothing, from out of whose nihilating, the fact of the work *is*. Earth cannot be determined as a self-concealing ontological giving. If it does mean this, it is no longer factical. Heidegger continues:

> The self-seclusion of earth... is not a uniform, inflexible staying under cover, but unfolds itself in an inexhaustible variety of simple modes and shapes... the sculptor uses stone... the painter... uses... colour.[52]

Earth 'as a whole' is now described as the source for the various modes of sensuous existence in truth-bearing artworks. Yet this generates a problem. The origin of the sensuous, thingly element of the work is, paradoxically, both a mode of earth as a whole and an ontic actuality disclosed by nullity of world. On the one hand, following *Being and Time*, Being discloses the factical 'that it is' of createdness from out of the Nothing. On the other hand earth as a whole brings the thingly element forth. It cannot be both. The move from earth as an ontic, sensuous, factical refusal to the spontaneity of an ontological self-concealing appears untenable. That this is the site of a tremendous difficulty in Heidegger's artwork essay has not been raised in an ontologically precise way in the interpretations of *Origin of the Work of Art*. Self-secluding earth as a whole is a form of ontological activity; it is in strife with world. Yet, as an apparent striving within the ontological itself, the distinctions between world/earth, truth/untruth and Being/being no longer possess the same essential content. The idea of earth as a whole introduces an untruth into Being itself. Therefore, Being can no longer mean the 'unconcealedness of what is'. Yet, as Heidegger writes in *Origin of the Work of Art*, Being *is* the Nothing of the world of men, the existential truth or unconcealedness of beings. Truth (Being) is also untruth because Being must establish itself in a being. Untruth on the other hand is the facticity of inauthentic dissembling or authentic refusal. In this regard, as a site for the happening of truth, the artwork does not house or contain the strife between earth and world: it *is* that strife. Indeed, the difference between the sensuous material being of the work and the Nothing of world starts the strife.[53] The sensuous materiality of the earth disclosed in and through the work-being of the work must therefore be the originary ground for the meaning of the concept of earth. As Heidegger writes, it is from the earthy character of the work itself that the concept of earth 'as such' and things of the earth, come-to-be.[54] Hence earth, disclosed qua earth *in* and *through* the work, cannot be simultaneously grounded in the concept of earth 'as a whole' that is external to the work and that *gives* earthy material *to* the singular truth-bearing artwork. This move, attempted by Heidegger, appears phenomenologically suspect and methodologically unsound.

There are more problems. The instability of the concept of earth is further demonstrated in yet another meaning of earth that emerges from *Origin of the Work of Art*. Earth, as a 'silent call', is manifest, according to Heidegger, in the 'quiet gift of the ripening grain and its unexplained self-refusal in the fallow desolation of the wintery field'.[55] Earth, in *this* sense, is the sheltering agent of *phusis* or nature.[56] *Phusis* is the emerging and rising in all things, the growing and sprouting of tree and grass, eagle and bull, snake and cricket, whilst earth is 'that whence the arising brings back and shelters everything that arises without violation' – the soil of the peasant woman, for example.[57] That this is a different use of the concept of earth is clear. Earth is no longer the sensuous materiality of the colour of the painting but rather an element of the world of the peasant that is disclosed and finds a site *in* the painting. As an element *in* the world, alongside nature, the sky and divinities,[58] earth is also not, nor could it ever be, a form of transcendental activity in strife *with* world. Hence there is a threefold meaning of earth in *Origin of the Work of Art*, with each use of the concept both distinctive and ontologically incompatible with the others. Although Heidegger's artwork essay does not elaborate upon this third meaning of earth as a sheltering agent, there is further explication in other writings of the same period. Thus, Heidegger writes in *On the Essence and Concept of phusis in Aristotle's Physics B 1* (1939) that whereas artefacts, made things, require a *techne* for their *eidos* to be placed in a form, and so to appear, natural things place themselves into the appearance. The *eidos* of the being of nature brings itself into presencing and so generates itself. A plant, for example, instantiates itself into a particular form, such as leaves, in which and out of which other forms – blossom and fruit – are generated. Hence for Heidegger, *phusis* – the Being of natural beings – is the incessant 'being-on-the-way' of a 'not-yet' to a 'no-more' and this coming to presence and going away out of presence, Being as emergent appearing and not-Being as absence, is the becoming that constitutes the Being of *phusis*:[59]

> *Phusis*... the presencing of the absencing of itself, one that is on-the-way-from-itself and unto itself. As such an absencing, *phusis* remains a going-back-into-itself but this going back is only the going of a going forth.[60]

The absence or sheltering in the becoming of *phusis* is its 'going-back-into-itself' which goes back insofar as the Being of *phusis* is a going forth or presencing. For example, when the fruit comes to appearance on the plant, then the blossom is put away by the fruit, but the blossom, according to Heidegger, does not thereby disappear into an inconsequential nothingness. In the coming-to-be of the fruit, the absence of the blossom reveals itself. As a becoming shot through with the not-Being of the no longer now and not yet, *phusis,* in sprouting, emerging and arising out of itself is also a going-back-into-itself. The presencing of the present form is always the putting away or absencing of what went before and the anticipation of what-is-to-come. As such, according to Heidegger, every living thing in coming to life already begins to die and to retreat back into its seed as the source of life and death:

> ...while the plant sprouts, emerges and expands into the open, it simultaneously goes back into its roots, insofar as it plants them firmly in the closed ground and thus takes its stand. The act of self-unfolding emergence is inherently a going-back-into-itself.[61]

This closed ground is the sheltering agent of *phusis*, the whence of its going-back-into-itself: earth. However, the not-Being of earth, in the Being of *phusis*, *is* only in the presencing of this absence of not-Being. The not-Being in becoming is the presencing of a 'no longer now' or 'not yet now' and so merely the 'absence' of a non-present presence. Absence or 'earth', as the sheltering agent in *phusis*, is a mode of originary presencing, constituting the ever-decaying dissipation of the incessant welling up of Being. *Phusis* goes back into itself *as* earth only insofar as it is a self-productive, ceaseless bringing-forth of itself. Indeed, given that *phusis* is an element of world and world worlds, as Heidegger puts it, in Being, i.e. the presencing of the unconcealedness of what is, if earth is the absence of a sheltering in *phusis*, then it is necessarily derivative in relation to the presencing of self-showing Being.

Nonetheless, in regard to the ambiguous and threefold use of the concept of earth in *Origin of the Work of Art*, it is the third and final meaning which emerges as decisive in the later part of the corpus. With the work on poetry, dwelling and thinking, the concept of world in the artwork essay is further determined as the fourfold of sky and earth, divinities and mortals. Earth, as an essential element of the presencing of the fourfold, is thereby taken up into Being. Earth is described as follows:

> Earth is the serving bearer, blossoming and fruiting, spreading out in rock and water, rising up into plant and animal.[62]

Clearly a significant change has occurred in the content of the concept of earth. If earth is neither ontological spontaneity nor material sensuousness, it is with the idea of the fourfold not even conceived as a mere sheltering agent for *phusis*. The concealing character of earth has been entirely eradicated. Indeed, if earth is used to name one of the four of the fourfold, as a rising up, blossoming and spreading out, in all but name it has been utterly transformed into *phusis*. In the neutralising of the content of earth as a self-concealing, the general tendency of the corpus to found the concept of concealing in self-showing is made manifest.

By locating earth in the fourfold, Heidegger thus recoils before the unthought idea of ontological concealing. Yet, in the *Origin of the Work of Art*, Heidegger explicitly introduces – in the idea of the spontaneity of self-giving, concealing earth – that before which he recoils. The question of the innermost meaning of the problem of earth in the artwork essay, in *this* sense, remains unclarified and unanswered. However, though the problem *Origin of the Work of Art* generates cannot be resolved within the parameters of the essay itself, its origin and nature can be explained. To explain the duplication of the concept of earth is to understand further the nature of what is known as Heidegger's turn from the early to the later work. Earth, as sensuous materiality, is the factical, thrown ground of the work. As factical, earth is manifest in the Fact that the work *is*, and is not rather Nothing. As with the factical basis of authentic Dasein, this Fact of createdness is enigmatic.

On the other hand, earth as self-concealing giving is conceived as external to world, i.e. our understanding of Being. This resistance is not the resistance of ontic matter but of Being itself. Earth is not given: 'it gives'. The fundamental problem of earth in the artwork essay is the question of the manner, justification and nature of this becoming-ontological of ontic earth. The content of sensuous

materiality cannot be determined in such a way as to reach ontological activity. A break in the web of the text is required. This break, in fact, is what is called the 'turn' in Heidegger. Heidegger elaborates upon the meaning of the 'turn' in his *Letter on Humanism*:

> As ek-sisting, the human being sustains Da-sein in that he takes the *Da*, the clearing of being, into "care". But Da-sein itself occurs essentially as 'thrown'. It unfolds essentially in the throw of being as a destinal sending…. The human being is… "thrown" by being itself into the truth of being… Being is cleared for the human being in ecstatic projection. But this projection does not create being… the projection is essentially a thrown projection. What throws in such projection is not the human being but being itself, which sends the human being into the ek-sistence of Dasein that is his essence.[63]

In the turn, 'everything is reversed'.[64] The nature of this reversal is clear. In *Being and Time*, Dasein is a thrown projection insofar as it is both a factical being thrown in a world and understands this world in a temporal projecting of Being. Dasein understands itself as thrown in the having been of temporal worldhood and comes to itself *qua* thrown Being-a-basis from out of this disclosive projection. After the 'turn' the thrownness of factical being is reversed into the throwing of Being. This throwing gives the projecting of Dasein. There is reversal of the whole in that the structural relation in thrown projection is inverted. Rather than the Being of projecting disclosing our thrown, factical being, the throwing of Being *gives* the projecting of the human being. However, this inversion is not merely a simple flipping over. In 'turning' thrownness into throwing, the nature of factical, ontic being in-itself is taken up into Being, i.e. the ontological. Our thrownness is *activated*. The 'it gives' of temporal projection is reversed into the 'it gives' or 'it throws' of Being. The throw of Being gives the human being's understanding of Being: ontic *givenness* (thrownness) is reversed into ontological *giving* (throwing). The 'turn' is a step back into the truth of Being because the reversal 'turns' the question of the ontic-ontological difference into the question of the difference in Being *qua* Being. Being is no longer the Nothing of world *for* beings; as throwing, 'it gives' the gift of meaning or understanding. As such, the ontic-ontological difference is taken up into the fundamental difference *within* Being itself, as the immanent relation between Being and the Being of man. This relation constitutes the *Ereignis*.

The meaning of the duplication of earth in *Origin of the Work of Art* is now clear.[65] The elucidation of earth as sensuous materiality and as a non-sensuous, spontaneous self-concealing manifests in the unfolding of the essay itself not an already completed turn in Heidegger, but rather an attempt at turning. In the becoming-ontological of ontic earth, the very movement of the turning is evident. Sensuously given ontic earth is activated and animated as a spontaneous ontological giving. Nonetheless, the turning in the essay fails; it is not completed. This is because Heidegger does not properly determine the relation between the ontological gift-giving of earth and the preserver's understanding of world. This is not just an error or oversight on Heidegger's part. On the contrary, if earth *is* an ontological resistance, the entire apparatus of the early work is called into question. However, this apparatus – including the ontic-ontological difference – fatally pervades the very fibres of the artwork essay itself: *Origin of the Work of Art* is a ladder that must be thrown away. The ultimate result of the conceptual ambiguity within the Heideggerian text is a neutralisation of the radicality of earth by locating it within the fourfold conception of world. However, despite this retrograde step, in the later ontology of language the underlying affinity between distance and the spontaneity of ontological concealing manages once again to force itself to the surface of the corpus.

PART III
THE RHYTHM OF LANGUAGE AND
THE MEANING OF BEING

Chapter 6

The 'Speaking' of Language

The question 'what is man?' is further determined as the question of the possibility and nature of finite, pure receptivity. However, the idea of *a priori* ontological sensibility appears to entail that the finite subject both gives and receives Being independently of all empirical experience. This generates an antinomy: Being must arise and must not arise from the finitude of man. Early Heidegger attempts to resolve the aporia with the idea of the pure self-affection of Dasein. As has been demonstrated, this attempt fails; the idea of *a priori* ontological sensibility is contaminated by the intuition of ontic content. The antinomy appears intractable because the finite subject appears, necessarily, to have to give and not to give Being. In a Kantian register, the concept of the subject has the same meaning in the two conflicting judgements, yet two opposed predicates are asserted of it.

Later Heidegger, however, rather than addressing the antinomy on its own terms, re-casts the ontological concept of the finite subject that underpins and sustains it. This reformulation of the concept of the subject involves an existential elucidation of the primordial distance that constitutes the subjectivity of the self. Though Heidegger leaves the idea of spatial distance unthought, prioritising temporality in the analytic of Dasein, nonetheless the glimmer of an awareness of the radicality of the idea of distance bubbles to the surface in the late work on the *Ereignis*. Here the experience of distance is grounded in an intimate relation to the idea of concealing. The 'it' of the 'it gives' expropriates itself in the giving of distance. Distance is, consequently, experienced as an unfathomable depth or abyss. This inner depth manifests itself phenomenologically in the sublime feeling of intensity. The 'turn' in the nature of Being is evident most clearly in Heidegger's artwork essay: here there is an abortive attempt to invert the care-structure of existence. The meaning of earth, conceived as thrown factical ground, is reversed into the throwing of Being, i.e. ontological gift-giving. The sheer refusal of sensuous matter is elevated into the spontaneous self-concealing gift of Being. Man is not the 'it' giving Being to itself and receiving beings within this self-given horizon; the human being receives the 'it' giving Being – beings are experienced, after the 'turn', as a gift to man *from* the depths of Being.

Heidegger's re-casting of the notion of human finitude takes shape, therefore, through the introduction of an ontological distinction between the human being and Being in itself. The human being is not exclusively and simply the being that is ontic in that it *is* ontological. Rather after the 'turn' in Heidegger, the ontic-ontological difference that constitutes human finitude is taken up into, and repeated within, the ontological itself. A threefold relation thus arises between Being in itself, the Being of the human being, and beings. However, the nature of Being, as well as the way in which the human being experiences the gift that 'it gives', require greater phenomenological elucidation.

Fortunately, Heidegger explicitly points out the direction such an elucidation must take: a concrete interpretation of the *Ereignis* must determine what language *is* and the way in which Language gives:

> Saying, which resides in Appropriation, is *qua* showing, the most appropriate mode of appropriating.... . Saying is the mode in which Appropriation speaks.[1]

The *Ereignis*, the Event of Being, is manifest in what Heidegger calls the Saying or 'speaking' of language; saying is the most appropriate way in which Being gives. In order to understand the 'it gives' we must understand the way in which language 'speaks':

> To reflect on language thus demands that we enter into the speaking of language in order to take up our stay with language, i.e. within *its* speaking, not within our own. Only in that way do we arrive at the region within which it may happen... that language will call to us from there and grant us its nature.[2]

> Language speaks. If we let ourselves fall into the abyss denoted by this sentence... we fall upward, to a height. Its loftiness opens up a depth... to reflect on language means – to reach the speaking of language in such a way that this speaking takes place as that which grants an abode for the being of mortals.[3]

Human language does not, according to Heidegger, belong to us primarily as a tool for the communication and expression of inner thoughts and feelings. Rather, language gives to the human being from out of the fullness of an inner and intrinsic principle of life: it 'speaks' to us.[4] The 'speaking' of language to man is the way in which the truth of Being *is*. Though at first glance an odd expression, the idea of phenomena 'speaking' is not uncommon in philosophical discourse or in ordinary language. The idea is especially common in the field of art, though it is not restricted to it. Wittgenstein describes the way in which 'music speaks'[5] and uses this description to highlight the way in which music, rather than conveying particular emotions or feelings, 'conveys to us itself'.[6] Merleau-Ponty cites the experience of the artist Marchand, following Klee, as, in a moment of inspiration, feeling that the trees were 'speaking'.[7] Similar descriptions can also be found in the completely different ontic region of man's sporting existence.[8] All of these uses of the idea of the 'speaking' of entities involve the experience of beings that ordinarily appear either inanimate or at the very least lack the kind of animate life required for speech. Of course, Heidegger's conception of the 'speaking' of language does not refer to a certain kind of entity or specific region of beings, but to the speaking of Being itself. Meaning 'speaks' to us. Our understanding of Being is not a dead thing, a given, inanimate tool restricted to the purposes and needs of our material and pragmatic existence. Linguistic content possesses its *own* life.

However, given that the concept of the *Ereignis* is grounded in ontological self-concealing it is to be expected that the human being's reception of the 'speaking' of language also involves an element of withdrawal. Heidegger writes:

> Language, Saying of the world's fourfold... is, as world-moving Saying, the relation of all relations. It relates, maintains, proffers and enriches the face-to-face encounter of the world's regions, holds them and keeps them, in that it holds itself – Saying – in reserve. Reserving itself in this way, as Saying of the world's fourfold, language concerns us, us who as mortals belong within this fourfold world, us who can speak only as we respond to language.[9]

The 'speaking' of language is the giving that determines the fouring of the fourfold world, i.e. mortals, divinities, earth and sky. Language gives world, i.e. the human being's understanding of Being. Yet as giving, it is not exhausted in the nearness of the mutual presencing of the four regions. On the contrary, in the act of giving, language, Heidegger writes, holds itself in reserve. Concealing itself in the giving, language is therefore an existence exterior to the world it gives. As such, it is, for Heidegger, the 'relation of all relations': the originary relation of the expropriative self-concealing 'it' in the appropriative giving of the *Ereignis*. The expropriative nature of language is a self-withdrawing in 'speaking', i.e. that 'which must remain wholly unspoken, is held back as the unsaid, abides in concealment as unshowable, is mystery'.[10] Man speaks insofar as man receives, and responds to, the self-concealing 'speaking' of language, i.e. the inner, autonomous life of ontological content. In this regard, Heidegger, following Hamann, writes:

> ... is language itself the abyss? We speak of an abyss where the ground falls away and a ground is lacking to us... the sentence 'language is language' leaves us to hover over an abyss as long as we endure what is says.[11]

To endure the gift of language is to hover over the abyss of its groundless nature: as a self-concealing 'speaking', language opens up a depth within the soul of man. Nonetheless, it still remains unclear how the phenomenon of the 'speaking' of language is connected to the intrinsic self-concealing of Being. How can the autonomous life of the ontological content constituting the articulated totality of a linguistic community be experienced as withdrawing in giving its gift? Merely to assert that language is an abyss is in itself phenomenologically inadequate. However, following a familiar pattern, Heidegger recoils before this question as if before the elemental force of an animating unthought. The question of the expropriative, reserved source of the movement of Showing-Saying is, he writes, 'too premature' and 'asks too much'.[12]

The gift of language is not offered by a giver disclosing determinate content or information to man. To experience the 'speaking' of language is not to receive the revelation of a positive datum. Language is not: it is nothing that *is*. Rather, language, according to Heidegger, comes to be in the self-giving or holding sway of movement. This movement is what Heidegger calls the 'way' of language.[13] However, this movement of language is not arbitrary or haphazard. The giving of Being orders and binds ('appropriates') man in its giving: it has the force of necessity. Hence the movement by which language 'speaks' possesses within itself an essential element of necessity or purpose. A movement is purposeful if it appears to follow rules. A movement without purposefulness or rules is meaningless. There is no possibility of meaning in pure movement aside from the form and manner of the moving itself. Hence, a purposeful movement is a meaningful movement that manifests its meaning in an order that governs the way in which it moves. A movement that exhibits order is rhythmic. The idea of rhythm discloses the being of purposeful motion.

Rhythm, from the Latin *rhythmus* means symmetry or harmony and is derived from the Greek *rhythmos* defined as measure, shape, form or proportion. Rhythm gives purposefulness to the Being of movement, allowing the experience of movement to take on the appearance of meaningfulness. As Schelling rightly points out:

> ... in general, rhythm is viewed as the transformation of an essentially meaningless succession into a meaningful one. Succession or sequence purely as such possess the character of chance. The transformation of the accidental nature of a sequence into necessity = rhythm.[14]

The meaningfulness or purposeful character of movement exhibits a necessity in the order and relations that comprise this movement. Mere temporal succession, for example, is not rhythmic: only when beat and measure enter into and take over time-relations can we speak of a necessity in temporal unfolding. So too, in the 'speaking' of language, rhythm is the necessity or purposefulness that links the items, within a linguistic whole, of articulated ontological content. These items are, for the most part, words. Hence, the meaning of Being in the *Ereignis* is made concrete, it would appear, as the human being's immanent reception of the rhythm of language. At no time does Heidegger, recoiling before the question of the hidden source of the 'speaking' of language, explicitly elucidate and so make ontologically concrete the 'it' of the 'it gives' in terms of the concept of rhythm. Nonetheless, in a late seminar on Heraclitus, he makes the following remark:

> HEIDEGGER: In connection with what has been said concerning language, I would like to refer to the lecture 'Language as Rhythm' by Georgiades... he has spoken excellently about language. Among other things, he asks about rhythm and shows that rhythm has nothing to do with flow, but is to be understood as imprint. In recourse to Jaeger he appeals to a verse of Archilochus... "Recognise which rhythm holds men"... he cites a passage from Aeschylus' Prometheus "...in this rhythm I am bound". He, who is held immobile in the iron chains of his confinement, is "rhythmed", that is, joined. Georgiades points out that humans do not make rhythm; rather, for the Greeks, the rhythmos is the substrate of language, namely the language that approaches us. Georgiades understands the archaic language in this way. We must also have the old language of the fifth century in view in order to approximate understanding of Heraclitus. This language knows

no sentences… in the sentences of the archaic language, the state of affairs speaks, not the conceptual meaning.[15]

Rhythm is the ground or substrate of language. The rhythm of language approaches man and gives him his understanding of Being. Language is not made by man: as rhythm it is the form, measure or imprint which holds and orders man in its 'speaking', binding man to the giving of the 'it gives'. If Heidegger does not pursue the question of the rhythm of language in the seminar, nonetheless there is a further reference to the concept of rhythm in the lecture *Words*:

> Rhythm, rhythmos, is not flux or flowing but form… rhythm is what is at rest, what forms the movement of dance and song, and thus lets it rest within itself. Rhythm bestows rest.[16]

The 'speaking' of language is the giving of itself as movement. This self-moving is the 'way' of language. Rhythm is the *form* of movement. Form or imprint is the gathering of movement that allows it to rest within itself as a purposive self-moving. The linguist Benveniste corroborates Heidegger's observation in the Heraclitus seminar.[17] Benveniste demonstrates that although the word *rhythmos* is absent from the Homeric poems, it can be found in the Ionian authors and, as Heidegger also notes, in lyric and tragic poetry. Within the vocabulary of ancient Ionian philosophy, in particular Democritus, *rhythmos*, Benveniste argues, is a technical term that is used to specify a mode of the differentiation of things. There are three modes of differentiation – rhythm (form), inter-contact (order) and turning (position). Aristotle in his *Metaphysics* illustrates Democritus' point by applying these modes to the form, order and position of the letters of the alphabet. In Democritus, Benveniste similarly remarks, water and air differ from each other because of the form or rhythm that their constituent atoms take. In the contemporary Ionian prose of Heroditus, *rhythmos* is also used to denote form. Benveniste also demonstrates that the idea of rhythm as the distinctive form of human character, disposition and mood can be found in the lyric poetry of the early seventh century – in Archilochus, Anacreon, Theognis and Theocritus. So too in the tragedy of Aeschylus, Sophocles and Euripides, *rhythmos* is used to denote form, proportioned figure and arrangement. Finally, Benveniste suggest that Plato modifies his inheritance of the antique idea of *rhythmos* by converting the dominant notion of spatial form into the temporal notion of a numerically regulated measure. Rhythm is, after Plato, the order and form of temporal movement initially made by the human being in dance, but then applied to any continuous activity broken by metre into alternating intervals.[18]

However, what Benveniste does not mention, but which is implied in Heidegger's remarks, is that when rhythm is used to refer to the temper or disposition of a person in early lyric poetry, the idea is that rhythm or measure binds and grips the human being.[19] The form and order by which a person is rhythmed is to an extent out of their control. We do not give ourselves a certain temperament, rather a disposition sweeps over us – the origin of this temper lies beyond man. Plato, following this antique tradition, writes that the experience of rhythm is a divine gift and that the whole of human life has need of rhythm.[20] Similarly, in the *Republic*, Plato suggests that an early experience of musical rhythm helps cultivate a feeling of harmony within the soul of the guardians. However, in Plato a subtle shift appears to occur in the conception of rhythm. The human being is no longer rhythmed by an exterior and mysterious force: rather rhythm either in music or poetry must follow and conform to the spoken words, whilst the words themselves originate from the character of the speaker's soul.[21] Hence, for the Pre-Platonic thinkers and poets, the character or disposition of a person is a gift of rhythm, the human being is 'rhythmed'. In Plato on the other hand, the relation appears reversed. Character, i.e. intellectual virtue, gives rhythm. The good man gives himself the order and rhythm of his disposition. Correlatively, the idea of aesthetic harmony and rhythm disappears in the education of the philosopher-king: philosophical dialectic appears without intrinsic rhythm. Indeed, whether without an aesthetic intuition of rhythm the dialectician is able to perceive what Plato in the *Symposium* calls the ultimate *beauty* of the *logos* is questionable.

Nonetheless, by the time of Aristotle the idea of rhythm is largely restricted to the *numerus* or order of prose and verse composition. In *On Rhetoric*, Aristotle argues that the form of language must be rhythmical. If language is simply metrical it is monotonous; if it is devoid of rhythm it is unlimited, vague and unsatisfactory. Language, Aristotle writes, must have some limitation of boundary and rhythm gives it this. On the other hand, breaking the content of the concept of rhythm from out of its increasingly narrowly defined sphere, Augustine's *De Musica* takes up and reinvigorates the antique meditation on rhythm. According to Augustine, performing rhythm in the existential ease of bodily movement, such as walking and singing, and in the performance of perceptive rhythm in artistic craftsmanship cultivates a desire to become like and identify with the rhythm of *logos*; the rhythm of the divine, cosmic *carmen*.[22] This Augustinian metaphysics of Beauty, coalescing around the concept of rhythm, is the pitch and consummate jointure of the Greek traditions of Pythagorean proportion and NeoPlatonic *eros*. The rhythm of the *cosmos* stretches from the ease of bodily movement, to perceptible reason, to an unhearable, ineffable rhythm of the spheres. As both a principle of order and erotic delight, this experience of divine rhythm is quenched and inflamed in the fires of Christian faith.

However, it was not until the much later aesthetic tradition in German thought, stretching from Hamann and Schiller, through Schlegel and Novalis, to Humboldt, that the specific ontological relation between the phenomenon of language and the idea of rhythm is addressed. Though this tradition is the fertile soil from out of which Heidegger's own work emerges, he often fails to admit the extent of his debt to it. For example, Heidegger describes Humboldt's work as, on the one hand, continuously stimulating and yet, on the other hand, he relegates it to contemporary Leibnizian metaphysics. Heidegger argues that Humboldt's conception of *energeia* means, essentially, the activity of the subject.[23] This remark, however, does not do justice to the range and penetrating power of Humboldt's work on language. Indeed, according to Humboldt, far from arising from the subject:

> Language... arises from a depth of human nature, which everywhere forbids us to regard it as a true product and creation of peoples. It possesses an autonomy that visibly declares itself to us, though inexplicable in its nature and, seen from this aspect, is no production of activity but an involuntary emanation of the mind, no work of nations but a gift fallen to them by their inner destiny.[24]

> The *bringing forth of language* is an *inner need* of human beings, not merely an external necessity for maintaining communal intercourse but a thing lying in their own nature, indispensable for the development of their mental power and the attainment of a world-view.[25]

Language, for Humboldt, arises in autonomy solely from itself, its inner life principle does not proceed teleologically toward a set goal, but from an unfathomable cause.[26] There is an ineliminable 'dark unrevealed depth'[27] in language; it is a 'fathomless abyss'.[28] Beauty, rather than being a civilised ornamentation, perfects the essence of language. It results from the entwining of the rhythm of sound with the logical eurhythmy of thought.[29] Language-production, hence, tends towards rhythm; rhythm or 'regulated freedom' is the innermost and essential form of language.[30] Humboldt's conception of rhythm therefore extends over both the sensuous and non-sensuous realms of existence. The sensuous essence of languages resides in sound:

> If language, by its origin from the depths of man's nature, did not also enter into true and authentic combination with physical descent why... would the native tongue possess a strength and intimacy so much greater than any foreign one... This obviously [depends on] the very thing that is least explicable and most individual, its sound.[31]

Sound and tone comprise the 'musical element' of language.[32] Heidegger offers a remarkably similar judgement:

> It is much more important to consider whether, in any of the ways of looking at the structure of language we have mentioned, the physical element of language, its vocal and written character, is being adequately experienced.... Vocalisation and sounds may no doubt be explained physiologically as a production of sounds. But the question remains whether the real nature of the sounds and tones of speech is thus ever experienced and kept before our eyes. We are instead referred to melody and rhythm in language and thus to the kinship between song and speech.... It is just as much a property of language to sound and ring and vibrate, to hover and tremble, as it is for the spoken words of language to carry a meaning... we Germans call the different manners of speaking in different sections of the country modes of mouth.... These differences do not primarily grow out of different movement patterns of the organs of speech. The landscape, and that means the earth, speaks in them, differently each time... body and mouth are part of the earth's flow and growth in which we mortals flourish and from which we receive the soundness of our roots.[33]

Both Humboldt and Heidegger suggest that the sound of the words constituting the totality of a language are an essential element in its existence. However, the individuating tendency of a particular sound-pattern is something that resists scientific-physiological analysis. Conceived as earth, ontic sound and tone are, both thinkers agree, ultimately inexplicable. However, Humboldt also extends his analysis of the idea of rhythm to the non-sensuous existence of language. This existence is the spirit of a language, the living breath that animates it.[34] Here Humboldt is clearly following Kant's *Critique of Judgement*, in which poetic genius is said to require both the freedom of spirit or *Geist* and, in an implicit criticism of *Sturm und Drang* aesthetics, the constraint of the correctness, richness and metre of language. These latter elements – grammar, tone and rhythm – comprise what Kant calls the body of the poetic work.[35] So too, for Humboldt, sound, as well as the grammar and rules of a linguistic tradition, constrain the mental substance or spirit of language. Language-production is as much a re-shaping of what is already-there, as it is a creating *ex nihilo*.[36]

Nonetheless, non-sensuous spirit also manifests a kind of rhythm – 'logical eurhythmy' – that involves an order and force in the arrangement and system of pure thoughts. Heidegger, on the other hand, fixated as he is on poetry and perhaps aware of the shadow of Hegel, does not offer an analysis of the correlative idea of non-sensuous rhythm. According to Humboldt, logical rhythm is above all revealed in prose; prose discloses the whole living growth of thought. Whereas poetry is inseparable from music, prose lives exclusively within the element of language. Indeed, Humboldt argues that prose is not derived from an original poetry but is equiprimordial with it. In fact, Humboldt writes, following the essential tendencies of the Jena Romantics, prose is the highest peak that language can attain in the forming of character:[37]

> However infinite and inexhaustible within itself, the sphere of the poetic is nevertheless always a *closed* one, which does not take in everything... thought, unfettered by any external form, can move onward in free development to every side both in grasping the particular and in constructing the universal Idea. To that extent the need to cultivate prose is rooted in the abundance and freedom of intellectuality.[38]

> ...science demands a *prosaic* garb: the mind deals exclusively with the objective and with the subjective only insofar as the latter contains necessity... it is seeking truth.[39]

The philosophical prose of Aristotle, Kant and Schelling, Humboldt suggests, exhibit the sublimity of language, revealing within it a higher seriousness and strength.[40] The capacity for logical rhythm – the form and systematic order of mental content – depends, according to Humboldt, upon the efficacy of an inner linguistic sense. This efficacy varies from language to language, but it is the stress-timed rhythm of the English language that according to Humboldt most of all conveys the intellectual energy and force of thought. The ground and root of this ordering force, however, is always unfathomable.[41] The ontic inexplicability of sound and tone is here matched by the inexplicable non-sensuous rhythm of thought. The latter is what in a Heideggerian register might be called the ontological rhythm of Being. This determines the innermost content of the idea of the rhythm of language.

The connection between the phenomenon of the 'speaking' of language and the intrinsic self-concealing of Being is now clear. Rhythm is the form of the movement of language. The movement of self-giving – the 'speaking' of language – is received as purposefully ordered as it flows back into the hidden form of its giving. Rhythm hides or conceals itself in the sense that no reason can be given to account for its giving. No determinate conception lies at the source of the rhythmic movement. Rhythm refuses itself. Simply, *there is* rhythm. 'It gives' rhythm: rhythm gives itself. Rhythm manifests the necessity of an ordering *for* the receptivity of man, whilst concealing the nature of this self-manifesting *from* man. As the self-concealing form of the movement of language, rhythm is received from out of an unfathomable depth in the human being. Rhythm is not conceptually represented but felt: it is the form and order of the aesthetically intuited intensity of Being. The feeling of the rhythm of language is not the soul of language, loosely intermediate between sensuous body and non-sensuous spirit, but the radical, ontological source for meaning. Man thus receives his understanding of Being as the gift of the rhythmic 'speaking' of language. If Heidegger recoils before the question of the expropriative self-concealing of the 'speaking' of language then it is not surprising that there is also recoil before the idea of rhythm, given that rhythm is pre-eminently a hidden form.

The finite receptivity of man experiences rhythm in the sublime, unfathomable depth of an ordering and purposeful 'speaking' of language. Language 'speaks' from out of the abyss of man's own human nature. Language is not, according to Heidegger, an activity of man whereby inner feelings and thoughts are communicated from one mind to another mind in linguistic utterance. Language, for the traditional understanding, expresses and externalises inner thought in speech and writing: letters are signs of sounds, sounds of mental experiences and experiences of things. Language, according to this interpretation, gives utterance to what the human being pictures to himself and this picture corresponds to the real world. As Heidegger argues, the traditional understanding explains the phenomenon of language by recourse to another phenomenon – the mental interiority that accompanies speech.

However, in regard to Heidegger's recoil before the phenomenon of the rhythm of language, it is instructive to see how far he is thrown back upon the traditional understanding that he criticises. Indeed, although *Being and Time* criticises the idea of language as the 'conveying of experiences, such as opinions or wishes, from the interior of one subject into the interior of another',[42] nonetheless the early work remains *within* the traditional understanding of language insofar as it still conceives the phenomenon as a form of communication. According to Heidegger, the existentiale of understanding discloses Dasein's potentiality-for-Being and discourse, the articulation of the intelligibility of Being-in-the-World is the significant articulation of understanding. The articulation of discursive speech is existentially prior to both the hermeneutical 'as' of interpretation in which the understanding appropriates itself understandingly, seeing a particular ready-to-hand item of equipment 'as' something for such and such a purpose and to the apophantical 'as' of assertion, in which an object is pointed out and properties are predicated of it.

However, discursive speech, the articulated, as Heidegger puts it, 'speaking forth' of the understanding, is not necessarily a form of verbal utterance. Hearing and keeping silent, for example, are modes of discourse. These modes of authentic discourse articulate meaning, i.e. that wherein the intelligibility of something maintains itself, and this 'speaking forth' of meaning is communication:

> Discourse which expresses itself is communication. Its tendency of Being is aimed at bringing the hearer to participate in disclosed Being towards what is talked about in the discourse.[43]

The communication of discourse is not the avowal of inner thoughts, but a making-explicit of something that has not been taken hold of. In discourse the existentiale Being-with becomes explicitly shared in that it *is* already but is unshared in that it has not been appropriated.[44] Hence, authentic communication is the articulation of Being-with-one-another understandingly.[45] In this context language, according to early Heidegger, has its existential foundations in discourse. Language is a totality of words ready-to-hand within the world, which, for the most part, are used to express discourse in linguistic utterance. In this regard language, for Heidegger, is the inauthentic correlate of discursive speech. Dasein is delivered over to the totality of words in which the significance of the world is deposited and must fight its way through the chatter of idle talk to get back to the silent 'speaking forth' of genuine Being-with. Language in early Heidegger is not the unique mode of the giving of Being, but is a totality of ready-to-hand entities in the world, alongside other entities. On the other hand, authentic discursive speech does not convey inner experiences to another mind. Nonetheless, it is still understood as a communication of meaning, in that it makes explicit the shared, already-given understanding of Dasein's Being-with. Hence, *there is* the 'speaking' of discursive speech insofar as the meaning of the world has already been disclosed and understood.

Conversely, in later Heidegger, the 'speaking' of language *gives* the totality of articulated significance, i.e. the human being's idea of world. The silence of the 'speaking' of language is not the making-explicit of an already-given and implicit understanding, but a movement of giving exterior to our horizon of intelligibility. Language *is* in its rhythmic 'speaking'. The rhythmic ordering of the 'speaking' of Language says nothing. It does not disclose the inner or make-explicit an already-understood meaning of Being, but is received as the compelling feeling of a rhythmic ordering in the articulation of meaning. Rhythm, as the feeling of a purposive movement in the relations of articulated significance in discourse, is received as the hidden, self-concealing form unifying finite ontological content and so binding the experience of man.

Nonetheless, if the human being's horizon of intelligibility is not simply disclosed in a special linguistic capacity possessed by man, but is received as a gift from the rhythm of language, the question remains as to the concrete nature of linguistic meaning and how this is to be ontologically related to the purposeful self-moving of language. Such an ontological elucidation would prepare the ground for an analytic of the nature of the receptive Being of man and for a clarification of the way in which man belongs to Being. If discourse is the articulation of meaning in early Heidegger, there is no correlative conceptualisation of the nature of the grammar of human discourse after the later 'turn' to the 'speaking' of language. The way in which the 'speaking forth' of man is 'rhythmed' by Being remains opaque.

Chapter 7

Human Nature and *Sensus Communis*

Language 'speaks' to the human being in the form of a purposeful feeling of immanent necessity in the unfolding of ontological content. This form is the non-sensuous rhythm or life of language. The concealing of Being is rooted in the phenomenological experience of rhythm – no determinate reason lies at the heart of the giving of rhythm. Simply: *there is* rhythm. As the Pre-Socratics thought, the rhythm and order of Being gives character to the human being; character is a gift received from Being. Humboldt, following this tradition, determines spirit not as a constituting subjectivity but rather a gift offered from the 'speaking' of language. Language 'speaks' to us, i.e. Being gives, *as* the spirit that orders and appropriates the human being. However, the ontological relation between language and the human being remains obscure: how is the grammar of a linguistic community related to the giving of language? What is the nature of this community, if our understanding of Being is determined as a gift?

Humboldt conceives the formation and ordering of the human being as *Bildung*. Generally speaking, *Bildung* means a process of formation or setting up; specifically it can also mean education, i.e. initiation into the rules and practices of a culture. According to Humboldt, there is *Bildung* in the reception of Being: through this ontological intuition our character is formed. The rhythm of Being that gives character, Humboldt suggests, constitutes the *nature* of the human being. The gift of character is intuited in the form of a rhythmic movement received from human nature. Nature is intended here neither as a wholly objective nor wholly subjective phenomenon: it is the nature *of* man that gives *to* him the gift of rhythm. Nature is, in this sense, more precisely determined as the second nature of a form of life. The basis of this form of life is language. Language is the second nature that forms the being of man. Human nature, hence, is not something static and predetermined:

> Since the development in man of his human nature depends on that of his language, the very concept of the nation is thereby directly given, as that of a body of men who form language in a particular way.[1]

Language gives the form of the community, i.e. the spirit and character of a 'body of men'. This aesthetically perceived second nature or *Bildung* moulds and shapes human nature, determining what and how man *is*. The Humboldtian account of the origin and nature of *Bildung* resting in an aesthetic form granted by language is sharply opposed to the description recently offered by McDowell in *Mind and World*. Contrary to Humboldt, McDowell, using Aristotle's account of ethical character, describes *Bildung* or second nature as an initiation into conceptual capacities in which the human being is opened up to the rational demands of an ethical community.[2] The conception of *Bildung* is vital for McDowell because he uses it to re-enchant the conception of nature bequeathed by the Enlightenment, in which the space of reasons and the domain of nature are understood to be mutually exclusive realms of existence. The problem that arises as a consequence of the disenchantment of nature is that our understanding of how the human mind is related to the world oscillates between two equally unsatisfactory poles: coherentism and the Myth of the Given. Coherentism, according to McDowell, argues that although experience is causally relevant to a subject's beliefs and judgements, it has no bearing on their status as justified or warranted.[3] Rather, only a belief can count as a reason for holding another belief. Thus, the world that is experienced in operations of receptivity can in the coherentist picture of experience only causally influence but not rationally constrain our empirical thinking. The difficulty that follows from coherentism, McDowell suggests, is that the very possibility of empirical content, i.e. that our judgements and beliefs are about how the world *is*, becomes mysterious. This, he stresses, is not an epistemological, but rather a metaphysical or ontological question. The result is that the spontaneous sphere of thinking, the space of reasons, does not appear to bear upon the outside world at all: our thought is, as McDowell puts it, seemingly frictionless. Without the rational constraint or friction of the reality disclosed in the receptive operations of human experience, the very fact of empirical knowledge becomes questionable.

According to McDowell, the traditional response to the problems generated by coherentism is to move to an equally untenable Myth of the Given. The idea of the Myth of the Given expresses the need for rational constraint on our thinking by something outside it. However, the given that is supposed to introduce this friction on thought is an extra-conceptual item of experience, i.e. a bare, sensory presence. This bare presence is manifest to us as a brute impact from the exterior.[4] However, such an impact upon the operations of spontaneity cannot be the ground for the justification of a belief or judgement but only an exculpation: we are exempt from offering a reason or possible justification for thinking such and such. The Myth of the Given, therefore, also presents us with an unsatisfactory picture of experience: it does not succeed in doing what it is supposed to do. A result of the failure of the Myth of the Given and thus of the attempt to constrain and limit the space of reasons is to swing again toward the frictionless spontaneity of thought depicted by coherentism. It would appear to be impossible to have rational constraint in empirical thinking and spontaneity, i.e. relations of possible justification, all the way out.

McDowell offers a way out of this impasse by re-thinking the idea of nature upon which it is based. Both the Myth of the Given and coherentism assume that the space of reasons and the domain of nature are mutually exclusive, the latter constituted by causal relations. The realm of lawlike nature appears, after the scientific revolution, intrinsically meaningless. It cannot, therefore, rationally constrain our thinking. There is, hence, a dualism in this pervasive idea of experience; human receptivity intuits the extra-conceptual causal impacts of the realm of nature, which offer a form of external but not rational constraint. Human spontaneity, on the other hand, subsists separately from operations of receptivity within the space of reasons. McDowell attempts to overturn this dualistic conception of experience by demonstrating that, if the natural, receptive capacities of the human being are understood to include the element of spontaneity then the anxiety which gives rise to the theoretical oscillation dissipates. Hence, in the spirit of Wittgenstein, McDowell, trying to avoid theory-construction, offers a kind of therapy for a philosophical anxiety. On the other hand, following Kant, he also presents something that looks very much like a 'transcendental argument' to make his case: if empirical content is to be possible (X), something else (Y) must be the case. Indeed, after *Mind and World*, McDowell has explicitly referred to the transcendental nature of his method.[5]

McDowell attempts to show that the only way to have both rational constraint on thinking and spontaneity all the way down, and thus to avoid the dualism of a conceptual content given in the space of reasons and an extra-conceptual content given in the realm of law, is to conceive of our operations of receptivity as themselves conceptually structured. The human being does not simply receive empirical items of sense-data. In perceptual experience, we intuit the fact that things are thus and so: deliverances of receptivity already possess conceptual content. This already-given conceptual content rationally constrains what we think, i.e. the content of our judgements and beliefs. Hence, the human being's operations of receptivity intuit the manifold, already-given conceptual content that constitutes its idea of world. The repository, according to McDowell, citing Gadamer, of the conceptual content comprising the world of man is language:

> Now it is not even clearly intelligible to suppose a creature might be born at home in the space of reasons. Human beings are not: they are born mere animals and they are transformed into thinkers and intentional agents in the course of coming to maturity. This transformation risks looking mysterious. But we can take it in our stride if, in our conception of *Bildung* that is a central element in the normal maturation of human beings, we give pride of place to the learning of language. In being initiated into a language, a human being is introduced into something that already embodies putatively rational linkages between concepts... before she comes on the scene. This is a picture of initiation into the space of reasons as an already going concern. ...Human beings mature into being at home in the space of reasons, or, what comes to the same thing, living their lives in the world; we can make sense of that by noting that the language into which a human being is first initiated stands over against her as a prior embodidness of mindedness, of the possibility of an orientation to the world.[6]

Language is the second nature of the human being. In perceptual experience operations of receptivity intuit the already given, articulated conceptual content that constitutes this second nature. Thus, inheriting and working within a linguistic tradition is a central element in any plausible and satisfactory conception of human experience. If nature is determined as second nature or *Bildung*, then to intuit the exteriority of the natural, real world is not to receive extra-conceptual sensory data. Rather nature, the world of the human being, is already conceptually articulated. It is already part of the space of reasons. Nonetheless, McDowell thinks there is present in this conception of experience a rational constraint missing from coherentism. How the world *is*, i.e. how it has already been linguistically articulated in the tradition of a particular form of life, constrains and regulates the content of our judgements and beliefs. Hence, this content can be unproblematically understood to be genuinely empirical.

In fact, though McDowell cites Gadamer in stating his conclusions, he is equally close to early Heidegger. The operations of receptivity that inherit an already-given linguistic tradition are described in *Being and Time* as the 'thrownness' of Dasein. Dasein is always thrown into a world not of its own making; this world constrains and determines its factical existence. According to Heidegger, as for McDowell, the human being does not intuit items of extra-conceptual sensory data and then interpret this data in terms of a particular belief system or conceptual scheme. Rather man 'hears' the motorbike, 'sees' the crackling fire; in other words, the human being intuits facts in its perceptual experience. These facts are aspects of the perceptible, already significant world within which it lives. Sensory experience, therefore, is already pervaded with meaning, or, as Heidegger puts it, with a pre-ontological understanding of Being. On the other hand, if early Heidegger's conception of inauthentic experience is similar to McDowell, his conception of authentic experience might be said to swing back to a Myth of the Given. Dasein comes face to face with the sheer Fact that it is and this Fact is phenomenologically manifest in the experience of the sensory presence of extra-conceptual, unintelligible matter. This material presence is a bare Given to which Dasein must submit: to reach the ontic real is to hit bedrock in the giving of reasons.

In McDowell's conception of experience there is no gap between mind and world, i.e. between thought and Being:[7]

> The fact that experience is passive, a matter of receptivity in operation, should assure us that we have all the external constraint we can reasonably want. The constraint comes from outside *thinking*, but not from outside what is *thinkable*. When we trace justifications back, the last thing we come to is still thinkable content; not something more ultimate than that, a bare pointing to a bit of the Given.[8]

> This talk of impingements on our senses is not an invitation to suppose that the whole dynamic system, the medium within which we think, is held in place by extra-conceptual links to something outside it... . The impressions on our senses that keep the dynamic system in motion are already equipped with conceptual content.[9]

The Hegelian background to McDowell's conception of experience is here explicit. The idea of the unboundedness of the conceptual conforms, according to McDowell, to Hegel's remark 'In thinking, I am free because I am not in an other'. This statement conveys the same point as Wittgenstein's remark 'We – and our meaning – do not stop anywhere short of the fact'. To this list may be added Heidegger's remark in *Being and Time*, 'Being "is" Dasein's understanding of

Being'. However, there are at least two problems that arise in regard to McDowell's conception of experience. First, it is not clear that the idea of conceptually structured operations of receptivity assures us that the McDowellian picture of experience yields the kind of external constraint he demands. As Kant realised, part of the idea of human reception, i.e. the ontological essence of finitude, is that we are dependent upon and in relation to an exterior, distinct existence. McDowell argues that this demand for exteriority is satisfied in the idea of the reception of already-existing conceptual content. However, in this case, we receive in experience the already given spontaneity of thought. Reception, as in early Heidegger, is grounded in a prior form of what might be called congealed spontaneity, i.e. the thinkable. The human being receives as external the articulated significance of a linguistic tradition or world into which it has been thrown. Yet the intuited content remains disclosed *within* the spontaneity of understanding or space of reasons. This is not so far from coherentism as McDowell implies. The difference, of course, is that on McDowell's Hegelian conception of experience, the space of reason embraces the idea of the natural and the correlative sensibility of human experience, which had been previously occupied by the scientific idea of law.

Nonetheless, the anxiety remains that the possibility of the kind of content McDowell demands, a content that describes how the world actually is, remains elusive on the picture of experience he presents. World or Being is the already-given articulated content of a tradition. Rather than world or Being in itself opening up new and surprising aspects of experience, the forms of traditional experience disclose the nature and possibility of world and Being. There is nothing exterior to the thinkable, not even the 'motion' that drives the dynamic system of thought. Hence, it would appear that there still remains inadequate constraint on our empirical thinking – the limits of thought are those that it has spontaneously given to itself. Yet without a limit and so understanding itself as dependent upon something else, thought is no longer finite. The pure, *a priori* receptivity of human existence is thereby lost. McDowell does not think this criticism of his idea of conceptually structured operations of receptivity is plausible because he believes that the only alternative is the Myth of the Given. For McDowell, any limitation of the unboundedness of the conceptual must lead to the idea of non-conceptual content and this idea, in turn, must revert necessarily to the idea of a given, sensory presence to which one can only 'point'. The problem, as already stated, is that the kind of content to which McDowell turns cannot yield the specific kind of constraint that he is after.

However, McDowell presupposes that non-conceptual content is exclusively constituted by bits of the sensorily given. Yet this is not necessarily the case. Indeed, the phenomenon of the rhythm of language yields an idea of content that is both non-conceptual and non-sensory. The content of Being is not conceptual, i.e. it is not the articulated significance of the human being's understanding of Being. Yet this content remains ontological: it is not an item of empirical experience intuited by the corporeal sense organs. Rather, the content of Being is the feeling of a purposeful movement ordering and shaping linguistic content. The ground of this rhythm or motion is not determinate: the human being cannot say precisely why certain patterns of development and kinship appear necessary within the linguistic whole. Ontological content, thus, does not offer relations of rational justification to account exhaustively for our judgements and beliefs. Yet some beliefs and judgements are rooted in this kind of content. This is not however exculpation. The non-conceptual content of Being is not a sheer Given to which one points; as an intuited intensity, it is a gift that one expresses. To express this content is not to teach a rule, but to exemplify the way a pattern and movement within language grips us. Consequently, our relation to this kind of content is neither causal nor rational; rather it is given in an affectively structured operation of receptivity. The intuition of the rhythm of language is aesthetic. The content of the 'speaking' of language cannot be exhaustively determined according to reasons, it can only be shown or exemplified.

Because Being is the felt rhythm of non-conceptual content that limits the possibility of the conceptual, it offers the requisite constraint missing in McDowell's conception of experience. The movement of language, rooted in human nature, limits and binds, as an exterior force, the thinkable content of our understanding of Being. This is the friction or constraint of Being in itself as 'it gives' to man. It is the transcendental correlate to the ontic Real missing in early Heidegger. As a purposeful movement, this exterior constraint holds and orders our system of thought – though we do not know and can never fully explain what it is. From this perspective, the Being in itself of the rhythm of language originally constitutes the idea of world. Our world or form of life is not primarily a system of rational linkages between concepts or given determinate rules of behaviour. Rather, the originary form of life is an aesthetically perceived, rhythmically unified field of experience. The conceptual content that constitutes this field of meaning is manifest as a gift because, in the felt intuition of its intrinsic purposefulness, it appears to have its own movement, direction and life. In and through this life, language 'speaks' to the human being. Contrary to McDowell, the originary *Bildung* is not initiation into conceptual capacities but, first and foremost, the aesthetic intuition of the form and movement of spirit. Spirit moves and animates our understanding of Being, though proximally and for the most part we are oblivious to it. To participate in the community of speakers, and so to acquire *Bildung*, is to understand that language is not simply a tool of communication or a system of determinate rules, but an aesthetically perceived, living gift.

Indeed, this conception of a rhythmic field of experience brings together elements from orthodox empiricism and rationalism. In the rhythmic current of a form of life, the uniform and homogeneous regularity of Humean, empirical association is penetrated by the underlying 'force and vivacity' of a free, external purposefulness. Hence, in the upsurge of freedom, the habitual horizon of regularity, the second nature of a sedimented tradition, takes on the appearance of rhythm. Rhythm is the becoming-free of regularity. Rhythm is free because it exhibits a movement that appears purposeful; however, rhythm is a free regularity because this freedom is not universally determinate or determinable. As with the empiricist idea of experience, the field governing our experience of objects is a loosely connected fabric of associations that is open to modification. However, against empiricism, the unfolding of this fabric contains a necessity that goes beyond the subjective purview of custom or the present impressions of sense. The 'empirical' associations are present in the very nature of things. This constitutes the objectivity of our form of life: ontological content moves itself. 'It gives' us the linguistic rules that make up our understanding of Being.

The motion, therefore, that belongs intrinsically to the idea of ontological sensibility is an aesthetically intuited purposeful movement that arises from the depths of our form of life. This rhythmic movement rooted in human nature (Being) gives motion or activity *to* the subject. As early Heidegger implicitly suggests, rhythm does not simply offer the intelligible horizon of our form of life. Rhythm also unifies the forms of intuition – space and time. As their unitary ground, 'it gives' the phenomena of time and space from out of itself. The intuitions of time and space are thus rooted in the experience of rhythm. The originary gift of nature to the human being is manifest, therefore, in the *a priori* reception of a rhythmically unified field of experience within which the human being encounters beings. The rhythm of human nature forms the intuitive and intelligible horizon within which an empirically receptive experience of beings is possible. On the other hand, McDowell's attempted re-enchantment of the concept of nature fails. Second nature is riven with unbounded conceptual content. For later Heidegger, conversely, the human being *a priori* receives second nature or language in the aesthetic intuition of an affective self-ordering movement. This movement is the felt order underlying our linguistic articulation of conceptual content. However, nature, *as* spirit, is not a sheer given; 'it gives' the ontological relation between mind and world. Indeed, though McDowell cites Wittgenstein in outlining his Hegelian conception of experience, there are other elements within Wittgenstein's work on aesthetics, music and rule-following that are remarkably similar to later Heidegger.[10]

Thus, in later Heidegger's ontology of language, to understand the 'speaking' of language requires the capacity for a reception of non-conceptual content. This capacity, hence, is not conceptually structured; it is a form of aesthetic perception. Nonetheless, it refers to a transcendental aesthetic, i.e. an ontological idea of receptivity. The reception of non-conceptual content is not empirical; the content is not a sensory given. Rather, as an intuited intensity, the non-conceptual content is a gift; it is received from the movement of human nature that constitutes our form of life. Heidegger's idea of ontological sensibility in fact is already manifest in a thread that runs through the historical tradition and which is referred to in the notion of *sensus communis*. In this context, Gadamer offers a useful historical account of the notion of *sensus communis* in *Truth and Method*, tying it also to the notion of *Bildung*. Indeed, these two ideas, together with the ideas of judgement and taste, constitute, according to Gadamer, the guiding concepts of the humanist tradition. The concept of *Bildung*, Gadamer explains, originated in medieval mysticism; it evoked the tradition according to which man carries in his soul and cultivates the image of God after whom he is fashioned. The idea of cultivation, whose equivalent in Shaftesbury is the idea of formation, continues through Herder and Humboldt to Hegel. However, this idea is also, Gadamer suggests, tied to the notion of 'common sense'. Following Vico, this sense gives the human will direction, not as the abstract universality of reason but as the concrete universality represented by a community.[11] It is close to the Aristotelian notion of practical knowledge, *phronesis*. Shaftesbury, following the Stoics, understands by *sensus communis* a sense of and love for the community, a social virtue with a moral basis. Hutcheson and Hume take up and develop this idea, which later serves as a foil to Kantian ethics.

According to Gadamer, the third historical manifestation of the idea of *sensus communis* appears in the work of the Pietist Friedrich Christoph Oetinger (1702-1782). For Oetinger, man is receptive to common, sensible truths, which, in perceptual experience, as with the Aristotelian common sensibles, unify the five corporeal senses. These truths are received through a manifold of irresistible, natural instincts and tendencies – the whole of which make up our *sensus communis*. The original basis of our common sense is our natural existence or life, and life itself, Oetinger argues, is a gift from God. Accordingly, though Gadamer does not point this out, the Pietist conception of *sensus communis* steps beyond the humanist tradition. The common sense in both form and content is a divine gift; through the *sensus communis* man reaches *beyond* man. This constitutes the 'inhuman' ground of human sensibility. Oetinger's account of common sense is closest to that which can be extracted from later Heidegger. The difference, however, is that, for Heidegger, our capacity for ontological intuition is a gift not from a divine giver, but rather, within the bounds of aesthetic immanence, from life itself. Through the *sensus communis* we receive the non-conceptual content that *is* life. It is life that, through *Bildung*, animates and moves us.

However, for Oetinger, the human being shares with all living things the *sensus communis*. Here, Oetinger departs radically from McDowell. For McDowell, the conceptually structured operations of receptivity that constitute his idea of sensible experience are exclusive to human beings. This gives rise to the second difficulty that is generated by his elucidation of finite experience. The problem, as McDowell rightly points out, is that the scientific dis-enchantment of nature has separated the domain of reason from that of nature and, consequently, the spontaneity of our understanding from the sensibility of our natural, animal existence. The result is a distortion of the Aristotelian idea that human beings are rational animals, i.e. that our reasoning power is part of our sensible, animal life. McDowell's ambition is to recapture this Aristotelian intuition by bringing understanding and sensibility, reason and nature, back together again and so overturning the metaphysical split that has formed in the conception of the human being.[12] The danger, McDowell argues, in any philosophical anthropology that is concerned with the relations of human beings to animals, is that we are tempted into committing ourselves to a version of the Myth of the Given. For example Evans, on McDowell's reading, argues that judgements of experience are based on non-conceptual content, which we share with animals. Humans, however, convert this content into conceptual form:

> The idea is that mere animals enjoy perceptual experience in which the world strikes them as being in a certain way, and the only difference our understanding makes for us is that we can impose conceptual form on the already world-

representing but less than conceptual content that, like them, we receive in experience.[13]

On this picture we share with animals the non-conceptual content that makes up the world that we inhabit. This world is disclosed in the extra-conceptual sensibility of our perceptual existence. The benefit of this determination of experience is that it is immediately apparent that there are important respects in which humans can be understood to participate in animal life. However, McDowell rightly rejects this picture of experience. It is complicit, he thinks, in the metaphysical dualism that we are seeking to overcome: animals, like us, receive the Given, whilst we receive it and put it into conceptual shape. The human being is then a composite of non-conceptual content (animal) and conceptual content (rational). McDowell's response, on the other hand, is to emphasise the differences between animals and humans. Animals, he writes, following Gadamer, inhabit an environment within which they respond to a succession of biological imperatives; humans live in a world in which they are free from the needs of mere biological existence. The world is disclosed in a greater array of knowable detail than any creaturely environment, e.g. in the richness of the human being's visual field, which conveys within it more than is a matter for simply coping with animal needs.[14] Hence, humans do not share nature with animals: nature, i.e. the conceptual content of the human world, is received as already meaningful. In this McDowell essentially repeats a remark made by Heidegger in his 1929-30 lectures on the *Fundamental Concepts of Metaphysics*: man is world-forming, whereas the animal is poor in world.[15] Early Heidegger, like McDowell, excludes animals both from a share in Being and from the manifestness of beings.

The problem, however, is that on this McDowellian conception of experience, it is all but impossible to determine the way in which humans *share* a natural existence with animals. The difference between human and animal life is articulated as a reflex from the untenable dualism of non-conceptual and conceptual content. However, the price of overcoming this metaphysical split is to negate the domain of the Same within which there *is* this difference. Without this Same, it is unintelligible that the reason of human beings could remain a part of natural, animal life. The idea of nature appears devoid of anything identifiably natural, i.e. genuinely sensible. To insist on the animality of human existence goes hand in hand, therefore, with the claim that there is more to the idea of receptivity than its being conceptually structured. The difficulty is to insist on the Same, whilst avoiding the temptation of suggesting that this Same is constituted by the sharing of a given, non-conceptual content.

However, a way out of this impasse is suggested by the notion of non-conceptual content offered by later Heidegger. Humans and animals, following Oetinger, enjoy a *sensus communis*. However, they do nor share something perceptually given; spirit is not given, 'it gives'. Humans express the non-conceptual content of spirit in the unique conceptual articulation of a characteristically human language. Expression is not the conversion of something already intuitively there. Rather, it is the particular way something is received, from the ground up. Spirit does not hover about as a given thing, waiting to be actualised in different ways by different animals: it *is* only in its expression.

Animals express Spirit differently, in a language not recognisably conceptual, but which, in the higher mammals at least, is still perceivable *as a language*. The expression becomes more remote from us in cold-blooded, reptilian life. The point is, however, that it is a matter of qualitative gradations within the Same. Hence, the language communities of humans and animals are radically distinct, they are distanced as if by an abyss, yet they share a common root, expressed and performed by each in a different way. This difference is manifest between and within natural kinds and *between* and *within* the collection of language-groups that comprise the human species.

Hence, on this conception of experience, humans and animals share life (Being). Life is the underlying Same within which there is the expression of difference: animals and humans repeat the Same, differently. Yet the content of life is not a non-conceptual Given; it is not something already there which we shape conceptually. Rather, conceptuality *is* the way life is expressed by human beings. In the activity of expression we receive the order and movement of conceptual content that 'it gives' to us. Naturally, it is a distinct question whether it is a unique trait of human animality to understand life as a gift and to be able to repeat and return this gift. In this case, the power of reason does not detach us from our natural, sensible existence; on the contrary, it would then be the consummation and perfection of animal life.

Chapter 8

Inspiration and Genius

The human being receives second nature in the aesthetic intuition of an affective self-ordering movement. This movement is the felt order underlying our linguistic articulation of conceptual content. The whole of this articulated content or grammar is to be conceived as a gift from nature. Nature is manifest in the second nature of an aesthetically bounded field of experience (form of life). This form is intuited in the manifestation of a free regularity or rhythm. The necessity of rhythm is not rooted in the subjective, habitual associations of a custom: it is the power of objective nature. On the other hand, the purposeful freedom of rhythm is not determinable according to purposes. The ground and wellspring of the linguistic community remains unfathomable. As Heidegger puts it: Being withdraws in the gift that 'it gives'. The content intuited by the human being is non-conceptual: Being is the depth of intensity. Aesthetic intuition of the form and movement of ontological content constitutes our originary *Bildung*. To be formed in this way is not to learn an array of determinate rules but to be 'appropriated' by the giving of the *logos*. However, if *Bildung* is granted to us by language itself it remains thus far undetermined how man receives and returns the gift. What is the precise ontological structure of the form of the expression by which the belonging of man to Being is manifest?

In order to clear the approach for an adequate response to this question, it is illuminating to contrast Heidegger's account of ontological content with Hegel's. This, however, can only be carried out in a comprehensive way after Heidegger's non-Hegelian interpretation of the origin and movement of ontological content is traced back to elements within Kant's *Critique of Judgement*. Indeed, this chapter argues, the analytic of man in later Heidegger involves an ontological clarification of the finite existence of genius in Kant's *Critique of Judgement*, analogous to early Heidegger's analytic of the finitude of Dasein grounded in the *Critique of Pure Reason* and presented in *Kant and the Problem of Metaphysics*. Thus, early Heidegger remains within a conception of finitude largely inherited from the *Critique of Pure Reason,* in which Being 'is' Dasein's understanding of Being. Later Heidegger, conversely, turns from this analytic of finitude, though never explicitly and with full comprehension, by introducing a distinction into the ontological conception of finitude between Being and the human being. This distinction is made concrete by Heidegger, drawing upon Kant, as the difference between nature (Being) and genius (human being). However, in order to grasp in its full ontological breadth the existential structure of genius that Heidegger incorporates into his later philosophical anthropology, it is first necessary to offer a provisional interpretation of the precise role Kant's analytic of genius plays within the *Critique of Judgement* as a whole.

The purpose of the *Critique of Judgement* is, explicitly, a critique of the power of judgement. This critique is necessary, Kant writes, not only because judgement contains an *a priori* principle of its own but also because, following the faculty psychology of his day, all the soul's powers can be reduced to three: the cognitive power, the feeling of pleasure or displeasure and the power of desire. Hence, Kant suggests, we must presuppose that the critique of judgement is concerned with the power of the soul that lies in between desire and cognition, just as judgement itself mediates understanding and reason. However, in spite of these external concerns, the other, fundamental problem around which the *Critique of Judgement* coalesces is the problem of, as Kant puts it, the immense gulf that opens up, after the *Critique of Pure Reason* and the *Critique of Practical Reason,* between the domain of the concept of nature and the domain of the concept of freedom.[1]

A domain is a realm of objects for which there is *a priori* legislation in the powers of understanding or reason. The theoretical understanding performs legislation through the concept of nature. Legislation through the concept of freedom is performed by practical reason.[2] The concepts of nature posit the theoretical notion of nature as such as the sum total of objects of possible experience (i.e. as appearances) and correlatively point to the supersensible substrate of phenomenal nature as merely an undetermined transcendental 'X'. On the other hand, the concept of freedom allows its object – the moral law – to be represented as a supersensible thing-in-itself for which, nonetheless, there is no intuition to be found in sensible nature. Hence the great gulf Kant describes. The problem is that implicit within the concept of freedom is the possibility that the purpose enjoined by its laws can be actualised in the world of sense, so that the performance and realisation of moral duty might also be in harmony with the happiness involved in living a sensuously existent human life.[3] The gulf between the two worlds becomes a problem, then, insofar as freedom is to pass over into and have some influence upon the domain of nature; this problem would be resolved if it were possible to conceive of a transition from nature to freedom. The question of the possibility of a transition from nature to freedom is not simply conceived by Kant in terms of a transition from sensible nature to supersensible freedom, but rather, more specifically, from an entirely undetermined supersensible substrate of nature as such (bare 'X') given by the understanding, to the determination of this supersensible substrate through the *a priori* practical law of freedom.[4] Only by determining the undetermined substrate of nature on the basis of the concept of freedom is it possible to think of a unity of the two domains and so the possibility that the effects of both will harmonise in sensible nature, though each is grounded in an entirely different kind of legislative activity.

In order for a transition of this sort to be possible, from the undetermined substrate of nature to a determination of this substrate by reason, the supersensible substrate of nature as such, Kant concludes, has to be conceived as determinable. It is this demand for the determinability of the supersensible that understanding cannot fulfil, necessarily leaving the substrate of phenomenal nature – the thing in itself – wholly undetermined. Nor can reason fulfil this demand. Reason is determinative, i.e. it acts according to purposes. Yet a solution to the problem requires a preparation of nature's substrate as *determinable* by purposes; however, a purpose cannot make something determinable *for* purposes. Kant writes in this regard: 'judgement, through its *a priori* principle…provides nature's supersensible substrate with determinability by the intellectual power'.[5]

Hence, for Kant, the *a priori* principle of the power of judgement provides nature's supersensible substrate with determinability. This principle, Kant writes, is the concept of the purposefulness of nature; the *Critique of Judgement* interrogates the origin and justification of this *a priori* principle. However, the concept of the purposefulness of nature can be taken in two ways, each way corresponding to a separate element of the critique of judgement. The concept of the purposefulness of nature can be understood as a subjective purposefulness rooted in aesthetic judgement or an objective purposefulness rooted in teleological judgement. However, as Kant suggests, only aesthetic judgement belongs essentially to the critique of the mental powers of the subject. Whereas aesthetic judgement contains an *a priori* principle that judgement by means of the feeling of pleasure or displeasure has itself legislated, teleology relies upon reason's concept of a purpose. Teleology therefore cannot provide an *a priori* principle for representing objective purposes in nature. Both kinds of judgement are reflective, but it is (aesthetic) judgement's *a priori* principle of the formal, subjective purposefulness of nature that takes precedence within the critique. This reflective *a priori* principle of nature, employed in an aesthetic judgement of taste, is formal in that what is reflected upon is the form of the manifold in empirical intuition (in the imagination) as it relates to the power of concepts in general (in the understanding). It concerns a purposefulness of nature because in judgements of taste the form of the beautiful thing appears as commensurate with, i.e. in lawful or purposive harmony with, the power of cognition. It is a subjective principle because it refers merely to the nature of the object as the subject presents it and reflects upon this presentation. Finally, this subjective, formal purposefulness of nature is without purpose because no concept of perfection lies at the basis for judging an object beautiful. Rather, the beauty is felt in the indeterminate feeling of pleasure that arises in reflection upon the free harmony of the form of the object with the lawful power of concepts.

The *a priori* principle of the subjective purposefulness without purpose of nature, which lies at the ground of aesthetic judgements of taste, is, according to Kant, the route whereby the transition from nature to freedom becomes possible.[6] In order for the transition to work, judgements of taste have to disclose the transcendental substrate of nature as determinable by the intellectual power. To put the point another way, there has to be a trace of freedom in the principle of nature on the basis of which judgements of taste are possible. A judgement of taste, Kant argues, is based upon a feeling of pleasure that the object judged beautiful arouses in us, but, though based on feeling, the judgement nonetheless demands universal assent. Because of this demand the feeling cannot be private but rather is a manifestation of the harmony of the form of the beautiful object presented in imagination with the cognitive power in general that is shared by all human beings.

The deduction or justification of judgements of taste ends with a reference to the *sensus communis*, the common sense. This common sense, which Kant also describes as an 'inner sense'[7], is a sense insofar as it senses the effect that the indeterminate, harmonious activity of the relation between imagination and understanding has on the mind. The effect of this relation is manifest as the inner feeling of a purposeful state of mind in which the mental faculties participate in a play that is both free and regular. The *sensus communis* is presupposed as the ground for the autonomy of pure judgements of taste if the demand for universal assent contained within these judgements is to be justified.

However, in the Kantian corpus the idea of the common sense refers merely to the subjective conditions for the power of judgement whose principle is the formal, subjective purposefulness of nature. This principle of nature contains no reference to the transcendental or ontological substrate of nature. What counts, according to Kant, in judging something beautiful is not what nature is, nor what purpose it has, but merely how man receives it, i.e. how man presents it and reflects upon this presentation. So it follows from the concept of the subjective purposefulness of nature contained within the judgement of taste that, as Kant writes, '…it is we who receive nature with favour not nature that favours us'.[8] However, in that case, it is impossible to disclose the transcendental substrate of nature itself as determinable, and so for any transition from nature to freedom to take place. This is because the *a priori* principle of pure judgements of taste refers merely to the subjective effect that the relation between imagination and understanding has on the mind, regardless of the existence or purpose of nature itself. Kantian judgements of beauty are a kind of self-affection. It is for this reason that immediately after the discussion of judgements of taste Kant suggests a variety of interests are additionally connected with these aesthetic judgements. These interests are not however the determining basis of judgements of taste, given that these are disinterested. The interests may be empirical, fulfilled for the most part in fine art, and referring to the human inclination toward sociability, which judgements of taste facilitate by allowing for the communication of the feeling of pleasure that is aroused in the perception of beauty. Or the interests may be intellectual. Intellectual interest is above all manifest in a direct interest in natural beauty in which nature is loved not just for its form but also in and for itself, i.e. in its existence, in that it is understood to provide purposefully beautiful products for man in order to further his ultimate moral purpose.[9]

It is on the basis of this latter intellectual interest connected with judgements of taste that Kant shifts his ground in the later sections on the antinomy of judgements of taste. A judgement of taste, Kant argues, must refer to a concept or it could not lay claim to universal validity and yet it must not refer to a concept because judgements of this kind are not theoretically demonstrable.[10] Previously the problem had been resolved by making reference to the indeterminate subjective, though still universal, ground of taste conceived as the *sensus communis*. Now, Kant suggests, the concept to which judgements of taste must refer is reason's transcendental concept of the supersensible, the idea of the supersensible substrate of humanity, i.e. the 'ultimate purpose given by the intelligible element of our nature', which, Kant concludes, is the 'morally good'.[11]

Only insofar as we refer the beautiful to the morally good does our liking for it include a claim to everyone's assent.[12] In this case there clearly is a transition from judgement to freedom, conceived as the *a priori* law of reason, a transition that purely disinterested, though autonomous, judgements of taste could not supply. But Kant has not explained or justified the move he makes from the principle of the indeterminate, subjective purposefulness of nature, upon which judgements of taste are based, to the idea of the intelligible supersensible substrate of this same principle of nature upon which judgements of taste are based in the sections on the antinomy. Only if this move is explained can there be a genuine transition from nature to freedom. Yet the move itself revolves merely around the initial connection of interest to taste. At best, Kant's explanation takes the form of an assertion that in judging an object beautiful the demand for the universal communicability of the feeling of pleasure is 'in addition' a duty in which man takes an interest in the existence of the object. Yet, as Kant remarks, this interest presupposes an already solidly established interest in the morally good.[13]

If the transition from nature to freedom presupposes the connection between taste and interest, given the fact that this seemingly external connection is not itself explained, it would appear that the transition is not grounded in the movement of the things themselves but is merely asserted. On the other hand, if it is possible to locate a reference to the supersensible, intelligible substrate of nature *within* aesthetic judgement without determining this as the morally good but rather as the determinable supersensible 'something' underlying taste, then the transition may still be possible. Indeed, Kant, echoing his description of the work of the transcendental imagination in the *Critique of Pure Reason,* writes in the *Critique of Judgement* that the source of the indeterminate idea of the supersensible underlying taste in the human being is a mystery that is concealed in its origins and which one cannot grasp, but only point at.[14] Kant writes,

> Judgement finds itself referred to something that is both in the subject himself and outside him, something that is neither nature nor freedom and yet is linked with the basis of freedom, the supersensible, in which the theoretical and practical power are in an unknown manner combined and joined into unity.[15]

Judgement in this context makes a necessary reference to the supersensible that is neither nature as such disclosed by the understanding nor freedom determined by practical reason, but which combines and joins both into a unity, i.e. allows for a transition from the one to the other such that a unity between them is possible. The question is: first, what kind of judgement is involved here? Second, is it possible to elucidate the transcendental and existential commitments that it contains without contaminating the bounds of aesthetic immanence with the introduction of elements from the external, moral domain?

Indeed, though Kant does not explicitly admit that this is the case, it is his analysis of genius that provides answers to these questions. Though influential contemporary interpretations of the *Critique of Judgement* insist on the parergonal nature of Kant's discussion of genius,[16] it is not merely a coincidence of the work's architectonic that the passages on genius lie in between the analytic of aesthetic and teleological judgement. In judgements of taste, it is the subject who receives beauty with favour, insofar as the predicate beautiful is attached to the object solely on the basis of a subjective reflection upon a given presentation of a manifold.[17] Hence, the purposefulness of nature is subjective, it refers to the conditions of presentation – the harmonious relation between imagination and understanding – enjoyed by the aesthetically judging subject. However, conversely, the genius is 'nature's favourite'.[18] The relation of favour between nature and genius is natural in that nature gives the innate mental predisposition of the genius, i.e. his *ingenium* or character. On the basis of this natural talent the genius is able to produce original art. Genius is that through which nature gives the rule to art.[19]

The character of the genius, then, on the basis of which the genius has an original productive ability, is a gift or favour from nature. The creative ability, derived from character, is the animating principle in the mind of the genius that Kant names spirit.[20] Spirit, consequently, manifests the favour of nature received by the genius: it is to the inspiration of the guiding spirit of the genius that his original ideas are due. The idea of the creative ability of genius grounded in the natural gift of spirit clearly does not involve a principle of the subjective purposefulness in which the subject favours nature. On the contrary, nature itself favours the subject; the subject is favoured or is received with favour. Hence the relation of favouring manifest with the phenomenon of genius reverses the relation of subject and nature found in pure judgements of taste.

Thus, pure judgements of taste have as an underlying principle the subjective purposive of nature without purpose. The principle of judgement involved in the work of genius, however, does not understand nature as subjective, i.e. in terms of the subject's reflection upon the presentation of the form of an empirical intuition. In the perception of beauty the subject receives with favour the presentation of nature that it has given to itself. Genius, on the other hand, receives the gift of spirit as a favour from that which receives genius with favour. Only insofar as the genius receives the gift offered by nature is it allowed into the subjectivity through which alone it can judge or create. Hence, nature cannot be understood as subjective, because 'it gives' the being of the self. Rather, the principle of nature is determined as an objective purposefulness because the working of nature *through* the genius manifests a natural, objective constraint upon the ideality of the aesthetically judging subject.

On the other hand, this principle of the objective purposefulness of nature manifest in the artwork of genius does not contain explicit reference to determinate purposes. If it did, the principle would have its ground in teleology and, therefore, in reason's concept of a purpose. As Kant reminds us, though art to an extent depends upon a concept of the object, i.e. its purpose, and so a judgment of artistic beauty involves a comparison of the intuited manifold with the perfection contained in the concept, nonetheless the fine art of genius because it receives its rule from nature is *not* to be judged strictly according to deliberate purposes or intentions.[21] Indeed, Kant proceeds to argue that the work of genius expresses aesthetic ideas, i.e. ideas the aesthetic attributes of which, presented by the imagination, contain more in them than can be determined by a single concept or purpose or linguistic expression.[22] If, therefore, aesthetic ideas are supposed to exhibit concepts they nonetheless also go beyond them and, as Kant puts it, 'set the power of intellectual ideas in motion' and 'make reason think more'.[23] Aesthetic ideas, therefore, manifest the spirit of the genius's natural character in that they possess and incite a purposeful momentum, the largely ineffable feeling of which quickens the cognitive powers.

The genius, Kant proceeds to write, does not produce art by means of determinate rules and so cannot explain how he created the work or what the work exhaustively means.[24] Kant is quite clear here: 'the rule must be abstracted from what the artist has done, i.e. from the product'.[25] The being of the artwork itself comes to the fore in Kant. The role of art in the *Critique of Judgement* is not simply reduced to the discipline of taste or to the transcendental subjectivity of genius: there is already in Kant the beginning of an ontology of the work. The objectivity of Nature underlying the principle of original, artistic creation is therefore mirrored in the principle underlying judgement of the artwork of genius. Far from inaugurating an impoverished, experience-based aesthetics and reducing art in various ways to human subjectivity, Kant makes central the intimately related ideas of artistic creation as expression of spirit and the being of the work itself as exemplary, a solitary, unique and irreducible Example. There is of course an internal relation between the two ideas. A work is exemplary because it manifests the concrete and singular expression of spirit through which genius receives and returns the gift of his naturally given character. In order to judge the work, taste is not sufficient. As Kant puts it, to follow the example of the work of genius is to be aroused by the spirit of the work and to re-express this spirit in an original way.[26] In other words, to *repeat* the Same of the work *differently*. Hence, ultimately, to judge the work of genius is to *be* a genius: to enact or express spirit rather than to imitate or describe it.

Hence, creating and judging inspired art involves an underlying principle of the objective purposefulness of nature without determinate purpose. This principle lies in-between the aesthetic pure judgement of taste (subjective purposefulness of nature without purpose) and teleological judgement (objective purposefulness of nature with purpose). Nature is objective in that 'it gives' the mode of subjectivity of genius as a favour or gift rather than being conceived only in terms of subjective reflection upon a given presentation. Yet this objective purposefulness is without purpose because no determinate concept or rule lies at the heart of the natural talent of genius in artistic creation; the work cannot be fully explained – it is irreducible, a solitary example that requires an original repetition or enactment of its underlying spirit.

The question remains however: how is Kant justified in moving from the principle of the subjective purposefulness of nature in aesthetic judgements of taste to the idea of a supersensible substrate underlying this purposefulness, without thereby determining this idea as the 'morally Good'? The answer can be found in the way in which Kant conceives the relation between spirit and genius in the context of that art which, according to Kant, is pre-eminently the work of genius: poetry. In poetry, the imagination, Kant writes, creates another nature out of the material that actual nature gives it and thereby 'may even reconstruct experience' and so 'surpass nature'.[27] Crucially, in poetic creation, Kant suggests, the imagination, feeling itself to be a very great power, is 'free, spontaneous and independent of natural determination' and has:

> the ability to contemplate and judge phenomenal nature as having aspects that nature on its own does not offer in experience... and hence poetry lets the mind feel its ability to use nature on behalf of, and as it were a schema of, the supersensible.[28]

It has already been established that, for Kant, the key to solving the mystery of the ability of taste is the indeterminate idea of the supersensible in us and that Kant conceives of this idea as that of the morally good. However, the aesthetic ideas of inspired poetry, also, Kant writes, involve the idea of the supersensible in that they strive to emulate reason by offering completeness in the exhibition of concepts that cannot belong within phenomenal nature.[29] If the archetype of taste, as Kant puts it, is reason's indeterminate idea of a maximum, then it is precisely in the inspired poetic art of genius that this idea is first and foremost experienced. The archetype of taste is phenomenologically perceived in the indeterminate feeling of totality aroused by the sublime expansion of the mind experienced in the reception, and exhibition, of aesthetic ideas. Of course, if genius in the act of creation is inspired, in the sense of intuiting the purposeful, free movement of inner spirit, then it would be expected that the feeling of creation is existentially related to the feeling of sublimity, given that judgements of the sublime involve the experience of an inner purposefulness beyond empirical, natural determination. Indeed, the feeling aroused in poetic creation is also described by Kant in a similar way to that of the sublime. The genius feels a great inner power whose ground and origin, as a favour from nature itself, is nonetheless concealed.[30] The inner purposefulness similarly arises in the feeling of the sublime and in poetic creation from a violent, rupturing use that is made of phenomenal nature, including our own, to reveal a transcendental freedom within the subject. However, in the context of genius, the feeling of sublimity prompts not humanity's moral vocation to be judged sublime, but spirit, the gift of the subject's original inner nature. The idea of genius is here stripped down to its pure essence, purified of the external accruements pertaining to the moral-practical domain. Spirit is an underlying, free purposefulness within the unfathomable, sublime depths of genius that neither determines the supersensible through the *a priori* law of practical reason nor leaves the supersensible wholly undetermined. Rather, in the act of poetic creation, the subject experiences its supersensible substrate as an inner purposefulness whose ground nonetheless conceals itself.

That Kant is open to this interpretation of the work of genius is clear from a remark he makes in section 57:

> In products of genius, art (i.e. production of the beautiful) receives its rule from nature (the nature of the subject) rather than from a deliberate purpose... we must judge the beautiful... according to the purposive attunement of the imagination that brings it into harmony with the power of concepts as such...the subjective standard for that aesthetic but unconditioned purposiveness in fine art that is to lay claim to everyone's necessary liking... can only be supplied by that which is

merely nature in the subject... namely the supersensible substrate of all his powers.[31]

As Kant here explicitly argues, what is nature in the subject, which gives the rule to art, i.e. nature itself, is in fact the supersensible substrate of the creative power of genius. The favouring of man by nature is the reception of an inner, supersensible purposefulness that is nonetheless objective in that it is intuited as exterior to the being of the subject. Given that the character of genius according to Kant is an original proportional attunement of the imagination and understanding, a proportion or relation that is received from nature as the subject's transcendental substrate, it becomes clearer why Kant also calls the harmonious activity between imagination and understanding a kind of spontaneity.[32] Kant however fails to conceive the *sensus communis* as receptive to an underlying, free power of (human) nature and narrows down its meaning and scope to merely subjective, empirical experience. The curious thing about the spontaneity intuited in a reconstructed conception of our common sense, however, is that it represents the activity of the transcendental (nature) working in man and yet, nonetheless, this is an inner purposefulness that is necessarily intuited or received. In other words, it is a purposefulness *in* the subject that comes to it *from without* as the manifestation of its natural being. Spirit, consequently, makes sensible the supersensible thing-in-itself. Thus, the aesthetic reception of spirit is the transcendental mystery underlying aesthetic judgement remarked on by Kant and which, he suggests, as with the transcendental imagination in the First Critique, refuses all comprehension. As Heidegger writes in the context of his interpretation of the *Critique of Pure Reason*, there is here manifest a fundamental recoil by Kant before an animating unthought lying beneath the textual architectonic. Thus, with and beyond Kant, the idea of the indeterminate, supersensible essence of man is disclosed in the gift of Spirit. The inspired art of genius is the point at which transcendental freedom breaks through into the world. The poetic work, thereby, is an irreducible example or Event that reconstructs and transforms natural experience.

Here, then, there is revealed the possibility of a genuine transition from nature to freedom. The art of genius is the manifestation of an objective purposiveness of nature. The genius experiences an inner transcendental freedom or power in the imaginative, sublime act of poetic creation. This free, inner purposiveness is the gift with which nature favours genius. The created work allows the indeterminate sublime feeling of absolute totality to shine forth in the phenomenal world. This supersensible freedom underlying the phenomenon of the artwork is neither wholly undetermined, as it is with the understanding, nor is it determined by moral reason. The work is both a manifestation of objective nature and a disclosure of nature as commensurate with the freedom of purposes. There is not a principle or determinate concept of reason underlying this natural purposiveness of the work and of artistic creation. Thus, the supersensible freedom manifest in the work of genius is determinable according to the purposes of practical reason, but the transition is possible only because of the infinite determinability (spirit) of the substrate underlying the artwork. As Schelling puts it, this is the 'unconscious infinity' of art. Within the bounds of aesthetic experience, spirit is manifest in the work as the gift from the self-concealing natural being of genius. Thus the gift of spirit is thought not in terms of a purposeful Giver but solely in terms of a giving and receiving. To determine this giving in terms of determinate purposes would be to think the Giver of the gift, i.e. the *a priori* self-legislative activity of the practical Self. But this would be to 'step beyond the bounds' of the aesthetic domain. Yet, only because the nature of aesthetic immanence offers itself as determinable in this way, is the possibility revealed for a transition from sensible nature disclosed by the understanding to supersensible, determinate moral freedom under the moral law. Schiller understood this point very well; see, for example, his twentieth letter on the aesthetic education of man.

Genius, therefore, is the mode of subjectivity that allows for a transition from freedom (mind) to nature (world). The ontology of later Heidegger retrieves the Kantian conception of the relation of favour between genius and nature.[33] Heidegger, however, following Herder and Humboldt, broadens Kant's idea of the spirit of the art of genius to include the idea of second nature. Hence, the second nature or linguistic community of the human being, as with the art of genius, manifests a free purposefulness, i.e. it is an embodiment of mindedness. The world as a whole has the appearance, according to Heidegger, of a work of art. Consequently, the object of aesthetic intuition, i.e. of transcendental aesthetic, is not a narrowly circumscribed aesthetic idea but, in fact, embraces the totality of the ontological content that constitutes our experience of world. Indeed, the totality of ontological content is an aesthetic totality – the idea of world *is* an aesthetic Idea. Spirit, *Geist*, underlies the second nature of our form of life. The purposeful mindedness of the idea of nature constituting this form of life is not, however, wholly determinate, i.e. conceptually articulated and articulable. Rather, the purposeful mindedness of our form of life *gives* our understanding of Being.

Consequently, the mind is related to world in Heidegger in a way analogous to the relation of genius to the work of art in Kant: an act of inspiration or aesthetic intuition underlies the human being's relation to Being. The principle, extracted from the *Critique of Judgement*, underlying this intuition of the favour or gift of Being is that of an objective purposefulness without purpose. To put the point a different way, our understanding of Being is based upon a teleological principle without a determinate *telos*. The rhythm of our second nature is the external 'for the sake of which' that gives linguistic meaning. Meaning is not constituted primarily by the use we make of words but rather by the way in which words appear to have a life and purposeful movement of their own. Words, if we let them, order and arrange themselves into relations of kinship and mutual accord: they 'speak' to us from out of an exteriority that is both purposeful and unfathomable.

Later Heidegger's analytic of the existentiality of genius, however, conceives the subject that gives and creates world not as the artist-poet but rather as the inspired thinker. The aesthetic idea of world is a product of thought in the sense that the original thinker repeats in a unique way the spirit animating our entire form of life. In the work of thought the thinker gives the form of the aesthetic idea that constitutes our experience of world. As such, it is the thinker, not the artist, who intuits our understanding of Being as a gift of second nature. The receptivity of authentic thinking lets the rhythmic self-ordering of linguistic content 'speak' to us. In arguing this, Heidegger is in fact tying together two loosely connected threads that run through the First and Third Critiques – the idea of the genius receiving the gift of nature and the idea, found explicitly in the *Prolegomena*, that metaphysical thinking also belongs to the human being as a gift or favour from nature. As Kant writes in the *Prolegomena*, metaphysics is to be conceived as a natural disposition of the human being because it is placed in man by nature itself. The natural predisposition of human reason bears metaphysics as a 'favourite child'.[34]

Just as, for Kant, a philosophical critique of pure reason illuminates the transcendental underpinnings of our natural disposition for metaphysics, so too, for later Heidegger, an analytic of the conditions of philosophical thought uncovers the existential structure underlying the gift we all receive from nature. The difference is that, in later Heidegger, the limit that metaphysical 'critique' gives to natural experience is not curtailing and disciplining, but enabling. Thinking opens up new forms of experience: in intuiting the movement of spirit the inspired thinker transforms our idea of world. This is the ontological basis of the originality and freedom of the thinker. Thinking is disclosive in a twofold sense: it reveals new modes of finite experience and, in the transformation or event that re-forms our form of life, it also manifests the shared act of inspiration that underlies our everyday existence. Hence, thinking is the authentic form of subjectivity that intensifies and uncovers the *sensus communis* that we all, though for the most part unknowingly, participate in. In the work of thought the linguistic community both gathers and finds itself.

On the basis of the preceding, provisional existential analytic of Kant's *Critique of Judgement*, we are now in a position to contrast Heidegger's conception of the origin and movement of ontological content with Hegel's. Hegel, like Heidegger, makes central to his metaphysics the idea of the living, autonomous essence of ontological content. The determinations or pure self-movements ('souls') of conceptual content together comprise the Rhythm of the Notion.[35] Rhythm is, according to Hegel, the immanent form of self-moving content, i.e. of the thing itself. Philosophical science offers an exposition of the way this determinate content moves spontaneously of its own nature. The effort of science is 'strenuous' because, Hegel writes, it requires the expositor giving up the freedom involved in being the moving principle of the content and the submerging of this subjective freedom into the self-moving life of objective Spirit. However, though Hegel contrasts this sinking of freedom into Spirit with the non-method of artistic inspiration, nonetheless, in his *Lectures on Fine Art*, the inspired person, like the philosopher, is said to be '...completely filled with the theme' and is '...animated by the rationality of the inherently true content of the subject-matter'.[36] The difference between art and philosophical thought, according to Hegel, is that artistic inspiration involves the giving of the form for the formation of the theme that has taken hold of the inspired person. This subjective element, missing in Science, is what he calls the living activation of the theme. Hence, in the act of inspiration, Hegel writes, there is a unity between immersion in objective content and the transformation of this content in the natural, subjective element of feeling and intuition. This, Hegel writes, is the essence of genuine originality. The inspired work, enjoying a strict interconnection of parts as if the thing in itself has united them, gives character. Thus, the work of art, according to Hegel, is not created from the resources of a fully-fledged subjectivity but rather yields both an intensification of subjective existence and an extension of the scope and depth of objective, social life.

Heidegger, conversely, though agreeing with Hegel that ontological content has its own, inner principle of life, offers a radically different account of the relation between this content and the act of inspiration. Hegel removes the act of inspiration from a determination of the rhythm of the Notion because the inspired person is said to give the form of ontological content. This introduces, he thinks, an unacceptably subjective element into the Notion. Later Heidegger, conversely, suggests that Being 'is' the form of the natural element of feeling and intuition that constitutes our second nature. To be inspired is to receive the rhythm of human nature: this rhythm gives the form of ontological content. Hence the movement of rhythm belongs to a 'subjective' element of human existence – as Hegel also suggests. But, as Hegel does not admit, this subjective element of our second nature is also manifest as 'objective' in that 'it gives' the form of the content *to* the inspired person. The language that constitutes our second nature has its own life and purposefulness, over and above our subjective needs and concerns. It is in the aesthetic reception of the movement of objective, second nature that the inspired person gives form to Being. Thus, the nature of the subjectivity of the inspired person and the relation of the subject to the objective movement that it intuits, determine the way in which later Heidegger re-casts the Hegelian interpretation of the relation between the human being and Being. However, following his radicalisation and unification of the Kantian analytic of genius and the idea of the metaphysician as a child of nature, the inspired person is not, according to Heidegger, an artist but a thinker. Against Hegel, there is an ineradicably subjective, inspired element in the philosophical thinking of the human being. Thinking is a gift from Being. Conversely, the purposeful life or Spirit of the Notion needs the thinking of the human being to *be*. This comprises what Heidegger calls the originary belonging of man and Being. The gift of *Geist* and the act of inspiration are, thus, the concrete, phenomenological ground for determining adequately the relation of gift-exchange between the human being and language.

Thus, to consolidate: later Heidegger, implicitly grounding his ontology in the *Critique of Judgement*, provides the foundations for an aesthetic idea of experience; i.e. an idea of the limits of experience as aesthetically bounded. This is the enabling limit that rhythm gives: not a limitation and legalistic curtailing of experience but the boundary or form that *gives* it – as the ancient Greeks, before Aristotle, realised.[37] By incorporating elements from Kant's analysis of the relation of nature and genius into a wider and more general conception of human experience, later Heidegger also attacks the very metaphysical foundations of transcendental idealism. In a Kantian, dualistic conception of experience the relation of the subject to the object in itself cannot be conceived. This is because, according to Kant, it is incomprehensible how the properties of the object in itself can be in harmony with the representations of the subject. The relation of subject to objects-in-themselves must be, in this case, based on 'inspiration'.[38] For Kant, the answer to this dilemma is to determine the relation between subject and object on the basis of *a priori* forms of intuition that order a given empirical manifold of intuition. The price, however, is that we can know *a priori* objects as appearances, but not as they are in-themselves. However, in order to overcome the Kantian dualism of appearance and thing-in-itself and at the same time to retain the idea of *a priori* pure intuition, the form of ontological intuition, paradoxically, can neither be in the subject nor external to it. If the form of intuition is in the subject *a priori*, the object is not represented as it is in itself but merely as it appears. If the forms of intuition are external to the subject and a determination of the object in itself, they are no longer *a priori*. In this case the relation between subject and object depends upon the actual presence of the empirical object for it to be determined.

However, later Heidegger shows the way out of this impasse in the Kantian idea of experience. Rhythm gives *a priori* the content of space and time to human beings; it is the intuited form of time-space, yielding an aesthetically unified ontological horizon within which beings can appear. Against Kant, time and space, in this sense, are not simply located in the faculties of the transcendental subject. Hegel rightly criticises Kant for not sufficiently appreciating that space and time are external universals.[39] Nonetheless, Hegel goes too far in externalising the pure forms of intuition into the mechanics of wholly objective nature.[40] On the other hand, resting in a position between Kant and Hegel, it is human nature that, in the ontology of later Heidegger, gives time-space. Hence, the human being does not give the form of intuition to things; things are not, consequently, appearances *for* the finite self. Human nature gives form to beings through the ontologically receptive human being. Second nature, our form of life, in this sense, is the ontological correlate to the ontic Real missing in early Heidegger. The second nature of man is the Real of Being in that, as Rhythm, it refuses or resists the human being's understanding of Being.

This conception of the ontological Real provides the constraint that McDowell's picture of experience demands but cannot fulfil. It is not a brute, sensory given but rather the aesthetically perceived constraint or limit that forms the boundary of our second nature. The rhythm of our form of life is, thus, the felt resistance of an indeterminate, purposeful movement underlying our articulation of conceptual content. Man cannot exhaustively explain why Rhythm gives. This ontological refusal is not, as in early Heidegger, the unintelligible, sheer sensory weight of ontic sensation, resisting and cancelling the ontological horizon within which it appears. Being gives the understanding of Being to man and conceals itself in this giving; this is the Rhythm or in-itself of Being. It is not a mute unintelligibility dependent upon what it resists, but the hidden gift-giving source of meaning. The human being experiences things in themselves from out of the *a priori* intuited horizon of Being in itself: the horizon determines the relation of subject and object. Being and the beings of 'real', natural experience touch in the expanse opened by human nature; the second nature of our form of life brings man back to things. Things, thus, are no longer appearances for us: we experience them as they are in themselves. The dualism of transcendental idealism is overcome. McDowell, on the other hand, tries to overcome this dualism by following Hegel and, as a result, remains within the frictionless, infinite ideality of conceptual content. Hence, later Heidegger both completes and annuls Kant's Copernican Turn. The human being experiences the Real of ontic existence not by clawing back the empirical, but *through* the Ideality of Being to the transcendental Real in-itself of Rhythm. Though he uses the term pejoratively Kant is right, and follows a tradition beginning with Plato, in describing the *a priori* aesthetic intuition of Rhythm as a kind of 'inspiration'. The aesthetic act of inspiration is the existential root of the *a priori* relation of mind and world.

However, the idea of second nature entails a purposefulness of spirit without a determinate or determinable purpose. There is no teleology of nature in later Heidegger or a dogmatic interpretation of nature as created by a transcendent, supreme Giver. The latter would allow for a pre-established harmony of subject and object in that the human being and beings are elements of a unified creation, correspondent, ultimately, to the divine ideas. This move to pre-critical Realism would neutralise Kant's Transcendental Idealism. Nonetheless, the price of this interpretation is a collapse into onto-theology. Conversely, in the ontology of later Heidegger, nature gives. The giving of nature is not explained as the giving or causing to-be of a most perfect, divine being, but as the offering by human nature of the unfathomable gift of Rhythm. The source of this giving remains immanent. No principle of reason lies at the heart of the giving of Rhythm; why Rhythm gives remains mysterious. The depth in man remains, hence, unfathomable. Language is an abyss because the human being cannot determine why or how 'it gives' in the way in which it does. Simply, Rhythm gives; *there is* Rhythm. Alternatively, neither is Being conceived as the ground for beings, a given horizon within which beings are and which, consequently, is given *for* beings as the condition for their possibility. Rather Being is in itself a *gift* offered to man from out of the abyssal depths of language. The human being's understanding of Being is not a nihilating Nothing that both gives and is cancelled by the actuality of the ontic: it releases beings as they are in-themselves, disclosing a living depth in ontic existence mirroring the depths of Being disclosed in the nature of man.

Later Heidegger, therefore, in providing the foundations for a fully concrete resolution of the antimony of ontological sensibility, does not fall back into onto-theology. The question posed at the end of chapter one was: what is the nature of the relation between the human being and Being, if this ontological relation involves both a giving and receiving of Being within the *a priori* immanence of finite, sensible experience? In later Heidegger's conception of experience, human nature *a priori* gives to the human being the rhythmically bounded field of existence within which man encounters things-in-themselves. The finite self receives the Rhythm of Being as the gift of its nature; rhythm is the immanent form from out of which the spirit of Language 'speaks'. Hence, the idea of pure, ontological sensibility describes, essentially, the way in which the human being *a priori* intuits the nonsensuous movement of spirit; spirit unifies and aesthetically orders the subject's communal form of life. Spirit is not given: 'it gives'. The ontological sensibility or *sensus communis* of the finite human being *a priori* senses the giving of spirit; sensuous existence depends upon the pure reception of this non-conceptual ontological content for it to *be*.

In sum, Heidegger uses the Kantian analytic of genius and nature to re-cast the conceptual foundations of the finite subject underlying the antinomy of pure sensibility. If the finitude of the subject lacks a constitutive *a priori* relation to human nature, the human being is in an impossible position of both giving and receiving Being. If, on the other hand, an ontological distinction is introduced into human finitude between human nature and the self, then it can be shown that in the conflicting statements I) Being must arise from the subject II) Being must not arise from the subject, the concept of the subject is intended in two different ways. Being *a priori* arises from the subject in the sense that *human nature* gives; Being does not arise from the subject in the sense that *man a priori* receives the gift of Being from nature. The antinomy arises from a conflation of these two aspects of human finitude. Once a revised philosophical anthropology grounds the idea of human nature within an analytic of the human being, the paradoxical air surrounding the idea of *a priori* ontological sensibility dissipates and the antinomy is resolved.

Chapter 9

Thought and Expression

Spirit animates the second nature of our form of life. Radicalising Kant's analytic of genius in the *Critique of Judgement*, the idea of world is an aesthetic idea. The words that constitute the totality of language take on relations of kinship and accord; words are the aesthetic attributes that constitute the rhythmic movement of the unified whole. Conceived as rhythm, language orders itself. This self-ordering of language constitutes the intrinsic life of conceptual content: language 'speaks' to us from out of an infinite determinability or unconscious infinity. The mindedness or purposefulness that language (nature) embodies is aesthetic; as such, it bears resemblance to an autonomous work of art. The work of art that world resembles is a gift: language grants to us our understanding of Being. The relation between world and the human being is therefore grounded in an aesthetic intuition. This *sensus communis* is manifest phenomenologically in the act of inspiration; the human being inspires, breathes in, the life that spirit gives. The authentic mode of experience that discloses explicitly the existential structure underpinning our aesthetic relation to world is the act of thinking. Against Hegel, thinking is necessarily inspired; human nature (language) inspires the thinker. Nonetheless, the subjectivity of the inspired thinker still remains phenomenologically obscure in at least two respects. This chapter examines the concrete nature of both the act of thinking and the object of thought.

These questions are important because, although the antinomy of ontological sensibility is resolved in later Heidegger, the further problem noted in the early work regarding the unity of spontaneity and receptivity in the subject appears untouched. It seems that later Heidegger has merely reversed the earlier priority he gave to spontaneity: now man is exclusively receptive, without any genuine activity or spontaneity within the being of the Self. The unity of spontaneity and receptivity has again been lost. This appearance is, nonetheless, deceptive. Later Heidegger insists that man needs Being for his understanding of Being and, at the same time, Being needs man in order to to-be: the priority of gift-exchange in the later ontology of the *Ereignis* is clear. There is no simple, brute reception of Rhythm. The intuition of non-conceptual content occurs *in* and *through* the spontaneous enactment and performance of this reception.

The performative receptivity of the human being is existentially constituted in expression.[1] Expression is manifest in the inspired *act* of the thinker; thinking is not, according to later Heidegger, a mere passivity. Rather, as expression, thinking is the highest form of activity.[2] As such, it manifests the unified root of spontaneity and receptivity in the being of the subject. Expression, thus, is not the spontaneous, conceptual determination of a pre-given non-conceptual manifold, as if the faculties of understanding and sensibility are engaged in ontologically separable activities. Rather there *is* reception of Being only *in* the active expression of it by the human being. The thinker, therefore, does not receive Being in an identical way to others within the community, and then act upon the given manifold it has received. Rather the activity of thinking is from the ground up the most perfect kind of reception. Inspired thinking is heightened expression: it fully realises our capacity for receptivity. Expression realises our capacity for receptivity in the sense that, following Kant's analytic of genius, to comprehend and intuit spirit fully, the thinker cannot describe or imitate, but must repeat spirit differently. The most perfect reception of spirit is realised in the act that actively re-shapes and re-orders it. As Heidegger puts it, to receive a gift properly, one must return the gift – exchange gifts. We realise and perfect our *reception* of the gift of Being in the *act* of sending a gift back. A gift, after all, as the theologian Milbank argues, cannot be received without being returned.[3] Inspired thinking returns the gift to spirit in repeating differently, reforming, the idea of world that animates our form of life.

This, therefore, constitutes the ontologically precise structure of the form of expression by which man belongs to Being – expression is the spontaneous act in and through which the exterior giving of Being is received. The unity of this performed receptivity rooted in the being of man is manifest, concretely, in the heightened expression of philosophical thinking. Expression, therefore, is neither free, spontaneous creation from the resources of an isolated subjectivity nor the controlled externalisation of given, subjective content. On the contrary, expression is the perfected realisation of our capacity to receive. The intuited content expressed by thinking is non-conceptual; it is intuitively manifest to the thinker in the form of an unfathomable inner depth or intensity. Intensity, thus, is the gatehouse of Being. This content is not a sheer, given presence, or disordered manifold, separate from the activity of the self. As a gathered intensity, the sublime feeling of an inner purposefulness rooted in human nature *is* not, but gives. The heightened expression that constitutes metaphysical thinking receives and returns this gift, unfurling the intuited point of intensity into a line or plane

However, the act of thought that returns the gift of Being gives us *another* world – it is world-disclosing and community-creating. The act of philosophical thinking creates the work of thought that inflames and transforms the world. This transformation is what Heidegger calls an Event, *Ereignis*. In an Event, the form and shape of a moribund life are re-ordered; the indeterminate necessity and purposefulness of an underlying power of nature shatters the sedimentation of a fossilised tradition. Philosophical thinking, therefore, does not offer a scientific description of the phenomenologically fundamental constituents of our idea of world. It is an expression and not a description of Being. As such, ontology is ineliminably revisionary – it fails to describe the relation of man and world, not from cognitive inadequacy but because this relation is not cognitively constituted. Rather, re-ordering the relation between man and things, it repeats this relation differently in an original, synthetic act. The product of ontology is an aesthetic idea.

Philosophical thinking is disclosive, therefore, because only in the immanent re-birth genius offers is there insight into the originary act of inspiration by which the human being is related to the world. Normally, we cannot perceive the threads that tie us to it; in disrupting and re-ordering these threads, the thinker creates a space within which the gift of Being is disclosed. This gift, however, cannot be described or pointed at. In order to be experienced, it must be repeated anew. Thinking performs this repetition. Thus, an existential-ontological analytic of the subjectivity of genius and so an understanding of the way in which thinking transforms the world, discloses the hidden way in which the world *is* in ordinary experience. Thinking in the *Ereignis* is the authentic mode of existence that illuminates the existential structure of everyday life. Initiation into the mother tongue, entering the objective spirit of a community, is not to be primarily conceived along the lines of second language acquisition, in which we are taught a systematic array of grammatical rules for the use of words. Rather, the intuitive act of genius is a faint echo of the inspiration through which we all first receive the world. This inspiration is our first breath of life as human beings: the act of genius reminds us of this life – and reinvigorates it. Conceived as re-birth, it is the reclamation of the world.

Each philosophical work, therefore, is a unique totality and each act of genuine thinking a singular judgement. Letting the content of Being 'speak' in new and surprising ways, ontology is world-forming. This constitutes the ethical substance of philosophy: spinning out new funnels of spirit for the *sensus communis*, it offers a variation on our second nature, deepening and extending the character of man. To understand a work of genius, correlatively, is to enter into the particular 'speaking' of language that it enacts; to share the character that it manifests. The work and labour of thought, as such, offers a further individualisation of the character of a community, opening up a space within which a community of friends might take root and flourish. These manifold communities of spirit disclose irreducible perspectives on the whole: they represent the forms and shapes into which a community might evolve and extend itself. This is the artistic exuberance and plenitude of our human nature – some sparks fall on stony ground and wither in the dark, others kindle and glow.

Being, therefore, needs the ethical substance disclosed in the judging act of the inspired thinker. The unique, exemplary individuation of the 'speaking' of language that each ontological totality manifests is the finitude that constitutes philosophical thinking. Ontology, as later Heidegger puts it, is the spoken site within which Being 'speaks'. The rhythm of ontological content does not demand an absolute, Hegelian submergence of the finite in the spontaneous unfolding of the Notion but rather a unique, finite expression of this rhythm. This ontology of gift-exchange between finite and infinite, thinker and Being, represents genuine mediation. Neither element evacuates its essence into the other; each *is* in the originary relation of gift-giving and returning of gift. This is the gift-exchange that underpins Heidegger's ontology of the Event. However, the thinker's returning of the gift to Being is determined further by Heidegger as an offering of thanks:

> But the highest and really most lasting gift given to us is always our essential nature, with which we are gifted in such a way that we are what we are only through it. This is why we owe thanks for this endowment, first and unceasingly. But the thing given to us, in the sense of this dowry, is thinking. As thinking, it is pledged to what there is to be thought. And the thing that of itself ever and anon gives food for thought is what is the most thought-provoking. In it resides the real endowment of our nature for which we give thanks.[4]

> Such thanks is not recompense; but it remains an offering; and only by this offering do we allow that which properly gives food for thought to remain what it is in its essential nature. Thus we give thanks for our thinking. ...[5]

The essence of the human being is thinking. Here Heidegger remains Aristotelian: thinking constitutes the nature of the human being. However, thinking is a gift. Thinking that understands itself as a gift pledges itself to what is most thought-provoking. In this pledge, thinking offers thanks for the gift of thought. As the second passage makes clear, in offering thanks, the thinker allows that which gives the gift of thought to remain what it essentially *is*. The object of thought is not, therefore, wholly separate from the act of thinking. Without Being there is no gift of thinking for which to give thanks and without returning the gift of thinking in thanksgiving there is no gift of thought to be received. Each depends upon the other. Indeed, Heidegger's idea that true thinking takes us *beyond* the human being is also faintly Aristotelian. As Aristotle writes in book ten of the *Nicomachean Ethics*:

> ... the activity of intellect, which is contemplative, seems both to be superior in worth and to aim at no end beyond itself... and [since] all the other attributes ascribed to the blessed man are evidently those connected with this activity, it follows that this will be the complete happiness of man, if it be allowed a complete term of life.... But such a life would be too high for man; for it is not in so far as he is man that he will live so, but in so far as something divine is present in him...that thing which is proper to each thing is by nature best and most pleasant for each thing; for man, therefore, the life according to intellect is best and pleasantest, since intellect more than anything else *is* man.[6]

The nature of man, that which *is* man essentially, is the activity of intellect. But, paradoxically, the essence of man is *beyond* man: it is divine. Heidegger takes up this Aristotelian thought: the nature of man is thinking, but the ground of this activity reaches beyond the human being. In thinking, man surpasses man and touches Being. Being fulfils our human nature. It is in this surpassing of ourselves toward Being that we are happiest; this comprises the distinctive rationality of the human animal. In the surpassing and rupturing of world we experience the freedom bequeathed by our humanity.

The intuitive act of inspired thinking is, therefore, the perfection of our animal nature. Kant's correlation of genius and our instinctive, natural existence was called into question by F. Schlegel, who argued that it identified the art of genius with natural works constructed by things like insects and birds. This, however, misses the point: the act of intuiting spirit realises the unique kind of animal that we are – it does not amount to a sharing of animality across the species. What is shared with other animals is that the act of inspiration is a singular mode by which life is expressed – in a Heideggerian register, it is repetition of the Same. However, the expression of life manifest in the act of inspiration is unique to man. Repetition is an enactment of difference. Only man can be inspired – there can be no adequation of the Kantian conception of inspiration with the idea of a collection of brute inter-species instincts and drives. The consummate act of inspiration, however, is thinking. In thinking, i.e. aesthetically re-shaping and re-ordering the articulated content that determines our form of life, in offering new forms of experience, we become the animals that we uniquely are.

This, therefore, is the transfigured Aristotelian inheritance of later Heidegger: metaphysics belongs to human nature in the sublime act that intuits the inhuman essence of man (spirit) and so transforms our nature. Thus, the philosophical anthropology of later Heidegger moves beyond the early work in a decisive way. Early Heidegger articulates the natural disposition of man for metaphysics as the transcendence of Dasein. Consequently, the human being's metaphysical tendencies are restricted to the transcending of beings toward a pre-ontological understanding of Being. Rather than questioning the unconditioned beyond the boundaries of human understanding, Dasein questions the meaning of that Being, for whom, in asking the question of Being, Being is already understood. For later Heidegger, conversely, metaphysics belongs to human nature as a gift received by the inspired thinker. Ontology is a favour from nature. Thinking is not the elaboration of what is already implicitly understood; it is a gift received from that which refuses all comprehension. The thinker receives the gift in the most perfect way by repeating the gift of spirit differently. This is the act of man that returns the gift to Being. Being needs this act to-be; man belongs to Being in giving the gift that it has received.

Hence, as the expression of Being, ontology is a giving of thanks. This thanksgiving returns the gift of thought to Being: thanking is a thinking of that which allows thinking to give thanks. It may appear when Heidegger makes claims such as these that, if thinking is the thanking of Being for the gift of being able to think, then the object of thought is evacuated of all real content. The lectures delivered during 1951-2 and published as *What is Called Thinking* often encourage this appearance. However, the preceding interpretation of the *Ereignis* should alleviate this concern. Thinking is inspired because it receives the spirit that animates our understanding of Being and expresses this spirit differently. Expression re-animates and re-invigorates the mindedness or life that is embodied in the world. The object of thought, as such, is the totality of content that constitutes our idea of world. Thinking, on the other hand, is the act of recognition that experiences the world *as* other and perceives ourselves *in* the other: world is both the exteriority of Being and the free purposefulness of *our* human nature. The recognition of the world as an object that our second nature (Being) has given, however, is fulfilled in the act of inspiration or intuition. There is no conscious identification of thought and Being. World is *other* to us: it is a gift from Being. Full recognition of this is realised in the original activity that re-shapes the world bequeathed by human nature. World is a gift *received* as other in re-expressing the web of relations that bind us to it. Recognition of the object as belonging to *us* occurs only in a moment of differentiating ourselves *from* it. There is identity *in* difference. In giving thanks we return the gift that Being has given: we *repeat* the Same of subject (mind) and object (world) *differently.*

The totality of the objective content of world, however, is disclosed in the idea of world that has been determined and unified in the work of thought. Thinking gives thanks to Being by repeating differently the idea of world manifest in a work of thought that is already there. The already there-ness of thought constitutes what we call the philosophical tradition. An Event of Being, therefore, is the sublime moment and act that draws a solidified, traditional conception of world back into its aesthetic ground and repeats in an original way its underlying spirit. The idea of philosophy as the repetition and variation of the spirit underlying an earlier philosophical work is conceived by Heidegger as a thinking of the unthought of a particular thinker. Each authentic thinker, because they express Being in a unique way, taps into the spirit that underlies their form of life. Kant describes this as drawing from the 'wellsprings of Reason'.[7] In the *Ereignis*, therefore, the act of thinking experiences a relation to its own exteriority: spirit is the matter or passion upon which thought is shattered. Matter, pure intensity, is the transcendental Real upon which the finite thinker depends and to which he is bound. This later conception of authentic thinking is the fruit of the critique of the 'sensibility of reason' Heidegger demands in *Kant and the Problem of Metaphysics*. Shattered thought is passionate, finite: passion enables thinking to be what it is. The price of animating a conceptual field with spirit is that the inspired work is open to repetition of its underlying spirit by another work: indeed it is this potential for repetition and re-animation that makes a work both rare and great. A work without spirit cannot be repeated differently because it is not an original expression *of* spirit.

However, as later Heidegger argues, the gift of Being to man has been left suspended in the history of thought. Aside from the earliest Greek thinkers and not even then in a fully mediated way, the human being has failed to experience its understanding of Being as a gift. In the unfolding of the Western tradition, the concealing of the 'it gives' is itself concealed – Being has fallen into oblivion. This oblivion is due to the fact that each act of thought which constitutes a particular epoch in the history of metaphysics is not conceived as a unique expression of spirit. Spirit or Being is the Same that each thinker repeats differently. However, Heidegger argues, thinking prior to the *Ereignis*, has not understood itself to be the repetition and expression of Being. Thus, previous works of philosophy are in an external relation to their own form. Being gives the form by which the content of the philosophical object is ordered. To receive form from Being is to be inspired. Traditional thinking, however, understands philosophical thought and method as deeply antagonistic to the act of inspiration. Either the act of thinking gives form to a separate content, as in Kant, or, as in Hegel, the objective content gives itself the form by which it moves. In Heidegger, conversely, the act of inspired thinking gives form to the articulated object of thought by intuiting the gift that the movement of content, i.e. spirit, gives. The form of the object of thought is both radically external to us and at the same time a manifestation of the inner purposefulness of human nature.

When the act of thinking knows itself, it gives thanks. It gives thanks because the content of the world, which it recognises as an embodiment of mindedness, is nonetheless the purposefulness of an external existence to which thought is indebted. If thought recognised nature simply as the alienated presence of its own consciousness, in which the difference of subject and object is identified and sublated in an act of absolute comprehension, then the giving of thanks would not be intelligible. We cannot thank ourselves, as little as we can give a gift to ourselves. Thinking is not conceivable as thanking within the field of Hegelian ontology. However, for later Heidegger, thinking is in debt to Being. Thus, if philosophy is the history of thought finding itself then the process of discovery is 'completed' in the gift of thanks disclosed in the *Ereignis*, a gift that is endlessly repeated and repeatable. In giving thanks we *realise* our debt to Being.

From this perspective, the history of thought is analogous to Kant's description of the history of the art of genius. Each unique totality or ontology repeats differently what went before. For thinking the tradition is both enabling and constraining. In the historical relations between the systems of ontology, however, there is no rational dialectical necessity that can determine precisely why a later work supplants an earlier one. An expression of Being does not sublate the earlier work that it repeats anew. This is why each philosopher in the tradition always remains alive for us in a way that Newtonian physics cannot. Each work of philosophy is a repetition of the Same. As such each is accessible in the unique way that it *is* – despite the polemics launched against it by other thinkers. However, the repetition that each work enacts takes shape only in a re-ordering of the history of the expressions of Being that preceded it. Expression does not take place in a vacuum. A thread runs through the tradition, though the unravelling of this thread is not dialectical. Rather, it manifests an aesthetic purposefulness in which each expression of Being, like a theme in a musical work, offers a variation on the whole that is both necessary and yet utterly contingent.

The problem remains, however, as to the exact nature of the philosophical work in later Heidegger's conception of post-metaphysical thinking. Thinking, in fact, is quite different from what Heidegger names poeticising. Unfortunately, the fundamental differences between thought and poetry are often neglected in Heidegger studies. For example, Blanchot suggests that Heidegger's ontology of language is not sensitive to the relations between words and instead holds its attention on words considered on their own and 'concentrated in themselves'.[8] Blanchot concludes that Mallarmé's ontology must therefore supersede Heidegger's. Although Blanchot is right to highlight the distinction between words and relations between words, nonetheless Heidegger also makes this distinction within his ontology of language. Indeed, Heidegger articulates it precisely *as* the difference between thinking and poetry. The difficulty is that Heidegger's preoccupation with poetry, especially Hölderlin, often distorts and covers over his elucidation of the nature of thinking. However, against Blanchot, this does not entail that Heidegger has nothing to say on the essential traits of the act of thinking.

Indeed what he says appears very close to the kind of ontology of language Blanchot describes as Mallarméan.

There are at least three ways in which thinking differs from poetry: in act, object and origin. Poetry is a naming of things; it bestows the word.[9] Thinking does not name things: though Heidegger is not explicit, the preceding interpretation of the *Ereignis* suggests that his conception of the act of thinking is analogous to the creation of a Kantian aesthetic idea. The sense and feeling of the unity of the indeterminate totality that thinking gives is manifest in the relations of kinship and affinity between the words that it actively orders and forms. Thinking, therefore, is fundamentally a bringing into order and an act of relating rather than the naming of things. In addition, poetry names the holy in the sense that the naming of things allows a site for the presencing of the gods. Thinking, on the other hand, is not related to the divinities that comprise one element of the fourfold world. Rather, thinking says Being.[10] Thinking is the expression of the way language 'speaks' to us. The object of thought is the life and spirit underlying the conceptual content that constitutes our understanding of Being. This object is not, as in poetry, the ether of the holy within which a god may manifest itself. The object of thinking is strictly immanent. Finally, poetry names because it receives the word from the divinities: the unknown God, Heidegger claims, gives the measure for poetic composition.[11] On the other hand, the measure for thinking is not a hidden divinity. Thinking is a gift from the impersonal rhythm of Being; the inspired thinker is rhythmed and brought to order by Being. Being is not a Giver: as rhythm, it is the sheer movement of giving. One other salient difference, which goes to the heart of the distinction between poetry and thinking, is that thought works entirely within the non-sensuous domain. In the genuinely poetic work, the sensuous existence of sound and tone (earth) represent the ontic site for the happening of world. Philosophical thinking, however, deals exclusively with the meaning and content of words and does not make use of their sensuous form to order and articulate this content. The medium within which thinking works is, as Hegel argues, prose. Thinking must take place and be realised in the prose work; the inspired thinker is a prose writer.

As noted previously, for Humboldt, the prose of philosophical thought represents the sublimity and peak of language-production. Prose has a truth and objectivity that poetry lacks.[12] Nonetheless, for Humboldt, unlike Hegel, the logical eurhythmy of thought that prose realises is rooted in inspiration and feeling.[13] Humboldt's idea of the unique rhythm of prose echoes the remarks of the literary critic William Hazlitt, ten years earlier, on the requirements of a good prose style. The prose writer, for Hazlitt, must wait for the subject-matter to come of itself and must drift with the current, allowing the prose work to gain an elasticity and momentum.[14] The precision and weight of the form of the prose has its measure in the feeling of the subject, a feeling that is expressed in the common or natural order of words extracted and laid out in the composition. This feeling of the natural order of words discloses, according to Hazlitt, the rhythm and cadence of prose.[15] The task of the prose-writer is to reclaim the original simplicity, character and force of the English language that has become buried in the drive for a philosophical and universal language. This would, Hazlitt argues, allow us to understand that before becoming acquainted with extraneous models which spoil and adulterate the native cadence, we have enough to do to understand our own.[16]

However, despite the intimate relation between the activity of thinking and the writing of prose in the Romantic tradition, it is Adorno, in his reading of the essay as form, who offers the most philosophically satisfying interpretation of the prose work. According to Adorno, the prose essay does not offer an interpretation of its subject matter in the sense of removing an outer husk to find out what the author wanted to say, nor does it uncover any underlying psychological impulses.[17] The essential childlike play[18] of the form of prose frees up the objective wealth of meanings encapsulated in the phenomenon, the objectivity of which is reciprocated in the subjective expression of the interpretation itself. The power of the interpretation, Adorno writes, consists in the ability to give voice to the elements of the object in conjunction with each other.[19] However, though possessing quasi-aesthetic autonomy, the essay differs from art in that its medium is concepts. Nonetheless, the prose essay, according to Adorno, does not define the concepts, nor are the concepts primordial givens derived from a first principle.[20] Rather, they are introduced immediately when appropriate and as for Hazlitt are made more precise through their relationship to each other in the form of the immanent unfolding of the work. The form of the essay is not abstract or empty and thus separate from its content, however, because the concepts, received from the phenomenon, are already concretised as historical sedimentations of language. The essay reflects upon the immediate conceptual meanings and takes them further:[21]

> All its concepts are to be presented in such a way that they support one another, that each becomes articulated through its configuration with the others. ... But the elements crystallise as a configuration through their motion. The constellation is a force field, just as every intellectual structure is necessarily transformed into a force field under the essay's gaze.[22]

The configuration of the constellation of concepts crystallises through the motion introduced into the phenomenon by the prose work. This motion is the play or mobility of the mind, the process of what Adorno calls 'intellectual experience'.[23] This kind of experience, Adorno argues, feeds and sustains traditional thought although the memory of it is mostly eliminated in favour of the cognitive content of the result. So too, in Heidegger, the thinking experience which gives thanks is a recollection or remembrance.[24] To remember Being is to gather and express the motion or 'way' of language underlying the rigid order of our technologically framed linguistic field. Adorno and Heidegger also similarly argue that the model or archetype for the experience of movement in the prose work is anticipated in music. Language 'speaks' in the melodic mode.[25] The essay-form possesses the 'logic of music'.[26] In regard to this logic, Adorno writes:

> In such experience, concepts do not form a continuum of operations... the moments are interwoven as in a carpet. The fruitfulness of the thoughts depends

on the density of the texture. The thinker does not actually think, but rather makes himself into an arena for intellectual experience. ...[27]

The form of the essay offers a site and gathering point for the kind of thinking-experience Adorno and Heidegger relate. The essay does not describe this experience but enacts or performs it. The experience crystallised in the essay is recollected and expressed as the movement of the relations between concepts, in which there is manifest the precise order of an inner coherence and harmony.[28] Here, according to Adorno, is unveiled the constraint and play in the objectivity of language itself, an objectivity that is received and expressed in the force-field of the essay's constellation. Thus, Adorno's conception of the essay-form makes concrete and tangible the nature of the work of philosophical thought as implicitly envisaged by Heidegger.

For later Heidegger, each prose-essay bestowed in the finite act of the inspired thinker offers an aesthetic idea. This aesthetic idea repeats the spirit underlying the work of a previous thinker in a different, original way. Original repetition, thus, re-configures the conceptual field of a previous thinker, entering into and varying the originary experience that animated it. The concepts within a philosophical work, however, take on their own life; they 'speak' to us in the immanent, temporal movement of the unfolding prose. The temporal 'speaking' of Being is intuited from out of the unfathomable spatial depth of an inner intensity. This is the rhythmic time-space that the form of philosophical prose gives. The rhythm ordering the articulated content of the work offers the possibility of new forms of experience, it extends the scope of objective, social life and intensifies and deepens our subjective existence. The prose of thought, as such, bestows character. This is the originary *Bildung* into which the philosophical work initiates us. To write philosophical prose is to intuit the spirit underlying our form of life and to re-affirm this life. Inspired thinking returns the gift of life to life in the concrete, expressive act that resonates in the rhythm of a prose-work. In writing, we give thanks.

PART IV
THE TRUTH OF BEING AND THE
TRUTHFULNESS OF MAN

Chapter 10

A History of Truth and Truthfulness

Thinking is the act that identifies the object of thought (world) as belonging to us. World is the aesthetic idea that the free purposefulness of our second nature gives. The thinker intuits the life and spirit that animates our world in the act of repeating this spirit in an original way. Perfected reception of the world as an embodiment of our mindedness entails the act of differentiating ourselves from it. We recognise that the idea of world offered by our second nature (language) is fully intuitable *as* ours, as a gift offered to us, only in repeating and returning the gift to the *other* that gives it. This repetition of thinking is an act of thanksgiving. In thanksgiving we give thanks for the world that is ours; we reclaim the life that the world has lost. This reclamation of the world takes place in the site opened up by the work of philosophical prose. Ontology is revisionary. The singular judgement of the finite thinker opens up the possibility of new forms of experience; Being is the life in which human beings participate. This is the ethical substance bequeathed by philosophy.

However, according to later Heidegger, it is not simply the meaning of Being that is received as a gift by the human being. After the turn, the human being receives what Heidegger describes as the truth of Being. Yet, the literature on Heidegger does not explain why he shifts specifically from the concept of meaning to the concept of truth. Why is the idea of the meaning of Being not sufficient? What role does the concept of truth fulfil in the *Ereignis* that the concept of meaning cannot? Though the reason appears obscure, nonetheless, as Wittgenstein remarks, in ordinary language-use there are instances when the concepts of meaning and truth merge. For example, if I cry 'I *hope* she'll come' and say this with feeling, in such a way that the words are 'charged with my desire',[1] then it makes sense to suggest that the feeling gives the words both meaning and truth. Though the feeling does not give the individual words their meaning, it gives 'meaning' to them in the sense of a 'special ring' – it gives to the words their *point*.[2] It is on the basis of his observation that words can be spoken with feeling that Wittgenstein remarks that words are also deeds.[3] The concept of meaning merges with the concept of truth when our 'meaning' is charged with feeling: the expression of feeling in our linguistic behaviour gives meaning its purpose, i.e. its truth. Meaning is not simply given in the determinate grammar of a community or in a rule-governed, pre-ontological understanding of Being. The idea of the truth of linguistic expression, i.e. the true expression of feeling in language, merges into and elevates the idea of the meaning of linguistic use. After the turn the truth of Being is the expression, the feeling of purposefulness, which underlies our understanding of the meaning of Being. Meaning (use) 'turns' into truth (expression).

In a short paper entitled *Conversations on a Country Path about Thinking*, Heidegger remarks that the truth of Being is a 'hidden coming forth' from out of 'that which regions'.[4] That-which-regions Heidegger also describes as the giving of Being. Thus truth is a movement of giving. This movement is the life and way of truth. As such, truth is not the property of a proposition expressed in the truth predicate 'is true', in the sense of the correspondence of the true proposition to an extra-linguistic item in the world. Nor is truth the coherent relation that truth-bearers have to one another in the beliefs of a linguistic community, in which the criterion for truth is the rule for the evaluation of a belief as being true. The truth and movement of Being are, according to Heidegger, exterior to the rules and standards of the linguistic community. Nor is the truth of Being the pragmatic outcome of settled habits of action concerning what is useful in the manipulation of nature and the furtherance of the stability of human intercourse (Pierce). Neither is truth understood by Heidegger to be the redundant tool of an economy of expression, i.e. simply an expression of agreement between speakers (Ramsey). Rather the truth of Being appropriates and orders the human being's understanding of Being: it is an external movement to which the linguistic being of man is bound.

However, the truth of Being is not simply a movement but rather a movement that 'speaks' to man in the feeling of a purposeful order underlying the conceptual content determining his form of life. The origin of this feeling of the purposeful movement of the truth of Being is language itself, our second nature. The thinker receives the felt purposefulness of Being and, in the act of writing, returns the gift. The inspired thinker therefore is full of the truth. The life and movement of truth needs the receptivity of the human being to *be*; this constitutes the immanent relation within the nature of truth. The truth of Being needs the true expression of man. In expressing the truth of Being, the thinker receives the truth; he is full of the truth – inspired. The truthfulness of the human being intuits the feeling through which the truth of Being 'speaks' to us. Only in receiving the 'speaking' of language can man be full of the truth; only in being truthfully received by man can Being give the gift of truth. Truth is neither internal to the rule-giving, linguistic capacity of man, nor is it related to a wholly independent, extra-linguistic world. Truth is the rhythmic feeling of immanent purposefulness that gives meaning to us, i.e. that gives meaning its point, *telos*. The truth of Being allows us to use meaning purposefully – for this or that purpose. As such, Heidegger's conception of truth inverts the prioritisation of meaning over truth in contemporary philosophy of language.

The truthfulness of the inspired person, therefore, is the true expression of the 'speaking' of Being.[5] The truthfulness of man allows the truth of Being to-be. In ancient philosophy this idea of truth is named *aletheia*. It literally means unconcealing, bringing out of hiddenness. It can mean the truth of things and also the truthfulness of speech, being truthful. In the unfolding of the philosophical tradition, these two meanings of *aletheia* become sundered from each other. *Aletheia* is gradually used exclusively to mean a human being who speaks the truth, who is open and honest with himself and others. In the *Nicomachean Ethics*, for example, *aletheia* is used to describe the person who speaks and acts openly, who does not conceal his feelings and who is open in his hate and love.[6] Truthfulness here means the externalisation of an inner, subjective content, i.e. private feelings and thoughts. The Christian tradition consolidates this conception of truthfulness: truthfulness is a moral virtue, consummated in the act of confession. St. Thomas Aquinas provides the definitive classification and analysis of this idea of truthfulness. For Aquinas, the truthful man states that which concerns himself – truthfulness is a manifestation of the truth by one person to another, a moral debt. Replying to an objection that truthfulness is not a virtue because truth is the object of faith, Aquinas writes:

> Truth can be taken in two ways. First, for that by reason of which a thing is said to be true… taken in this way truth is a… certain equality between the understanding or sign and the thing understood or signified. … Secondly truth may stand for that by which a person says what is true, in which sense one is said to be truthful. This truth or truthfulness must needs be a virtue because to say what is true is a good act.[7]

According to Aquinas, truth is the adequation or equality of sign and signified thing. This medieval conception of truth, as Heidegger points out, is the ancestor of the modern correspondence theory of truth. However, as Heidegger also argues, the idea of truth as *adaequatio rei et intellectus* is grounded, for Aquinas, in the adequation of created things to the idea of them conceived in the divine intellect.[8] Only insofar as a being measures up to its essence can it appear, as how and what it is, for a human statement with which it is in accordance. Hence propositional truth is possible only on the basis of a material truth in which each species of being corresponds to the divine idea that forms it. This correspondence Aquinas determines as that between Creator and creation.[9] On the other hand, truthfulness is the virtue of saying 'what is true'. As Aquinas points out, it is possible to say what one believes is true, or what one truthfully thinks or feels and yet state a falsehood, as it is possible to intend to speak falsely, to deceive and yet to approximate to the truth. The act of speaking what one believes is true is, thereby, sundered from what truth itself is. There is truth without the truthfulness of man – truthfulness, the moral virtue of honesty to oneself and to others, presupposes truth in-itself as something already accessible. Truthfulness, a manifestation of the truth, is a mere act of will, a good act, whereas knowing the truth as such, for Aquinas, is an act of the intellect. Christian anthropology's classification of truthfulness as a moral virtue, thus formalised the meaning of *aletheia* that was already becoming dominant in Greek thought. This classification permeates Kant's decision to restrict the question of the nature of truthfulness to his *Anthropology from a Pragmatic Point of View* (1798). It remains in place up to the present day: see, for example, B. Williams, *Truth and Truthfulness: an essay in Genealogy* (2002) in which the value of truth is said to be contained in the basic virtues of Accuracy and Sincerity.[10]

However, Nietzsche rightly criticises this moral-Christian conception of truthfulness:

> Morality of truthfulness in the herd. "You shall be knowable, express your inner nature by clear and constant signs – otherwise you are dangerous: and if you are evil, your ability to dissimulate is the worst thing for the herd. We despise the secret and unrecognisable. – Consequently you must consider yourself knowable, you may not be concealed from yourself, you may not believe that you change." Thus: the demand for truthfulness presupposes the knowability and stability of the person. In fact, it is the object of education to create in the herd member a definite faith concerning the nature of man: it first invents this faith and then demands "truthfulness".[11]

> Within a herd, within any community, that is to say *inter pares*, the overestimation of truthfulness makes good sense. Not to be deceived – and consequently, as a personal point of morality, not to deceive!... In dealing with what lies outside, danger and caution demand that one should be on one's guard against deception: as a psychological preconditioning for this, also in dealing with what lies within. Mistrust as the source of truthfulness.[12]

As Nietzsche points out, the demand for moral truthfulness entails the knowability and stability of the person. The existentiality of the self is exhausted in the accessible and already given content that constitutes its inner experience. This morality of truthfulness, consequently, unveils a determinate concept of human nature: man simply *is* the actual manifold of inner, subjective experience to which he has transparent access. There is in this anthropology of man, no sense of our being unknowable, unfathomable. Without the idea of a hidden ground within the soul, the idea that we can *become* what we *are* has no purchase: the morality of truthfulness, hence, forbids change and self-overcoming. As Nietzsche also rightly points out, it is the phenomenon of mistrust, the possibility of pretence and deception – and the feeling of danger and anxiety that these generate – which demand a morality of truthfulness in the first place. However, this kind of morality cannot be simply restricted to a form of degenerate Christianity – a similar demand for truthfulness is prominent in the late Stoicism of M. Aurelius, in which the virtuous Roman is repeatedly said to possess a soul that is 'good, simple, naked, plainer to see than the body surrounding him'.[13] On the other hand, the antithesis of the good Roman is the person who acts a part, who coverts anything that calls for walls or coverings to conceal it, who needs a hole to hide in.[14]

However, if the moral demand for truthfulness arises from the fear and mistrust that follows from the possibility of pretence, this possibility, as well as the morality that flows from it, have also, as Nietzsche suggests, thoroughly pervaded our general conception of human experience. This Nietzschean thought is developed further by Wittgenstein. According to Wittgenstein, the possibility of lying and dissembling, when used to underpin and found our conception of thinking and feeling, culminates in a determination of the content of inner experience as essentially private:

'Thoughts and feelings are private' means roughly the same as 'There is pretending', or 'One can hide one's thoughts and feelings; can even lie and dissimulate'. And the question is, what is the import of this 'There is…' and 'One can'.

Under what circumstances, on what occasions, then, does one say 'Only I know my thoughts?' – When one might also have said 'I am not going to tell you my thoughts' or 'I am keeping my thoughts secret', or 'You people could not guess my thoughts'.[15]

Wittgenstein's point is that our being able to lie and dissimulate should not be used to determine a wider picture of human experience. In this picture, the first person is understood to have direct and certain epistemological access to the content of inner thinking and feeling, whilst the third person has merely inferential, indirect acquaintance with this content. Thus, experience is always private, the 'I' is the privileged locus of knowledge – leading, ultimately, to intolerable forms of scepticism. Hence, echoing Nietzsche, Wittgenstein remarks that the behaviour of feigning and pretending has eventually led to the concept of something inner, the 'soul'.[16] Yet the idea of the soul, Wittgenstein also stresses, is an outcome, not the origin, of this process.[17] On the other hand, highlighting the fact that pretence and dissembling are learned at a relatively advanced stage in the acquisition of a language, Wittgenstein attempts to undermine the concept of thinking as an inner and private process. Hence, for Wittgenstein, linguistic behaviour is a form of expression: it does not merely present a series of signs from which the third person can infer the character of the first person's inner content and experience. Rather, these forms of linguistic behaviour are the logically defeasible criteria for the application of, for example, sensation-concepts. Hence, the criterion for the truth of a confession is not to be identified with the criteria for a true description of a process, but rather with the special criteria of truthfulness,[18] i.e. the imponderable evidence of subtleties of glance, of gesture and of tone.[19] Wittgenstein thus overturns the stability and knowability of the self-certain 'I': the inner infuses the outer, our bodily animality, desire and suffering are the roots of thought. Thinking is a phenomenon of life.[20]

Later Heidegger's ontological conception of truthfulness works within this Wittgensteinian tradition: it is quite distinct from the idea of truthfulness as the externalisation of an inner, private content. Truthfulness is an expression of Being in-itself. Though Being is not ordinarily actively received as a gift, it is the public, shared ground of the linguistic community, whose content and form are intuited by our *sensus communis*. By determining the truth of Being in this way, Heidegger is attempting to recover an original sense of *aletheia*, involving both the idea of truthfulness, i.e. true expression, and the idea that the truth expressed concerns things-in-themselves. The problem with the interpretation of truthfulness as a moral virtue is that there is no longer any underlying ontological relation between 'speaking' the truth and the truth in-itself. Truth is sundered from its living relation to specifically human existence: it is a pure Object. As Nietzsche might say, by the modern period this Object has become a myth – it is redundant, an old tool that is

no longer useful. On the other hand, when truthfulness is sundered from the idea of the truth in itself, the act of being truthful is no longer disclosive. Truthfulness no longer has any relation to the truth of objective phenomena, i.e. how things actually are. It is a merely subjective, moral virtue, relegated to the will and guided by the intellect.

Heidegger's ontological conception of truthfulness tries to bring together both elements comprising the unified nature of truth that have become sundered from each other in the tradition. The other aspect of the ancient conception of *aletheia*, i.e. the objective movement and truth of things themselves, is faintly preserved in book three of Aristotle's *Metaphysics*:

> From these facts one might think that the only cause is the so-called material cause; but as men thus advanced, the things themselves showed them the way and joined in forcing them to investigate the subject... .When these men and the principles of this kind had had their day, as the latter were found inadequate to generate the nature of things, men were forced again by the truth itself [*aletheia*], as we said, to inquire into the next kind of cause.[21]

Here, *aletheia* is not, as in the *Nicomachean Ethics*, used in the sense of the morally virtuous man being honest and open. *Aletheia* instead refers to the truth itself, the things themselves. Yet a hint of the other meaning of *aletheia* shines though: truth is not simply a property inherent in our use of propositional language. Conceived as *aletheia*, truth shows the way – it forces the thinker to question and investigate the subject matter. In the manner in which Aristotle here describes *aletheia*, it has life and movement within itself. As *aletheia*, the truth 'speaks' to us. *Aletheia* is not used to refer to the morally commendable 'speaking' of man, the externalisation of inner feelings and thoughts. Rather, it means the objective 'speaking' of the things themselves. This speech constitutes the truth of what *is*.

The truthful, inspired person expresses the speech of Aristotle's things in themselves, *auto to pragma*. Truthfulness is the act that receives and gives voice to the 'speaking' of Being. Although elements within the New Testament and Augustine preserve this antique notion of *aletheia*, for the most part truthful expression comes to mean in the Western tradition the subjective externalisation of an inner, discrete content to which the first person has privileged access. The true content, however, of the unconcealing 'speaking' of truth is the truth in itself. The truthful thinker receives this content as objective – it arises from out of an unfathomable movement within the depths of human nature. Access to this content is given, therefore, not in the psychological state and private, mental process of the 'I' who forms it, but only in and through the work of thought itself. Correlatively, the act that receives Being is not the subjective avowal of an inner, given presence but the expression of a gift that the objective content itself gives. The second nature of the human being's form of life inspires and fills man with the truth; the act that receives this truth constitutes truthful expression. The finite truthfulness of man, therefore, *is* the way and life of truth. The truth of Being needs the truthfulness of the inspired human being to-be. The human being, conversely, must breathe in and inspire the gift of spirit in order to be full of the truth, to dwell in the truth. As Nietzsche puts it:

> Has anyone at the end of the nineteenth century a distinct conception of what poets of strong ages called *inspiration*? If not, I will describe it. – If one had the slightest residue of superstition left in one, one would hardly be able to set aside the idea that one is merely incarnation, merely mouthpiece, merely medium of overwhelming forces. The concept of revelation, in the sense that something suddenly, with unspeakable certainty and subtlety, becomes *visible*, audible, something that shakes and overturns one to the depths, simply describes the fact. One hears, one does not seek: one takes, one does not ask who gives; a thought flashes up like lightning, with necessity, unfalteringly formed... an instinct for rhythmical relationships which spans forms of wide extent – length, the need for a *wide-spanned* rhythm is almost the measure of the force of inspiration, a kind of compensation for its pressure and tension.... . Everything is in the highest degree involuntary but takes place as in a tempest of a feeling of freedom, of absoluteness, of power, of divinity.... The involuntary nature of image, of metaphor, is the most remarkable thing of all; one no longer has any idea what is image, what metaphor, everything presents itself as the readiest, the truest, the simplest means of expression. It really does seem, to allude to a saying of Zarathustra's, as if the things themselves approached and offered themselves as metaphors... . This is *my* experience of inspiration; I do not doubt that one has to go back thousands of years to find anyone who could say to me 'it is mine also'.[22]

The supreme virtue of Zarathustra, Nietzsche writes, is truthfulness.[23] As with Heidegger, the only previous manifestation of truthfulness, *aletheia*, occurs according to Nietzsche in the poets of the strong ages, the Pre-Socratics. These inspired poets 'speak' the truth. However, the opposite of the antique conception of *aletheia* is not the moral vice of lying, *pseudos*, telling falsehoods or concealing a guilty secret – i.e. choosing *not* to externalise subjective content. The withdrawing and withholding aspect of (un)truth is not keeping a secret we know from others – as it is in the act of lying. Concealing is not the opposite of revealing, as a moral vice is opposite to a moral virtue. Rather, *aletheia* itself hides; the gift of wide spanned rhythm is a mystery we cannot explain – 'we do not ask who gives'. This even Plato respectfully understood, despite his tirade against the lying poets. In being filled and inspired by the truth we experience the unfathomability of our finite existence, we are shaken to the depths. Being conceals itself in the sublime gift that 'it gives'. The concealing of untruth within the nature of truth is not, as in *Origin of the Work of Art*, the ontic refusal of sheer matter. Rhythm itself hides in the gift that 'it gives'. Truthlessness is not lying, but rather a refusal to listen to and hear the truth – the truthless person is not a liar because they have no content to lie about, they are the dispossessed. The truthful, inspired thinker, on the other hand, is possessed. Possession does not entail being completely denuded of selfhood by irrational drives, but rather being appropriated, brought into order. To be inspired, as Nietzsche puts it, is to be the force of truth incarnate. Truthful expression does entail being open, but openness conceived as honesty to the phenomena. Truthfulness is the capacity to receive the play and approach of the things themselves without prejudice, to listen in the right way. The truthful thinker lets language 'speak'; in so doing he becomes a mouthpiece of overwhelming and involuntary forces that, nevertheless, inspire a feeling of absolute freedom and power.

If an act of thinking truly expresses the 'speaking' of the *logos*, then the free-standing work of thought is brought into a rhythm and harmonious order – it has intrinsic life and spirit over and apart from the person who produced it. The order manifest within the inspired work *is* the instinctive consonance and rhythm of Being itself. A truthless work, conversely, is dissonant; it lacks order and rhythm in the unfolding of its content. In a metaphysical system that lacks truth the linkages between thoughts appear artificial and contrived; they are divested of the appearance of a natural objectivity. Relations of kinship are stretched too thin, the introduction of a new concept jars on the ear. In a work without truth, there is, as Nietzsche puts it, an absence of genuine rhythmical relations. Without rhythm and cadence the form of philosophical prose cannot reach the autonomy and necessity that an aesthetic idea of world demands: ontology becomes a literary exercise.

The act of the inspired person, therefore, is filled with the truth insofar as the expression of thought manifests the rhythm and order through which Being 'speaks' to man. Thought *is* expression when the subjective act of thinking lets the object manifest itself in and for itself: the inspired subject enacts the form that the movement of content has itself given. This content, however, is not wholly exterior to man: the act of Being is rooted in human nature. Unfortunately, after Kant, this purposeful inner activity within man is conceived as a collection of instinctive, unconscious drives, defined in opposition to the conscious ego. Contrary to this prevailing interpretation, the philosophical anthropology of later Heidegger re-casts the ontological foundations of the 'unconscious' act of human nature. The spontaneity of Being offers the thinking of man as a gift; thinking is indebted to the nature that gives it. To thank Being is not to lapse back into instinctive irrationality. Only when thinking knows itself can it give thanks to the purposeful movement that gives the conceptual content that constitutes its world. Being is the life that animates human reason: the inspired person recognises and expresses this life. The activity of Being within ourselves, therefore, which we receive and nurture, is not the brute force of unreason but the purposeful spontaneity and wellspring of life itself. A collection of sheer instincts and drives cannot give a gift, nor can a gift be intelligibly received from and returned to these instincts and drives.

However, despite the justified critique of the dogmatic morality of truthfulness, the nearest approximation to Heidegger's ontology of the act of Being within the human being is to be found in a certain strain of Christian anthropology. Heidegger writes:

> 'Disposition', man's heart, has a larger meaning than that given to it in modern speech; it means not merely the sensitive and emotive side of human consciousness, but the essential being of all human nature. In Latin it is called *animus*, as distinct from *anima*. In this distinction, *anima* means the fundamental determinant of every living being, including human beings... . Man so conceived is then ranked with plants and animals, regardless of whether we assume that rank

order to show an evolution, or classify the genera of organisms in some other way. Even when man is marked out as the rational living being, he is still seen in a way in which his character of organism remains decisive – though biological phenomena, in the sense of animal and vegetable beings, may be subordinated to that rational and personal character of man which determines his life of the spirit. All anthropology continues to be dominated by the idea that man is an organism. Philosophical anthropology as well as scientific anthropology will not use man's essential nature as the starting point for their definition of man.[24]

The basic characteristic of human nature, Heidegger continues, is the relatedness of man to Being. This relatedness to what is, because it constitutes the essence of man, is the measure for all else: it is not simply added to the already existing living being or *anima*. The idea of this ontological relatedness is determined by Heidegger as *animus*, an inner striving that is always determined by, attuned to, what is. *Animus*, meaning disposition, character, heart, passion or sensibility also means soul. Soul, Heidegger writes, is that in which spirit has its being, the spirit of spirit. It is, Heidegger remarks, essentially what Meister Eckhart, the Christian mystic, describes as the 'spark' of the soul.[25] Eckhart describes this activity or 'spark' within man in the following way:

> It is not that we should abandon, neglect or deny our inner self, but we should learn to work precisely in it, with it and from it… and… become used to acting without any compulsion. For we should concentrate on this inner prompting and act from it….[26]

> What is my life? That which is self-moving from within. But that which is moved from without is not alive. If we live with him then, we must also act with him from within so that we do not act from without. Rather, we should be moved by that from which we live, that is by him. We can and must act from our own inner self. And so if we are to live in him or through him, then he must become our own inner self and we must act from our own inner self.[27]

The self-moving life of the inner man is manifest not to a self-present ego, nor is it a collection of irrational, compulsive instincts defined in opposition to this ego. Rather the act that animates the human being from within comes to man from outside his subjectivity: we must release ourselves into this interior activity from which we receive life and spirit. Thus, intuiting and concentrating upon this inner prompting, we let ourselves be moved from within by a spontaneity that both belongs to us and gives to us the life that we live.[28] According to Heidegger, the *animus* of man is disposed toward this inner activity and life. Our life is not something bodily given to which is added the human being's capacity for thought. Rather, thinking fulfils our human nature; thinking receives and guards the spirit that Being gives. Man is disposed toward Being. This disposition is constituted by, as Heidegger puts it, the soul or heart of the human being. The notion of the heart, however, enjoys a venerable, if marginal, place within the Christian tradition. The Pietist Oetinger calls the *sensus communis* the 'heart' – it is that by which we receive the divine mystery of life.[29] The idea of the heart is also prominent, not just in Pascal, Schiller and Hölderlin, but also, to a lesser degree, in Nietzsche. Later Heidegger's determination of Being works within this tradition. The existentiality of the Self is not manifest in the cognitive 'I think' or the practical 'I act' but in the expression 'I live', 'I am alive'. To live is not to be certain of one's ownmost subjectivity as the most substantial in all existence. To live means to be alive, from the Anglo Saxon *on life*, meaning *in* life. The human being *is* insofar as it dwells and tarries in the life that Being gives. This is the original difference in the *Ereignis* between Being (life) and the Being of man ('I am alive'). Taking joy in the simple experience that life has no Why, that life simply *is*, we give thanks for living.

However, the Eckhartian conception of an interior spontaneity or spark that man must listen to and nurture, and which Heidegger draws upon in his later philosophical anthropology, is itself a descendent of an idea originally presented by St. Augustine. In *De Magistro*, Augustine writes:

> Regarding each of the things we understand, however, we don't consult a speaker who makes sounds outside us, but the Truth that presides within over the mind itself, though perhaps words prompt us to consult Him. What is more, He Who is consulted, He Who is said to *dwell in the inner man*, does teach. ...[30]

> When we deal with things that we perceive by the mind, namely by the intellect and reason, we're speaking of things that we look upon immediately in the inner light of Truth, in virtue of which the so-called inner man is illuminated and rejoices... when I'm stating truths, I don't even teach the person who is looking upon these truths. He's taught not by my words but by the things themselves made manifest within when God discloses them.[31]

Access to the truth requires an attentive listening to an inner teacher who dwells within the human being. This inner truth illuminates the objects of thought: it is the hidden part of the rational soul.[32] In this regard, Augustine remarks in the *Confessions*, 'let the person who can hear you speaking within listen'.[33] The truth of existence (Being) according to Augustine, as for Heidegger, is disclosed in the truthful, appropriate reception of the 'speaking' of the *logos* within the being of man. 'It gives' to us: in receiving the gift man is inspired. The inspired person is illuminated by the light that Being gives: they dwell within the truth, speak truthfully. To receive the activity of nature is not to be overcome by irrational impulses, but to open oneself up to new forms of experience, to *see* differently. However, Augustine and Eckhart go further: they name the Giver of the gift – the living Christ. Heidegger, on the other hand, refuses to do this. Nonetheless, the proximity of Heidegger to these Christian thinkers leads inexorably to another series of questions: what is the ontological relation between Augustinian faithful existence and the kind of immanent, aesthetic conception of experience presented by Heidegger? If the truth of Being is manifest in the inspired, truthful reception of the gift of an inner master, has ontology simply become a form of Christian anthropology? How are we to understand this refusal of Heidegger to name Being?

Chapter 11

Being and the Hidden God

There is a turn in Heidegger from the meaning to the truth of Being because our understanding of Being is grounded in the felt expression of the movement underlying the articulated significance of world. The truthful, inspired thinker expresses the truth of Being; ontological truth is manifest in the work of thought that offers a site for the 'speaking' of language to-be. This conception of truth is named *aletheia* in ancient philosophy: *aletheia* means both the truth of things in-themselves and telling or speaking the truth. The Western tradition emphasises the latter meaning – *aletheia* entails the moral virtue of speaking truthfully, being honest. The opposite of *aletheia* is *pseudos*, the moral vice of telling lies. The truth of Being and the truthfulness of man are ontologically sundered from each other – truthfulness no longer means being filled with the truth, i.e. it is no longer understood to be a form of disclosure. Later Heidegger attempts to bring back together these separated elements within *aletheia*: the truth of Being needs the truthfulness of the thinker, the thinker is inspired with the truth only insofar as he belongs to Being. The truth of Being is 'in' the truthful human being as the spontaneous act of life itself – following Augustine and Eckhart. This insight, however, raises a difficulty – what is the exact relation between a conception of inspired, philosophical thinking and the kind of faithful existence embodied in the Christian tradition of negative theology? Is the act of Being rooted in human nature experienced by us as the giving of a hidden God?

Heidegger, however, repeatedly emphasises that proper boundaries must be drawn between faith and thinking. In a theological discussion in 1964, Heidegger insists that theology must not borrow the categories of its thinking and the form of its speech from philosophy but must think and speak 'out of faith for faith with fidelity to its subject matter'.[1] In arguing this, Heidegger is merely restating a point he makes in 1927 regarding the relation between phenomenology and theology:

> In accord with the positum of theology (which is essentially disclosed only in faith) not only is the access to its object unique, but the evidence for the demonstration of its propositions is quite special. The conceptuality proper to theology can only grow out of theology itself.[2]

Thus, Heidegger insists that faith is always in genuine reflection understood to be the mortal enemy of philosophy.[3] However, he goes on to say that a right conception of the opposition between theology and philosophy nonetheless allows for the possibility of their community, as long as this communion is free from weak attempts at mediation.[4] It is important to bear this remark of Heidegger's in mind when examining the following famous passages taken from the much later *Letter on Humanism* (1946):

> In such nearness… a decision may be made as to whether and how God and the gods withhold their presence, whether and how the day of the holy dawns. …But the holy, which alone is the essential sphere of divinity, which in turn affords a dimension for the gods and for God, comes to radiate only when Being itself beforehand and after extensive preparation has been cleared and is experienced in its truth.[5]

> Only from the truth of being can the essence of the holy be thought. Only from the essence of the holy is the essence of divinity to be thought. Only in the light of the essence of divinity can it be thought or said what the word 'God' is to signify.[6]

Heidegger concludes that the idea of the thinking of the truth of Being is a kind of 'preparation' for the experience of divinity. The thinking that prepares for the object of faith is neither atheistic nor theistic:

> Not however because of an indifferent attitude but out of respect for the boundaries that have been set by what gives itself to thinking as what is to be thought, by the truth of Being.[7]

Heidegger is here explicitly concerned to differentiate the content of the object of thought (Being) from the subject matter of faith. To ignore this difference entails a transgression, in the shadow of Kant, of the proper bounds of human thinking. Heidegger, thus, remains silent on the question of the nature of God: following Luther, he writes, faith does not need the thought of Being. However, in response to this the French theologian Marion has criticised Heidegger's seemingly reverential silence toward an object considered beyond the limits of a thinking that knows itself. According to Marion, the true effect of Heideggerian ontology in relation to theology, explicitly in the *Letter on Humanism*, is to conceive of the experience of Being as an all-embracing horizon *within* which the object of theology must appear.[8] Heidegger's silence therefore is deeply misleading: rather than respectfully letting the content of faith move within its own bounds, a God that manifests itself must do so within the existential horizon of Dasein's understanding of Being. An idolatrous ontology therefore has already decided what and how God *is*. The concept of man's preparation of the coming of the gods is far from being a radical or original thought: to prepare for God is not a form of genuine receptivity but is already an act of determination and subordination. Being is, hence, Marion argues, the phenomenological foundation and screen for the coming to-be of the divine being.

Indeed, it is true that in his lecture on *Phenomenology and Theology*, Heidegger describes theology as an ontic science, whereas phenomenology is determined as ontological. Consequently, Heidegger argues, the believing of Christian ontic comportment remains ontologically determined as a concept of existence by the existentiality of pre-Christian Dasein. These existentialia comprise the neutral and invariant structure of existing on the basis of which there are ontic modifications, of which believing existence is one. Thus theology, a science of faith, is an ontic science whose object – the Crucified God disclosed in and for faith – is *a* being.[9] Thus, the analytic of Dasein, i.e. ontological science, must be used, Heidegger adds, to correct theology if it is truly to be a science and not just pure faith devoid of an implicitly comprehended but not explicitly disclosed understanding of Being. It would appear, therefore, that Heidegger's relation to theology is, at least in the early work, as Marion describes. Nonetheless, even in the early lecture important points have to be kept in mind. The relation between ontology and theology is *not* elaborated as one of subordination. For early Heidegger, although theology is an ontic science, it is unlike all other sciences of beings. Physics, for example, is the thematic objectification of a pre-scientific understanding of the being of nature. The basic concepts of physics – matter, space, time – determine the subject-area underlying the objects physics can take as its theme. These basic concepts, however, are themselves directed by a phenomenological, productive logic that discloses in advance the regional Being of the entities with which physics is concerned. The ontological content of theology, on the other hand, unlike physics, is not merely implicit. The object of theology disclosed through faith, *transforms* pre-Christian Dasein's mode of existence, such that ontic belief absorbs and 'sublates' the existentiality of Dasein.[10] Thus, Heidegger writes, the primary direction for the content of theological concepts is grounded exclusively in the singular experience of faith.

In faith, therefore, the truth of Being is utterly transformed. This is why theology is always the mortal enemy of philosophy: unlike all the other ontic sciences it sublates the human being's mode of existence. Marion errs, therefore, in suggesting the human being's understanding of Being is an anterior screen which regulates and controls the manifestation of the Christian God. As Heidegger repeatedly points out in stressing the boundaries of thinking, in faith everything is changed. This however is not to suggest that there is no relation between philosophy and theology. As Heidegger remarks in his *Letter on Humanism*, the experience of the truth of Being *prepares* our subjectivity for the coming of the gods. *Contra* Marion, this conception of preparation does not involve the idea of a pre-given horizon that anticipates and founds the divine presence. The preparation involved in thinking the truth of Being, if it is genuine, is a form of waiting that nonetheless does not pre-determine in any way the essence and nature of what is waited for.

Indeed, the Heideggerian concept of the preparation of the object of thought for theology, in which the presence of God transforms our experience of Being, in fact, echoes points made by Kant in the *Critique of Judgement*. According to Kant, in our experience of the whole of nature there are certain kinds of natural entities – organisms – that cannot be subsumed under the causal rule of the mechanism of nature. These organisms appear to possess an intrinsic ordering principle or a forming ability in which the existence and form of the parts depend on their relation to the whole, i.e. the purpose, of the organism. The purpose to which the living being is directed systematically unifies the form and combination of the manifold – this purposeful directness constitutes what Kant calls the formative force of a self-organising organism.[11] The concept for these kinds of objects cannot be given by the understanding but is dependent upon reason's concept of a purpose. The teleological purposefulness of natural beings, however, does not refer to a subject's reflection upon the form of the manifold it has presented to itself. The purposefulness is real;[12] the principle employed by teleology is, therefore, of the objective, material purposefulness of nature. We judge (reflectively) *as if* the beings within nature acted according to purposes. In judgements based on this principle effects are not caused mechanically – rather the cause's action is based on the idea of the effect. The idea or purpose is the underlying condition under which the cause can produce its effect.[13]

However, once nature has been judged teleologically, the natural purposes we find in organised beings entitle us to the idea of a vast system of purposes of nature, which includes the human being. In this case, the beauty we find in nature can be considered as an objective purpose produced by nature for man's benefit in order to further his culture, *humaniora*, and happiness.[14] From the perspective of teleological judgement, we do not, as in aesthetic judgement, judge beauty with favour – rather (similarly to genius) the opposite: we regard the existence of natural beauty as a favour *from* nature *to* us. However, as pointed out earlier, teleology cannot make the transition from freedom to nature because the principle upon which teleological judgements are based has already gone too far. Nature in itself is already determined as an objective system of purposes according to the specific kind of causality possessed by reason. On the other hand, aesthetic judgements of taste do not go far enough – the purposefulness of nature is entirely subjective without any reference to the transcendental concept of freedom underlying nature itself.

However, Kant argues, the teleological principle of nature demands an explanation of the production of organised beings that the idea of the mechanism of nature cannot provide. We need, therefore, the regulative idea of an intelligent world cause that underlies the system of purposes in nature as a whole and that acts according to purposes. This world cause, Kant argues against Spinoza, must contain the notion of an intelligent, original being that produces according to intentions. The result of the foregoing argument, Kant writes, is that teleology cannot find answers to its inquiries except in a theology – the principle of the objective purposefulness of nature inexorably culminates in the principle of the intentional causality of a supreme cause. The latter principle is subjective (reflective) and hence cannot be demonstrated or deduced objectively. Nonetheless, Kant writes, it remains an indispensable and necessary maxim of our judgement that attaches inescapably to the human race.[15] The principle is subjectively universal – it holds for the species of finite rational beings that we are, but not for the object itself nor for every cognising being. It is a regulative principle that is attached necessarily to '(human) nature'.[16] Hence, according to Kant, teleology is a preliminary 'propaedeutic' in relation to theology;[17] teleology allows us to 'feel the need for a theology'.[18] However, Kant adds as a caveat, the intentionality of this transcendent cause cannot be fathomed – we cannot call it wisdom or goodness. The nature of the divine understanding might necessarily determine it to produce certain forms, analogously to the compulsion of artistic instinct in animals. Our regulative idea of God, thus, is highly indeterminate, without many of the attributes normally predicated of divinity. On the other hand, Kant argues, moral theology adds the idea of wisdom to the supreme being and the determinate idea of the final moral purpose of man. Therefore, according to Kant, ethico-theology, not physico-teleology, is the proper ground for religion.

The Heideggerian conception of philosophy as a preparation for faith fits into the space Kant opens up between teleology and theology. To make a judgement regarding the truth of Being involves the teleological principle of the objective purposefulness of nature. Our form of life, human nature, acts according to purposes. Language 'speaks' to us; it is the spontaneous act and principle of life within the human being. The exteriority of life in itself (nature) is received as objective: it manifests itself as the inner feeling of a sublime and inhuman force. The 'speaking' of Being within the human being – Augustine's inner master – is the rhythmic form of our language and life. Language is manifest to the inspired thinker not as a voice disclosing private content accessible only to the 'I', but as the movement and spirit of the linguistic community itself. Thus the purposefulness of Being, our second nature, is teleological. Being in itself acts according to purposes and is not simply the subjective feeling resulting from reflection upon a self-given manifold. However, Being is teleological in a unique sense – there is no determinate *telos* or principle of reason explicitly driving its purposeful giving.

The teleologically perceived rhythm of Being prepares the thinker for faithful existence in the sense that it yields the field of subjective experience *within* which the thinker *may* determine the gift of Being as originating from a Giver. As Kant puts it, the inspired experience of the truth of Being makes us 'feel the need for a theology'. In thinking, the words and concepts we use appear to have their own life, the object of thought orders itself. Man lets the conceptual content animate and move itself. The ground for the life and purposefulness of this content cannot be found in the human being: it is received, i.e. perceived as a gift from nature. Our idea of nature, however, does not mean – as in orthodox teleology – the whole of living entities, but human (second) nature, i.e. the purposeful rhythm of our form of life. In faith, this immanent experience of the sublime movement and impersonal force of rhythm is transformed into the gift of a personal, transcendent creator. Human nature is then understood to be a gift from God. This creator may be hidden in its essential nature; following Nicholas of Cusa and Eckhart, we can only offer a conjecture as to *what* God is. However, faith determines *that* the divine giver *is* in a way that the sheer movement and giving of rhythm is *not* and can never be.[19]

Thus, the experience of being rhythmed by Being, as Augustine notes in *De Musica*, prepares the being of the self *for* the determination that faith offers. This possibility for determination constitutes the determinability of aesthetic immanence. Faith depends upon the determinability of the aesthetic domain (Being). But this dependence, against Marion, is not submission: in the act of determination faith utterly transforms the aesthetic domain, from the ground up. To think the truth of Being is to prepare for this determination of human nature by faithful existence. To determine what, if anything, is to be prepared *for* transgresses the appropriate bounds of thinking. If it did this, the domain of thought could no longer be what it essentially is. This is the communion that unites and the abyss that divides philosophy and theology. Teleology moves to theology, the abyss is spanned, when in the act of thinking the inspired, intuitive experience of the life and gift of spirit gives birth to the idea of a purposeful, loving Giver. In this moment, a moment that cannot be anticipated or predicted, we *do* ask who gives – the person of faith gives thanks, not to the terror and beauty of life, but to the God who elevates and sanctifies this life. The idea of preparation in later Heidegger, therefore, might also be called a teleological argument from inspiration. This would be appropriate if such an argument were to mean, not a rational proof and demonstration of the existence of God, but the idea of a preparation and cultivation of the soul, an existential propaedeutic.

Heideggerian ontology is, from this perspective, quite different from negative theology. Rhythm is the impersonal force of life that wells up in the inspired thinker. Language 'speaks' as the movement of an inhuman, sublime purposefulness that nevertheless emerges from the depths of human nature, our form of life. The manifestation of Being, thus, remains *within* the immanence of finite experience. In receiving the appropriating gift of rhythm, in listening to Being, no judgement is made as to the existence and nature of a transcendent giver of the gift. The 'It' that illuminates and gives life to the soul remains anonymous. 'It gives' as a sheer movement of giving, an act of Being rooted in the unfathomable abyss of language. We experience that, simply: *there is* order – order *exists*.[20] We do not give this order to ourselves – in the *Ereignis*, we receive order as a gift. Order, intended in this way, is not to be conceived as the ordering of beings: Being is not a given, epochal 'frame' that determines man as the orderer of all entities, including himself, as standing-reserve and resource. In the age of technology, the order by means of which the human being orders things is not yet perceived as a gift sent from Being *to* man. Order, consequently, takes shape as a given foundation, a *mathesis universalis*, for the experience and determination of beings. Here, in the characteristic manner of onto-theology, the order of Being is the ground for beings, but this order is itself grounded by that for which 'it gives' ground. The order of Being orders beings simply for the sake of ordering them.

In the *Ereignis*, on the other hand, we experience ourselves *as* ordered by Being: ontological order, thus, is not experienced as existing simply for the endless process of ontic ordering, regulating and securing. Order is received; it is a gift from the truth of Being itself. Within the immanent bounds of our finite existence, the gift of order from Being to the human being is experienced in the aesthetic intuition of rhythm. From out of the ontological real of rhythm, beings in-themselves 'speak' to us: we receive the order of things. In the swift change of aspects by which we perceive order – from mathematical frame to aesthetic rhythm, the world is transformed. This is what Heidegger means when he says that in extreme danger, the saving power also grows.[21] The merely illusory freedom the human being entertains in the age of technological reason is at this moment, according to Heidegger, echoing Marx, materially and spiritually realised. In the *Ereignis*, man is no longer alienated from his free relation to Being.[22]

The criterion, however, for judging whether Heidegger's isolation and purification of the domain of aesthetic immanence is justified is whether it is intelligible that there could be gift exchange within an immanent ontology between the impersonal gift of rhythm (life) and the human being. If a gift exchange such as this *is* intelligible, if language can be conceived as purposefully giving a gift without acquiring personality and being named as a Giver, then the site of metaphysics does not necessarily have to be evacuated, after the nihilistic age of technology, in favour of theology. Onto-theology, in this case, would not exhaust the possibilities of ontology. The preceding interpretation of the *Ereignis*, carving out a fissure between theology and metaphysical nihilism, has attempted to suggest ways in which such a conception of immanent gift-exchange might be seen as intelligible.

Conclusion

The human being belongs to the world in which it lives, though the threads that tie us to this world are not our bodily organs of sense. If this were the case the worldliness of our mind would depend upon a capacity to receive empirical content through the organs of touch, smell, taste, hearing and sight. It would follow that the content of mind describes how the world is, i.e. is genuinely empirical, only insofar as it receives discrete units of the sensuously given. These bits of the given, as McDowell argues, are not able to do the job they are supposed to do: they offer a causal but not justificatory relation of the content of mind to world. The bare presence of a unit of sense-data is not a reason for thinking 'thus and so'. The very ontological possibility of empirical content appears in jeopardy. A response to this problem might be to re-think the idea of nature that it implicitly presupposes: that nature is a realm of physical laws constituted by causal relations devoid of the spontaneity we normally associated with human rational reflection. If we can intelligibly determine nature as structured by relations of meaning with real non-sensory content, if we can 're-enchant' nature, then we are in a position to re-think the character of our belonging to the natural world in which we live. The task of re-thinking the idea of nature was first articulated in a radical way within the tradition of German thought stretching from Hamann and Herder, through the Jena Romantics and Hölderlin, to Schelling and W.V. Humboldt.

If nature is already structured with intelligible content then our relation to this content cannot be simply empirical. There is in us a capacity for ontological or transcendental intuition, a power of reception that cannot be identified with the empirical intuition of bits of sensuous content through the sense organs. This is what Kant realised, though his conception of this *a priori* content was restricted to the manifold of the spatial and temporal forms of pure intuition. McDowell, following Hegel, takes the idea of transcendental aesthetic a step further: it denotes a capacity for receiving conceptual content. Nature is already conceptually structured. Thrown into a world that is already there, we do not perceive unadulterated sensory content that we subsequently interpret internally according to our system of beliefs. We perceive facts, things that are 'thus and so'. The world is the totality of facts articulated in the second nature of a linguistic tradition. The human being belongs to the world insofar as he inherits the pre-given *Bildung* that allows him to think and act in a purposeful and oriented way. This is what early Heidegger calls a pre-ontological understanding of Being. Heidegger, however, more than McDowell, follows through Kant's claim that a transcendental aesthetic, i.e. a doctrine of *a priori* ontological sensibility, requires an account of the way in which the empirical content is ordered and arranged in spatial and temporal relations. Heidegger concludes that the self is transcendentally receptive insofar as it intuits the ontological horizon of the future that 'it gives' to itself. Ontological reception is pure temporal self-affection: the extension of the 'space of reasons' to include nature is temporally constituted.

However, in the move from Division I to Division II of *Being and Time*, Heidegger departs further from McDowell. The idea of experience involving conceptually structured operations of receptivity presupposes that there is present already an implicit understanding of Being: that the world already has conceptual content. Yet the idea of finite receptivity is determined essentially as the binding of man to an external, distinct existence upon which he depends. Any adequate conception of ontological sensibility must accommodate a notion of non-sensuous externality correlative to the 'real' existence of ontic matter intuited through our senses. However, both McDowell and early Heidegger determine the transcendental 'real' simply as the already given existence of conceptual content, i.e. the congealed spontaneity of our second nature. This does not yield the friction or constraint required for an adequate conception of ontological externality. The content of second nature is still *too* conceptual: there is no distance between the content of Being and the human being's understanding of Being. Unfortunately, without determining our second nature as sufficiently external and distinct from us there is no content available that we can genuinely be said to receive. Lacking the resistance of an intuitable object, our *a priori* power of intuition appears devoid of any determination that is recognisably receptive or natural. In the move from ontic to ontological sensibility the essential characteristics of the 'real' and of our finite dependence upon the 'real' have been lost. We are trapped within the frictionless dynamic of thinking and the thinkable: the idea of pure sensibility remains without concrete purchase. Yet the idea of *a priori* reception is crucial in any conception of experience that attempts to dispel the anxiety that thought bears no relation to how the world is. Early Heidegger follows through the logic of this position in Division II of *Being and Time* by moving from the idea of inauthentic to authentic experience. Whereas inauthentic existence remains within the inherited rules and standards of the community, the authentic human being comes face to face with the brute fact *that* it *is* – and is not rather Nothing. Authenticity reveals the sheer factical ground of human existence. Authentic man does not unthinkingly inherit the understanding of Being into which he has been thrown but rather intuits the present necessity of his actual situation from the exchange of future and past possibility. The authentic experience of ontic actuality offers the constraint and friction inauthentic existence lacks – but at a cost. Ontological content regresses to a sensuously perceived, material presence. The inexorable move from inauthentic to authentic experience, driven by the need for an external resistance that the idea of our finitude demands, lapses back into a form of the Myth of the Given. The thing-in-itself, its habitat destroyed by the relentless march of conceptual content into nature, takes refuge in the ontic real – the sheer refusal and resistance of matter. But the doomed flight of the thing-in-itself to the materiality of art is not without worth – it explicitly demonstrates the underlying tendency of the idea of finite experience shared by McDowell and early Heidegger to fall back into the metaphysical oscillation from which it was supposed to escape.

Matter however offers the thing-in-itself a barren and mute landscape without life or spirit. Later Heidegger 'turns' from determining the thing-in-itself as a given, thrown content to the idea that it throws or gives itself. This is the becoming-ontological of ontic existence, a becoming that transforms the ontic-ontological difference into the difference between Being and the Being of the human being. The thrown-projection of the care-structure of authentic existence is inverted. The human being's understanding of Being does not give the thrown factical given: rather the throw of Being gives to us our understanding of Being. Understanding is a gift – meaning is received from the giving of Being. Interpreted concretely, Being is the second nature of the form of life within which we live. Here Heidegger returns to the radical sphere of questioning first opened up by Herder. The activity of human nature is experienced as purposeful or meaningful but is not exhaustively determinable according to rational purposes. The principle on the basis of which we experience Being is teleological because it involves the idea of an objective purposefulness. Yet it retains an element of the aesthetic because this indeterminate objectivity is not grounded in a concept of reason. Without a determinate purpose driving it, the ontological content of (second) nature is non-conceptual. This non-conceptuality is manifest in what Heidegger calls the 'way' or movement of language. As such, the possibility arises of conceiving this ontological content as supplying the friction the sensibility of our finite reason demands. This in turn allows for an adequate conception of the human being's capacity for ontological sensibility. Later Heidegger's philosophical anthropology offers such a conception of experience; it goes beyond McDowell and the early work in at least two respects. The mode and form of the intuiting of second nature is aesthetic: nature 'speaks' to us in the rhythmic movement of language. Rhythm is the motion that animates and shapes our form of life: it orders the relations of affinity and kinship within the web of linguistic content that constitutes our second nature. Aesthetic intuition is not another supplementary corporeal sense but an inner, ontological sense – *sensus communis* – that unifies and regulates the disparate field of experience within which we encounter beings. Conceptual articulation and discrimination of ontic content presupposes the motion intuited through the *sensus communis*. This motion possesses intrinsic life; it moves or gives itself. Here Heidegger departs from the framework of Kantian finitude; the 'I' does not give form to things (phenomena). Rather the 'I' receives the intuitive form or time-space of beings from the purposeful giving of human nature. The rhythm of Being is the ontological or transcendental correlate to the ontic 'real' missing in early Heidegger: it is the external and distinct existence upon which we depend and to which we are bound. By introducing an ontological distinction into the finite ideality of the transcendental subject between second nature and the self, we fully reclaim empirical existence. The real of Being and of beings touch in the expanse opened up by human nature: our form of life brings us back to things.

The second way in which later Heidegger departs from McDowell and early Heidegger is in his conception of the kind of content that is aesthetically intuited by the human being. Rhythm is the form of intuition. The content of rhythm is non-conceptual. However, *contra* McDowell, non-conceptual does not mean non-ontological, i.e. a sensuously perceived ontic presence. Rather, the content of Being is concretely experienced as a non-sensuous intensity. The sublime experience of rhythm, of being appropriated by Being, opens up a depth of intensity within the human being. Distance is the schema or intuitive form that offers a discernable image for our experience of intensity. Space, subordinated to the temporal mode of intuiting, at this point reasserts its rights in Heidegger's transcendental aesthetic. Intensity is not a given presence: 'it gives'. Beyond orthodox empiricism, a feeling of intensity constitutes the subterranean necessity that drives and orders the movement and constellation of conceptual content. It binds us to the world, offering the friction and resistance that we need if the content of our mind can intelligibly be said to depend upon an external existence that is not merely causally efficacious. Intensity is not a private, psychological process that 'accompanies' conceptual content – we cannot point at and hypostatise intensity as if it were a phenomenon ontologically separate from our reasoning power. Rather, conceptual content *is* the expression of intensity, though for the most part we do not realise it. The gift of intensity animates and motivates the free spontaneity of our rational life and yet, beyond rationalism, withdraws from any principle of reason that deigns to comprehend its giving. The phenomenon of intensity elevates ontological content from meaning (use) to truth (expression). The truth of Being is manifest in the expression of intensity. Being no longer means our understanding of Being; rather the reverse – meaning is an expression of the 'speaking' of the *logos*. The inspired thinker is full of the truth insofar as he receives and expresses the sublime, inhuman feeling that intensity gives. In the reflected glow of the inspired work, Being manifests itself.

For the most part, we fail to experience the world as *our* expression of Being; the world makes no claim upon us, nor do we recognise our living bond with it. However, the work of thought – ontology – re-shapes and re-orders the content of decaying nature; thinking offers a variation on the limit rhythm gives, opening up new and surprising forms of experience. As such, the labour of thought allows us to reclaim the world we have lost, to recognise in the alienated other the outline of a gift that we have been given. In order to receive appropriately the gift of world we must return the gift. The harmony between man and things is not a pre-established given but living bond that must be repeated anew. Thinking receives the gift of human nature, the 'I' immerses itself in the life of its world, by thankfully reforming the second nature that 'it gives'. To live is to give back and renew the life that we are given. Ontology allows us to do this; it is the highest favour that nature gives to man. To write philosophical prose is neither to dismantle and unravel conceptual hierarchies nor simply to create 'new' concepts. Genuine thinking is neither absolute absorption within the object nor wilful creation from an unconstrained subjectivity. Expression is the act that receives the rhythmic form of intensity and gathers and realises this form, synthetically re-ordering the content of 'what there is'. As the expression of Being, the labour of philosophical thought is an artistic formation and individuation of character and a melodic extension of objective nature, our form of life. This is the ethical substance and promise of ontology – that a space will be opened for a community to take root and flourish, for a world to be born. Philosophy does not fly at dusk, it cries at dawn.

Notes

Introduction

[1] Heidegger, 'The Onto-Theological Constitution of Metaphysics', in *Identity and Difference*, trans. Stambaugh (Harper and Row, New York; 1969), 69-70

[2] For a detailed overview of Heidegger's notion of onto-theology, see Thomson, 'Ontotheology? Understanding Heidegger's *Destruktion* of Metaphysics', *International Journal of Philosophical Studies* vol. 8.3 297-327 reprinted in Dreyfus, H and Wrathall, M (eds.), *Heidegger re-examined*, vols. I-IV (Routledge; New York, 2002). Thomson, however, fails to show how the, as he puts it, 'deepest problem' in Heidegger's conception of onto-theology regarding the 'phenomenological explanation of the original onto-theological distinction', turns on the ontological distinction between understanding Being as ground and as gift. There is no need to assume with Thomson a pre-given, albeit contingent phenomenological numbness to the dynamic and to infer from this that the onto-theological tradition was not historically necessary. Rather, according to Heidegger, the early thinkers fail to experience the gift of Being, not from a deficiency of perception, but because Being refuses itself. As Heidegger puts it, the oblivion of Being is part of its essence. Correlatively, Thomson makes too clean a distinction between Thales and Anaximander (determined as onto-theological thinkers) and Parmenides and Heraclitus (determined as non-onto-theological). For Heidegger, Pre-Socratic thought *as a whole* neglects the concealing of Being and fails to think the essence of language, see *Early Greek Thinking*, trans. Krell (Harper and Row, New York; 1975), 26, 77. Elsewhere, Heidegger remarks that the earliest Greeks did not ground *aletheia* as ground, Heidegger, M *Basic Questions of Philosophy*, trans. Rojcewicz (Indiana University Press, Indiana; 1992), 99, 163. The difference between the new and the first beginning is that only in the *Ereignis* is the concealing of Being experienced in its truth. To put the point another way, it is only at the *end* of the historically necessary unfolding of the history of Being that Being discloses itself *as* epochal.

[3] Heidegger, *Hegel's concept of experience* (Octagon Books, New York; 1983), 135

[4] Heidegger, 'Overcoming Metaphysics', in *The End of Philosophy*, trans. Stambaugh (Souvenir Press, London; 1975), 106-7

[5] Heidegger, 'The Onto-Theological Constitution of Metaphysics', in *Identity and Difference*, trans. Stambaugh (Harper and Row, New York; 1969), 47

[6] See, for example, the following typical remark: 'Only from human being, that is, from the manner in which man grants the word of response to the claim of Being, can a reflection of its dignity shine forth to Being. In the timespan when Being delivers primordality to the Open and lets the purity of its freedom in relation to itself... be known and preserved, Being needs the reflection of a radiance of its essence in truth', in Heidegger, 'Recollection in Metaphysics', in *The End of Philosophy*, trans. Stambaugh (Souvenir Press, London; 1975), 76

[7] *KPM*, 29

[8] Ibid., 141

[9] Ibid.

Chapter 1: The Question of Man

[1] *BT*, 62
[2] *PI*
[3] *KPM*, Appendix 1, note one, 175
[4] Compare the introduction to *Being and Time* with the preface to the first edition of the *Critique of Pure Reason*
[5] Heidegger, *Aristotle's Metaphysics Theta 1-3: on the essence and actuality of force*, trans. Brogan and Warnek (Indiana University Press; Indianapolis, 1995), 30
[6] Aristotle, *Metaphysics* 998b21-27, *Complete Works*, Vol. II (Princeton University Press, Princeton; 1984), 1577
[7] Heidegger, 'Overcoming Metaphysics', *The End of Philosophy*, trans. Stambaugh (Souvenir Press, London; 1975), 88. At the time of writing *Kant and the Problem of Metaphysics*, Heidegger has not yet formulated his later critique of Kantian transcendental philosophy as grounded in the 'certainty of guaranteed representation', ibid.
[8] *KPM*, 8
[9] Ibid., 9-10
[10] Ibid., 10-11
[11] Ibid., 116-7
[12] Ibid., 117. 'Because Kant does not carry out the subjective deduction, the subjectivity of the subject for him continues to be guided by the constitution offered to him through traditional anthropology and psychology'
[13] Ibid., 1
[14] Heidegger, *Being and Time*, trans. Macquarrie and Robinson (Blackwell, Oxford; 1995), 228
[15] *KPM*, 148
[16] Ibid., 144-6
[17] Ibid., 18
[18] *CPR*, 92
[19] *CJ*, 29
[20] *BT*, 255
[21] *KPM*, 19
[22] Ibid., 64
[23] *CPR*, 66
[24] Allison, *Kant's Transcendental Idealism*, (Yale University Press, New Haven; 1983), 97
[25] *CPR*, 170
[26] Ibid., 111
[27] Ibid., 181
[28] Ibid., 23

Chapter 2: Time and the Will

[1] *KPM*, 133
[2] Ibid., 135
[3] Ibid., 39, 74-6
[4] Ibid., 99-100
[5] *BT*, 55
[6] *CPR*, 184
[7] *KPM*, 76

[8] Ibid., 213

[9] Ibid., 214

[10] Ibid.,135

[11] Ibid., 86-7

[12] *PI*, 97-99

[13] Ibid., 90

[14] Ibid., 98

[15] Ibid., 166-7

[16] Ibid., 87

[17] Ibid., 167

[18] *CPR*, 164

[19] Ibid., 109-112

[20] Ibid., 55

[21] *PI*, 254-6

[22] *KPM*, 52, 58

[23] Heidegger, M., *Metaphysical Foundations of Logic*, trans. Heim (Indiana University Press, Indianapolis; 1984), 166. See also 167-8 for confirmation that the phenomenon of transcendence is understood by Heidegger to be already implicit within *Being and Time*

[24] Ibid., 192

[25] *KPM*, 111

[26] *PI*, 250

[27] *BT*, 377

[28] Heidegger, M., *Metaphysical Foundations of Logic*, trans. Heim (Indiana University Press, Indianapolis; 1984), 211

[29] *KPM*, 109-112 and 'On the Essence of Ground', *Pathmarks*, ed. McNeill (Cambridge University Press, Cambridge; 1998), 133-5

[30] *BT*, 374

[31] Ibid, 355

[32] Heidegger, M., *Metaphysical Foundations of Logic*, trans. Heim (Indiana University Press, Indianapolis; 1984), 211

[33] Ibid., 215

[34] Neither the problem of ontological sensibility nor the way early Heidegger tries to resolve the problem by making use of the notion of pure self-affection have been sufficiently brought out in the literature on Heidegger's Kant interpretation. See, for example, Sherover, *Heidegger, Kant and Time* (University Press, Lanham; 1988), Macann, 'Heidegger's Kant Interpretation', in *Critical Heidegger*, ed. Macann (Routledge, London; 1996). Schalow, *The Renewal of the Heidegger-Kant Dialogue: Action, Thought and Responsibility* (State University, New York; 1992) suggests that Heidegger's use of the Kantian notion of pure self-affection entails that the self can no longer be located in the sphere of subjectivity and that Heidegger's retrieval of Kant therefore breaks the shackles of presence concealed in the humanist idea of the subject (201). On the contrary, this essay contends that the notion of pure self-affection tends for the most part to reinforce a metaphysics of subjectivity: the so-called 'otherness' of Being, according to Heidegger, is after all the spontaneously given horizon of intelligibility *within* which beings must appear. Weatherston, M. *Heidegger's Interpretation of Kant* (MacMillan, New York; 2002) rightly highlights the use Heidegger makes of the distinction between something intuited and the form of intuition (47) but does not offer an explicit explanation of how the concept of pure self-affection addresses the problem that this distinction in a priori intuition generates. Weatherston also correctly remarks in his conclusion that Heidegger's reading of Kant loses sight of pure receptivity and commits much the same error as he attributes to the Neo-Kantians by turning time and space into categories (174-5). However, these remarks are not followed through.

Weatherston's concluding inference, following the contemporaneous reading of the Kantbook by Heinrich Levy, that Heidegger's notion of the transcendental imagination is akin to Kantian intellectual intuition is wide of the mark. Spontaneity is able to 'get behind' receptivity and gain knowledge of the thing-in-itself as little as Dasein can 'get behind' its factical thrownness. The problem, *contra* Weatherston, is not Heidegger's alleged eradication of sensibility in the manner of an absolute idealism, but rather the specific (derivative) form that this sensibility takes in his conception of finite transcendence

[35] *BT*, 228

[36] Ibid., 255

[37] This should put into perspective Blattner's charge that Heidegger is essentially a Kantian temporal idealist, Blattner, 'Is Heidegger a Kantian Idealist?', *Inquiry* 37 185-201 reprinted in Dreyfus, H and Wrathall, M (eds.), *Heidegger re-examined*, vols. I-IV (Routledge, New York; 2002). In Heidegger's conception of experience, authentic Dasein experiences the sheer fact of the real that is 'already-there'. Unlike Kantian experience here the content of the real (for example the material sensuousness of art) is not conceptually determined prior to experience: it is an unintelligible, independent *given* that refuses the understanding of Being within which it appears

[38] *OWA*, 65

[39] Ibid., 66

[40] Ibid., 175

[41] *KPM*, 31 and *PI*, 283

[42] Ibid., 107, 137

[43] Ibid., 107

[44] Ibid., 108

[45] *PI*, 90

Chapter 3: Receptivity and Spatiality

[1] *CPR*, 244-256

[2] Ibid., 246

[3] Ibid., 35-6

[4] Ibid., 35

[5] Ibid., 246

[6] Ibid., 254

[7] *KPM*, 139

[8] *CPR*, 255

[9] Ibid., 331

[10] Ibid., 353

[11] Ibid., 352-3

[12] *KPM*, 140

[13] Ibid.

[14] Ibid., 135

[15] *CPR*, 77

[16] *KPM*, 140

[17] Ibid., note b, 170

[18] Heidegger, 'Time and Being', in *On Time and Being*, trans. Stambaugh (Harper and Row, NY; 1972), 23

[19] Heidegger, 'The End of Philosophy and the Task of Thinking', *Basic Writings*, ed. Krell. (Routledge, London; 1978), 385

[20] Heidegger, *History of the Concept of Time*, trans. Kiesel (Indiana University Press, Indianapolis; 1992), 224

[21] Ibid., 227

[22] *BT*, 419

[23] Ibid., 418

[24] Ibid., 421.

[25] Ibid., 346

[26] See chapter five for a detailed reading of Heidegger's 'Origin of the Work of Art'.

[27] Heidegger, 'Time and Being' in *On Time and Being*, trans. Stambaugh (Harper and Row, NY; 1972), 14

[28] Ibid., 13

[29] *BT*, particularly, 374, 378

[30] Heidegger, 'Time and Being' in *On Time and Being*, trans. Stambaugh (Harper and Row, NY; 1972), 14

[31] Ibid., 23

[32] Ibid., 16

[33] Ibid., 23

[34] Ibid., 15

[35] Ibid.

[36] Ibid., 15-16

[37] There have also been many papers on the status of space in Heidegger, for example Sefler, 'Heidegger's Philosophy of space', in *Philosophy Today* 1973 p. 246-254; Villela-Petit, Heidegger's conception of space', in *Heidegger studies* (Eterna Press, Oak Brook; 1988); Arisaka, 'Spatiality, Temporality and the problem of foundation in Being and Time' in *Philosophy Today* spring 1996 p. 36-45; Frodeman, 'Being and space: a re-reading of existential spatiality in Being and Time' in *Journal of the British Society for Phenomenology* vol. 23 no. 1 January 1992. However, none of these contributions to the 'problem of space' in Heidegger sufficiently interrogate spatiality in terms of the *entirety* of Heidegger's project or as the point of access for an analytic of pure receptivity in the *Ereignis*.

Chapter 4: Distance and Concealment

[1] Wittgenstein, L., *Philosophical Investigations*, trans. Anscombe (Blackwell, Oxford; 1998), 155

[2] Ibid., 182

[3] Ibid., 183

[4] Bergson, H., *Time and Free Will: an essay on the immediate data of consciousness*, trans. Pogson (Dover Publications, New York; 1913), chapter 1

[5] Deleuze, G., *Difference and Repetition*, trans. Patton (Athlone Press, London; 1994), 231

[6] Marion, *God Without Being*, trans. Carlson (University of Chicago Press, Chicago; 1995), 104

[7] Ibid.

[8] Ibid., 103

[9] Ibid., 104

[10] Heidegger, 'Time and Being', in *On Time and Being*, trans. Stambaugh (Harper and Row, NY; 1972), 18

[11] Ibid., 17

[12] Ibid., 15-6

[13] Ibid., 8

[14] Ibid., 9

[15] Ibid., 19

[16] Ibid., 22

[17] Ibid., 18

[18] Ibid., 12

[19] Ibid., 22-3

[20] Marion, *God Without Being,* trans. Carlson (University of Chicago Press, Chicago; 1995), 103

[21] *CJ*, 131

[22] Ibid., 115, 124

[23] Ibid., 129

[24] Ibid., 131

[25] A part of Heidegger's written reply (1970) to a series of questions from the editors of the collection of essays entitled *The End of Philosophy*, trans. Stambaugh (New York; Harper and Row; 1973). The question of the relation between 'expropriation' and the 'it gives', however, is not specifically asked by the editors but is *introduced as a question*, by Heidegger himself at the very end of the reply .

[26] *BT*, 51-55

[27] Ibid., 60

[28] Ibid., 395

[29] Ibid., 320

[30] Ibid., 320-1

[31] Ibid., 334

[32] Ibid., 318

[33] Ibid., 342

[34] Ibid., 357

[35] Ibid., 265

Chapter 5: Art and Difference

[1] For example, Guigon, 'Philosophy and Authenticity: Heidegger's Search for a Ground for Philosophising' in *Heidegger, Authenticity and Modernity*, ed. Malpas (MIT Press, Massachusetts; 2000). Pattison, G., *The Later Heidegger* (Routledge, London; 2000), 98

[2] *OWA*, 40

[3] Ibid., 29

[4] Ibid., 40

[5] Ibid., 19

[6] Ibid., 31-2

[7] Ibid., 22

[8] Ibid., 26

[9] Ibid., 29

[10] Ibid.

[11] Ibid., 19

[12] Ibid., 45-6

[13] Ibid., 25

[14] Ibid.

[15] Ibid., 27

[16] Ibid., 46-7

[17] Ibid., 69

[18] Ibid., 47

[19] Ibid., 48
[20] Ibid., 56
[21] Ibid., 65
[22] Ibid., 65
[23] Ibid., 66
[24] Ibid., 69
[25] Ibid., 62
[26] Ibid., 64
[27] Ibid., 53
[28] Ibid.

[29] That the strife between world and earth is in essence a re-description of the ontic-ontological difference appears to have escaped nearly all the interpretations of Heidegger's artwork essay. See, for example, Young, J. *Heidegger's Philosophy of Art* (Cambridge University Press, Cambridge; 2001), Pattison, G. *The Later Heidegger* (Routledge, London; 2000), Bernstein, J. *The Fate of Art* (Polity Press, Oxford; 1997). Gadamer, *Philosophical Hermeneutics*, trans. Linge (University of California Press, Berkeley; 1977) writes that the concept of earth is a new and radical starting point for Heidegger's transcendental inquiry and that 'there was no way to get from this hermeneutical limiting concept of disposition or moodfulness to a concept such as earth', 216-9. On the contrary, this interpretation of Heidegger's artwork essay argues that the concept of earth is not a new starting point but a re-description of the idea of factical thrownness encountered in Heidegger's earlier work. Kockelmans, *Heidegger on Art and Artworks* (Kluwer, Boston; 1985), rightly highlights the way in which the concept of earth is used in distinct ways by Heidegger in the artwork essay and in his later idea of the fourfold, but does not explicitly draw a connection between earth and Heidegger's early idea of the factical, ontic ground of finite existence. *Contra* Kockelmans, earth is not 'unrealised possibility' (153) but the experience of the highest form of actuality. As fully actual or real, the sensuous givenness of earth grounds the present Fact that the artwork *is* and is not rather Nothing. Earth gives the possibilities that constitute the world of man's existence, just the possibility of man's uttermost nullity discloses the present actuality of Earth

[30] *OWA* '...talk about the self-establishing of truth, that is, of Being... touches on the problem of the ontological difference.... . The whole essay... deliberately yet tacitly moves on the path of the question of the nature of Being', 86

[31] Ibid., 55

[32] Ibid

[33] For example, Guigon, 'Philosophy and Authenticity: Heidegger's Search for a Ground for Philosophising', in *Heidegger, Authenticity and Modernity*, ed. Malpas (MIT Press, Massachusetts; 2000), writes that unlike the artwork essay 'There was no place in *Being and Time* for the idea of something that remains totally opaque and defies comprehension', 96

[34] *BT*, 321
[35] Ibid., 330
[36] Ibid., 321
[37] Ibid.
[38] Ibid., 330
[39] Ibid., 175
[40] Ibid., 321
[41] *OWA*, 40, 65
[42] *BT*, 399

[43] *KPM* Appendix Five, '*finite knowing*... manifests itself to us in the fundamental experience of the *dependency upon what is given*. Everything remains as it was for the ancients, even if we conceive of designating this as finite knowing (to be sure, the finite

must then necessarily be explained differently, as "earthy"....' *'Thrownness'*, Heidegger
goes on to write, is 'the ground for the finitude of knowing', 208
[44] Ibid., 66
[45] Ibid.
[46] Ibid., 68
[47] Ibid., 75
[48] *OWA*, 75
[49] Bernstein, J. *The Fate of Art* (Polity Press, Oxford; 1997), 123
[50] *OWA*, 76
[51] Ibid., 48-9
[52] Ibid., 47
[53] Ibid.
[54] Ibid., 70
[55] Ibid., 34
[56] Ibid., 42
[57] Ibid., 34
[58] See especially Heidegger's description of the temple-work, 42-3
[59] Heidegger, *Introduction to Metaphysics*, trans. Polt (Yale University Press, New Haven; 2002), 121
[60] Heidegger, 'On the Essence and Concept of Physis', in *Pathmarks* (Cambridge University Press, Cambridge; 1998), 228
[61] Ibid., 195
[62] Heidegger, 'Building, Dwelling Thinking', in *Poetry, Language, Thought*, trans. Hofstadter (Harper and Row, New York; 1975), 149
[63] Heidegger, 'Letter on Humanism', in *Pathmarks* (Cambridge University Press, Cambridge; 1998), 249, 252, 257
[64] Ibid., 250
[65] Haar, M., *The Song of the Earth: Heidegger and the Grounds of the History of Being* (Indiana University Press, Indianapolis; 1993) offers the most incisive analysis of the concept of earth in the literature on Heidegger. Haar rightly points out that earth 'belongs to the factical limits of Dasein' (95) and means 'ontic facticity', an 'incontrovertible material density (96). Unfortunately, Haar does not see the connection between these two determinations of earth: in the experience of the actual, sensuous materiality of the artwork an ontic site is disclosed for explicitly grounding the factical possibilities of existence into which man is thrown. Despite this, Haar correctly writes that 'the Earth presents a striking analogy with the relation that holds in *Being and Time* between project (*Entwurf*)... and thrownness (*Geworfenheit*) or facticity' (100). He adds that the grounding of earth by the preservers of the work is 'in a way' of the 'same order as the retrieval by Dasein of its facticity' (101). Haar is quite right: the now of the authentically disclosed present of the work is analogous to Dasein's moment of vision in which man, in the Situation, comes explicitly face to face with his historical destiny. Unfortunately, these insights are not followed through. Haar concludes that earth is a nonpassive and powerfully enabling facticity whereas *Geworfenheit* can never ground the project (100). Hence, he writes, earth is 'transhistorical possibility' (102). The intractable problem that is generated by Haar's analysis of earth is that the ontic sensuousness of the earth is grounded *both* in its striving relationship with world (the ontological) and by a vague notion of non-historical earth in-itself that produces *modes* of earth from out of itself. The priority and relation between these determinations of earth are left undetermined. However, the interpretative confusion generated by Haar's account can be cleared up if these two determinations are *separated* and *then* the relation between them is shown. To make ontic facticity spontaneous (as clearly Heidegger tries to do - leading thereby to the separate notion of earth in-itself discussed by

Haar) is to *invert* the care-structure of existence. Earth is no longer ontic, *thrown* ground – 'it *throws*' as ontological spontaneity. In the relation between the two determinations of earth, in the becoming-ontological of ontic earth, the movement of *turning* is apparent in the Heideggerian corpus. The ontic-ontological difference is taken up *within* the ontological itself. This of course goes some way to *explaining* the problem generated by Heidegger's duplicated determinations of earth in the artwork essay: but it does not resolve the problem. The resources for such a resolution can only be found in the work that comes *after Origin of the Work of Art*

Chapter 6: The 'Speaking' of Language

[1] Heidegger, 'The Way to Language', in *On the Way to Language* (Harper and Row, New York; 1971), 135

[2] Heidegger, 'Language', in *Poetry, Language, Thought*, trans. Hofstadter (Harper and Row, New York; 1975), 190-1

[3] Ibid., 191-2

[4] Ibid., 190

[5] Wittgenstein, *Zettel*, ed. and trans. Anscombe, 2nd edition (Blackwell, Oxford; 1981), 28

[6] Wittgenstein, *The Blue and Brown Books*, 2nd edition (Blackwell, Oxford; 1993), 178

[7] Merleau-Ponty, 'Eye and Mind', *Merleau-Ponty Aesthetics Reader*, ed. Johnson, trans. Smith (Northwestern University Press; 1993), 129

[8] The current world snooker champion, often called a natural talent or genius, has described his highest need as 'letting the balls talk' rather than taking subjective pleasure in winning.

[9] Heidegger, 'The Nature of Language', in *On the Way to Language* (Harper and Row, New York; 1971), 107

[10] Heidegger, 'The Way to Language', in *On the Way to Language* (Harper and Row, New York; 1971), 122. References to the 'mystery' of language abound, see also, 111

[11] Heidegger, 'Language', in *Poetry, Language, Thought*, 191-2

[12] Heidegger, 'The Way to Language', in *On the Way to Language* (Harper and Row, New York; 1971), 126

[13] Ibid., 113, 130

[14] Schelling, *Philosophy of Art*, ed. Stott (Minnesota University Press, Minneapolis; 1989), 111. Schelling goes on to write that 'rhythm' is 'one of the most wonderful mysteries of nature and art' and that 'the ancients roundly attributed to rhythm the greatest aesthetic power', ibid.

[15] Heidegger, *Heraclitus Seminar*, trans. Seibert (Northwestern University Press, Illinois, 1993), 55

[16] Heidegger, 'Words', in *On the Way to Language*, 149

[17] Benveniste, E., *Problems in General Linguistics*, trans. Meek (University of Miami Press, Coral Gables; 1971), 281-7

[18] Ibid., 287

[19] That fact that rhythm could be used to refer to a human mood also suggests that Benveniste's clear-cut distinction between rhythm as Pre-Platonic spatial form and Platonic temporal interval is not as straightforward as it might first appear.

[20] Plato, *Protagoras* 326b and *Timaeus* 47d, in *Complete Works*, ed. Cooper, J.M. (Hackett, Indianapolis; 1997)

[21] Ibid., *Republic* 400d

[22] Augustine St., *On Music*, Writings of Saint Augustine, ed. Tagliaferro, Fathers of the Church (New York, 1947), 188

[23] Heidegger, 'The Way to Language', *On the Way to Language* (Harper and Row, New York; 1971), 118-9

[24] Humboldt, *On the Diversity of Human Language*, ed. Losonsky, trans. Heath (CUP; 1999), 24

[25] Ibid., 27. Here Humboldt is developing points made much earlier by Herder in his *Treatise on the Origin of Language* (1772). Language, Herder writes, is not added to our animal being as if it were a separate force. Nor is language a divine gift. Language is instead a gift from our own human nature; through the *logos* we become the animals we distinctively are. Herder, *Philosophical Writings*, ed. Forster (Cambridge University Press; 2002), 81, 128.

[26] Ibid., 26

[27] Ibid., 62

[28] Ibid., 146

[29] Ibid, 91, 170

[30] Ibid., 143-4

[31] Ibid., 59

[32] Ibid., 91

[33] Heidegger, 'The Nature of Language', in *On the Way to Language* (Harper and Row, New York; 1971), 98

[34] Humboldt, *On the Diversity of Human Language*, ed. Losonsky, trans. Heath (CUP; 1999), 35

[35] *CJ*, 171

[36] Humboldt, *On the Diversity of Human Language*, ed. Losonsky, trans. Heath (CUP; 1999), 49

[37] Ibid., 175

[38] Ibid., 171

[39] Ibid., 173

[40] Ibid., 173

[41] Ibid., 214

[42] *BT*, 205

[43] Ibid., 211-2

[44] Ibid., 205

[45] Ibid.

Chapter 7: Human Nature and *Sensus Communis*

[1] Humboldt, W.V., *On Language*, trans. Heath (Cambridge University Press, Cambridge; 1999), 153

[2] McDowell, *Mind and World* (Harvard University Press; 1998), 84

[3] Ibid., 14

[4] Ibid., 8

[5] McDowell, *Precis of Mind and World, Philosophy and Phenomenological Research* (vol. LVIII, no. 2, June 1998), 365

[6] McDowell, *Mind and World* (Harvard University Press; 1998), 125

[7] Ibid., 27

[8] Ibid., 28

[9] Ibid., 34

[10] Wittgenstein, *Culture and Value*, trans. Winch (Blackwell, Oxford; 1998): '"The repeat is necessary" In what respect is it necessary? Well, sing it, then you will see that it is only the

repeat that gives it its tremendous power. – Don't we feel then as though a model for this theme must in this case exist in reality, and as though the theme only approached it, corresponded to it, once this part were repeated.... And yet there *is* no paradigm there other than the theme. And yet again there *is* a paradigm other than the theme: namely the rhythm of our language, of our thinking and feeling...', 59

[11] Gadamer, *Truth and Method*, second edition, trans. Weinsheimer and Marshall (Sheed and Ward, London; 1989) 21

[12] McDowell, *Mind and World* (Harvard University Press; 1998), 108

[13] Ibid., 122

[14] Ibid., 119

[15] Heidegger, M., *Fundamental Concepts of Metaphysics*, trans. Walker (Indiana University Press, Indianapolis; 1995), 196

Chapter 8: Inspiration and Genius

[1] *CJ*, 14

[2] Ibid., 12-13

[3] Ibid., 15

[4] Ibid., 37

[5] Ibid

[6] For example, Ibid., 220

[7] Ibid., 75

[8] Ibid., 224

[9] Ibid., 165-170

[10] Ibid., 210-211

[11] Ibid., 228

[12] Ibid.

[13] Ibid., 167: 'But in terms of its kinship this interest is moral, and whoever takes such an interest in the beautiful in nature can do so only to the extent that he has beforehand already solidly established an interest in the morally good. Hence if someone is directly interested in the beauty of nature, we have cause to suppose that he has at least a predisposition to a good moral attitude'

[14] Ibid., 214: 'As for the subjective principle – i.e. the indeterminate idea of the supersensible in us – as the sole key for solving the mystery of this ability concealed from us even as to its sources, we can do no more than point at it; but there is nothing we can do that would allow us to grasp it further'

[15] Ibid., 229

[16] See Allison, *Kant's Theory of Taste* (Cambridge University Press, Cambridge; 2001)

[17] *CJ*, 224

[18] Ibid., 187

[19] Ibid., 174

[20] Ibid., 181

[21] Ibid., 175

[22] Ibid., 184

[23] Ibid., 183

[24] Ibid., 175

[25] Ibid., 177

[26] Ibid., 187

[27] Ibid., 182

[28] Ibid.

[29] Ibid., 183

[30] Ibid., 185

[31] Ibid., 217

[32] Ibid., 63: 'This sensation, whose universal communicability and judgement of postulates is the quickening of the two powers (imagination and understanding) to an activity that is indeterminate but... nonetheless accordant: the activity required for cognition in general'

[33] Heidegger, 'Letter on Humanism', in *Pathmarks* (Cambridge University Press, Cambridge; 1998), 241

[34] Kant, *Prolegomena to Any Future Metaphysics*, trans. Hatfield (Cambridge University Press, Cambridge; 2003), 107

[35] Hegel, *Phenomenology of Spirit*, trans. Miller (Oxford, Clarendon Press), 36

[36] Hegel, *Aesthetics: Lectures on Fine Art*, trans. Knox (Oxford, Clarendon Press; 1998), 281-98

[37] On the Pre-Socratics see Heidegger, *Heraclitus Seminar*, trans. Seibert (Northwestern University Press; 1997), 55. For Plato, see *Republic* 396-404 and *Timaeus* 47c7-e2

[38] Kant, *Prolegomena to Any Future Metaphysics*, 34 (...sie mußte denn auf Eingebung beruhen)

[39] Hegel, *Lectures on the History of Philosophy* vol. 3, trans. Haldane (University of Nebraska Press; 1995), 434

[40] See section entitled 'mechanics', in Hegel, *Philosophy of Nature*, trans. Miller (Oxford, Clarendon Press; 1970)

Chapter 9: Thought and Expression

[1] On the idea of 'active reception' from a theological perspective – to which this interpretation is indebted – see *Truth in Aquinas,* ed. Milbank (Routledge, London; 2001), 57-8 and Milbank, J., *The Word Made Strange* (Blackwell, Oxford; 1997), 50, 195. However, departing from the theological perspective, brilliant as it is, this interpretation of the *Ereignis* argues that a coherent conception of active reception can be located within the aesthetic domain of Heideggerian immanence. In this sense there is not an exclusive choice, pushed by Radical Orthodoxy, between metaphysical nihilism and a theology of love. Philosophy has the resources to overcome 'bad' metaphysics without becoming faith.

[2] Heidegger, 'Conversations on a Country Path about Thinking', in *Discourse on Thinking: a translation of Gelassenheit*, trans. Anderson (Harper and Row, New York; 1966), 61-2

[3] Milbank, J., 'Can a gift be given? Prolegomena to a future Trinitarian metaphysic', in Modern Theology, Jan. 1995 vol 2 issue 1.

[4] Heidegger, M., *What is Called Thinking?*, trans. Gray (Harper and Row, New York; 1968), 142

[5] Ibid., 146

[6] Aristotle, *Nicomachean Ethics*, 1178a1-8

[7] Kant, *Prolegomena to Any Future Metaphysics*, trans. Hatfield (Cambridge University Press, Cambridge; 2003), 5

[8] Blanchot, M. *Le Livre à Venir* (Paris: Editions Gallimards, 1959), 320, cited in Bernstein, J., *The Fate of Art* (Polity Press, Oxford; 1997), 139

[9] Heidegger, 'Postscript to "What is Metaphysics"', in *Pathmarks* (Cambridge University Press, Cambridge; 1998), 237, and Heidegger, *Elucidations of Hölderlin's Poetry*, trans. Hoeller (Humanity Books, New York; 2000), 59

[10] Heidegger, 'Postscript to "What is Metaphysics"', in *Pathmarks* (Cambridge University Press, Cambridge; 1998), 237

[11] Heidegger, '...Poetically Man Dwells...', in Heidegger, M., *Poetry, Language, Thought*, trans. Hofstadter (Harper and Row, New York; 1975), 222

[12] Humboldt, W.V., *On Language*, trans. Heath (Cambridge University Press, Cambridge; 1999), 170

[13] Ibid., 170-1

[14] Hazlitt, 'On the Prose-Style of Poets', Hazlitt, *The Fight and Other Writings* (Penguin; London; 2000), 393

[15] Ibid.

[16] Hazlitt, 'Old English Writers and Speakers', *The Plain Speaker* (Dent, London; 1934), 312

[17] Adorno, 'Essay as Form', in *Notes to Literature*, trans. Nicholson (Columbia University Press, NY; 1992) p. 4

[18] Ibid.

[19] Ibid., 5

[20] Ibid., 12

[21] Ibid.

[22] Ibid., 13

[23] Ibid.

[24] Heidegger, M., *What is Called Thinking?*, trans. Gray (Harper and Row, New York; 1968), 139-141

[25] Heidegger, 'On the Way to Language', *On the Way to Language* (Harper and Row, New York; 1971), 135

[26] Adorno, 'Essay as Form', in *Notes to Literature*, trans. Nicholson (Columbia University Press; NY 1992), 22

[27] Ibid., 13

[28] Ibid., 16

Chapter 10: A History of Truth and Truthfulness

[1] Wittgenstein, L., *Philosophical Investigations*, trans. Anscombe (Blackwell, Oxford; 1998), no. 546

[2] Ibid., no. 545

[3] Ibid., no. 546

[4] Heidegger, M., *Discourse on Thinking: a translation of Gelassenheit*, trans. Anderson (Harper and Row, New York; 1966), 81

[5] An alternative account of truthfulness is given by Han-Pile, 'Nietzsche and the "Masters of Truth": The Pre-Socratics and Christ', in *Heidegger, Authenticity and Modernity*, ed. Wrathall (MIT Press, London; 2000). According to Han-Pile, Nietzsche uncovers an archaic understanding of truth as truthfulness in the Pre-Platonic philosophers in which the words and deeds of a thinker are true because they are rooted naturally in the personal excellence of the character of their author. The argument proceeds that Goethe, for Nietzsche, represents a modern revival of the archaic understanding of truth – deprived of an instinctive unity given by nature, the modern artist must create himself in order to be able to create. The integrity of the self is restored through artistic work on the self: this 'grand style' is the existential condition for any claim to authenticity, 183. There are some issues that such a conception of truthfulness must address, however. The most pressing is whether a conception of style is able to withstand the comprehensive critique Heidegger presents in his

lectures on Nietzsche: '… in the grand style nascent law grows out of original action, which is itself the yoke… . The grand style is the active will to Being, which takes up becoming into itself'. Heidegger, M., *Nietzsche*, trans Krell vol. 1-2 (Harper and Row, San Francisco; 1979-87), 134-5. There is additionally a danger that a Nietzschean-Foucauldian conception of style has been read back into Pre-Socratic thought. For example, in Foucault's reading of Stoicism, truth is transformed into a 'permanent principle of action' whereby 'aletheia becomes ethos', Foucault, 'Technologies of the Self', in *Ethics: subjectivity and truth*, ed. Rabinow, trans, Hurley (New York Press, New York; 1997) 239. So too for Han-Pile 'aletheia depends on ethos', 169; truthfulness is a 'purely active' phenomenon, 171

[6] Aristotle, *Nicomachean Ethics*, Book 4 Section 3

[7] Aquinas, *Summa Theologica*, ed. Pegis (Hackett, Indianapolis; 1997) Q109 Art. 1 p. 1654-1655

[8] Heidegger, 'On the Essence of Truth', trans. Sallis, in *Pathmarks* (Cambridge University Press, Cambridge; 1998), 138-9

[9] Ibid.

[10] Williams, B., *Truth and Truthfulness: an Essay in Genealogy*, (Princeton University Press, New Jersey; 2002). A respect for truth entails doing the best you can to acquire true beliefs (Accuracy) and saying what you believe (Sincerity), 11. Sincerity, Williams writes, is a disposition to make sure that one's assertion expresses what one actually believes (96) and Accuracy entails the virtuous resistance to self-deception in any truth-acquiring method of inquiry. Accuracy is different from Sincerity in that it involves the idea of true information or more simply, 'the truth' (126). Williams proceeds to criticise Detienne's thesis that there is an archaic conception of *aletheia* which is not opposed to lying, *pseudos*, and which therefore does not mean the moral virtue of 'telling the truth', i.e. not deceiving. Rather, Williams argues, *aletheia* refers not to people but to their communications; communications are true because they are correct, informative and reliable (273). Hence, *aletheia* allegedly comes very close to the range of considerations Williams associates with the quality of Accuracy. Truthfulness is therefore the communication of true information that has already been accurately acquired. Williams' conception of truthfulness as such remains within a form of Christian anthropology: without the objective and independent truth of 'what there is' there is nothing for our subjective truth-telling to be in accordance with. Truthfulness is here a moral (liberal) disposition that has a purely formal, methodological import separate from the substantive content of 'what is true'. The relation between 'speaking' the truth and truth in-itself is sundered; the original, Pre-Socratic unity in the conception of *aletheia* is lost. On the revival of this archaic understanding of truth, see the early Christian thinkers, particularly St. Augustine, as well as the use of *aletheia* in the New Testament, especially the Gospel of St. John

[11] Nietzsche, F., *The Will to Power*, trans. Hollingdale (Vintage, New York; 1968), no. 277

[12] Nietzsche, F., *The Will to Power*, trans. Hollingdale (Vintage, New York; 1968), no. 278

[13] Aurelius, M., *Meditations*, trans. Farquharson (Oxford University Press, Oxford; 1998), 90

[14] Ibid., Book III, 7-8

[15] *The Wittgenstein Reader*, edited Kenny (Blackwell, Oxford; 1997), 215

[16] Wittgenstein, L., *Last Writings on the Philosophy of Psychology,* trans. Luckhardt (Blackwell, Oxford; 1999) Vol. 1, 123

[17] Ibid.

[18] Wittgenstein, L., *Philosophical Investigations*, trans. Anscombe (Blackwell, Oxford; 1998), 222

[19] Ibid., 228

[20] Hacker, *Wittgenstein* (Phoenix, London; 1997), 55

[21] Aristotle, *Metaphysics*, A17-B11

[22] Nietzsche, F., *Ecce Homo*, trans. Hollingdale (Penguin, London; 1992), 72-3

[23] Ibid., 98

[24] Heidegger, M., *What is Called Thinking?*, trans. Gray (Harper and Row, New York; 1968), 148-9

[25] Ibid, 149

[26] Eckhart, *Selected Writings* (Penguin, London; 1994), 45

[27] Ibid., 190

[28] For a comparison of Heidegger and Eckhart, see Schurmann, R., 'Heidegger and Meister Eckhart on Releasement', in Dreyfus, H. and Wrathall, M. (eds.), *Heidegger re-examined*, vols. I-IV (Routledge; New York, 2002). Schurmann unfortunately does not follow through the comparison in an ontologically radical fashion by explicitly fusing the Eckhartian 'spark' of the soul with the immanently conceived 'it gives' of Being

[29] Gadamer, *Truth and Method*, second edition, trans. Weinsheimer and Marshall (Sheed and Ward, London; 1989), 29

[30] Augustine, St., *Against the Academicians and The Teacher*, trans. King (Hackett, Indianapolis; 1995), 139

[31] Ibid., 141

[32] Ibid., 96

[33] Augustine St., *Confessions*, trans. Chadwick (Oxford University Press, Oxford; 1998), 227

Chapter 11: Being and the Hidden God

[1] Heidegger, 'Phenomenology and Theology', in *Pathmarks* (Cambridge University Press, Cambridge; 1998), 55

[2] Ibid., 49

[3] Ibid., 53

[4] Ibid.

[5] Heidegger, 'Letter on Humanism', in *Pathmarks* (Cambridge University Press, Cambridge; 1998), 258.

[6] Ibid., 267

[7] ibid.

[8] Marion, *God Without Being*, trans. Carlson (University of Chicago Press, Chicago; 1995), 69-70

[9] Heidegger, 'Phenomenology and Theology', in *Pathmarks* (Cambridge University Press, Cambridge; 1998), 41, 43

[10] Ibid, 51

[11] *CJ*, 253

[12] Ibid., 241

[13] Ibid., 244

[14] Ibid., 260

[15] Ibid., 279, 282, 285, 256

[16] Ibid., 286

[17] Ibid., 381

[18] Ibid.

[19] Eckhart, M. *Selected German Sermons*, trans. Walshe (Watkins, London; 1979) Sermon 1.

[20] Foucault appears to have genuine insight into this Heideggerian conception of the *Ereignis* in the preface to *The Order of Things*: between the primary codes of a culture and the philosophical reflection upon these codes is a middle region, a 'pure experience of order': we perceive in this region the fact that *there is* order. The experience of pure order

for Foucault is also an act of separation and deviation from the empirical orders prescribed for it by its primary codes: in this experience we discover the possibility of different kinds of order. Our codes of language, perception and practice are here criticised and rendered partially invalid. Hence this experience 'liberates order itself'. The similarities between Foucault's analysis and Heidegger's notion of the Event are striking. Han-Pile rightly highlights these similarities, *Foucault's Critical Project: Between the Transcendental and the Historical*, trans. Pile (Stanford University Press, California; 2002), 55. Han-Pile also interestingly states that this proximity to Heidegger may have offered Foucault a third way to resolve the dilemma according to which order should reside either in the gaze of the transcendental beholder or in things, 57. In this case the historical *a priori* in Foucault is analogous to the Heideggerian epoch of Being. Unfortunately, Han-Pile rejects this analogy because she argues, firstly, it is impossible to identify order with Being. The experience of things as orderable pertains only to specific epochs of Being. This argument, however, relies upon too restrictive a notion of order, determining it specifically as the ordering of objects. It neglects the different *kinds* of order present in, for example, aesthetic perception of the beautiful, the form of rhythm, the process that regulates and secures resource in the age of technology and so on. Han-Pile's second reason for dismissing the idea of Heideggerian strands in the preface is that for Foucault there is a pure experience of order and this raises the spectre of a revival of the humanist tradition, a 'sudden coming to consciousness', 59, that it is precisely the intention of the later, anti-humanist Heidegger to avoid. Again, this argument appears too hasty: though the mode of subjectivity involved here certainly requires ontological elucidation, experience is not *per se* humanistic. As this essay has argued, even in the Heideggerian *Ereignis* – and the anti-humanism it entails – there is still a relation to human subjectivity, Being still *needs* the human being

[21] Heidegger, 'The Question Concerning Technology', in *The Question Concerning Technology and Other Essays*, trans. Lovitt (Harper Torchbooks, New York; 1977), 28
[22] Ibid., 27, 32

Bibliography

Adorno, T.W., 'The Essay as Form', in *Notes to Literature*, trans. Nicholsen (Columbia University Press, New York; 1992)

Allison, H., *Kant's Transcendental Idealism* (Yale University Press, New Haven; 1983)

Aquinas, T., *Basic Writings of Saint Thomas Aquinas*, Volume One, ed. Pegis (Hackett Publishing, Indianapolis; 1997)

Aristotle, *The Complete Works*, vol. 1-2 (Princeton University Press, Princeton; 1984)

Augustine, *On Music*, Writings of Saint Augustine, ed. Tagliaferro, Fathers of the Church (New York; 1947)

——, *Confessions*, trans. Chadwick (Oxford University Press, Oxford; 1998)

——, *Against the Academicians and The Teacher*, trans. King (Hackett, Indianapolis; 1995)

Aurelius, M., *Meditations*, trans. Farquharson (Oxford University Press, Oxford; 1998)

Bernstein, J., *The Fate of Art*, (Polity Press, Oxford; 1997)

Bergson, H., *Time and Free Will: an essay on the immediate data of consciousness*, trans. Pogson (Dover Publications, New York; 1913)

Deleuze, G., *Difference and Repetition*, trans. Patton (Athlone Press, London; 1994)

Dreyfus, H., *Being in the World: A Commentary on Heidegger's 'Being and Time', Division 1* (MIT Press, Cambridge, Massachusetts; 1991)

Dreyfus, H., and Wrathall, M. (eds.), *Heidegger re-examined*, vols. I-IV (Routledge, New York; 2002)

Gadamer, H-G., *Philosophical Hermeneutics*, trans. Linge (University of California Press, Berkeley; 1977)

——, *Truth and Method*, second edition, trans. Weinsheimer and Marshall (Sheed and Ward, London; 1989)

Guignon, C., (ed.), *The Cambridge Companion to Heidegger* (Cambridge University Press, Cambridge; 1993)

Hazlitt, W., *The Fight and Other Writings* (Penguin, London; 2000)

Hegel G.W.F., *Aesthetics: Lectures on Fine Art*, vol. 1-2, trans. Knox (Clarendon Press, Oxford; 1975)

——, *Science of Logic*, vol 1., trans. Johnston (Allen and Unwin, London; 1966)

——, *Logic: Part One of the Encyclopaedia of the Philosophical Sciences*, trans. Wallace (Clarendon Press, Oxford; 1975)

——, *Phenomenology of Spirit,* trans. Miller (Oxford University Press, Oxford; 1977)

——, *Lectures on the Philosophy of Religion*, vol. 1-3, trans. Brown (University California Press, Berkeley; 1984-5)

Heidegger, M., *Discourse on Thinking: a translation of Gelassenheit*, trans. Anderson (Harper and Row, New York; 1966)

——, *What is Called Thinking?,*, trans. Gray (Harper and Row, New York; 1968)

——, *Identity and Difference*, trans. Stambaugh (Harper and Row, New York; 1969)

——, *On the Way to Language,* (Harper and Row, New York; 1971)

——, *On Time and Being,* trans. Stambaugh (Harper and Row, New York; 1972)

——, *'Art and Space'*, trans. Seibert in *Man and World* (Feb. 1973 vol 6 1.)

——, *'Letter to Richardson'*, in Richardson, *Heidegger: through phenomenology to thought,* (Nijhoff, The Hague; 1974)

——, *Early Greek Thinking*, trans Krell (Harper and Row, New York; 1975)

——, *The End of Philosophy,* trans. Stambaugh (Souvenir Press, London; 1975)

——, *Poetry, Language, Thought,* trans. Hofstadter (Harper and Row, New York; 1975)

——, *The Question Concerning Technology and Other Essays,* trans. Lovitt (Harper Torchbooks, New York; 1977)

——, *Nietzsche,* trans. Krell vol. 1-4 (Harper and Row, San Francisco; 1979-87)

——, *Hegel's Concept of Experience* (Octagon Books, New York; 1983)

——, *Metaphysical Foundations of Logic,* trans. Heim (Indiana University Press, Indianapolis; 1984)

——, *Schelling's Treatise on the Essence of Human Freedom,* trans. Stambaugh (Ohio University Press, Ohio; 1985)

——, *The Basic Problems of Phenomenology,* trans. Hofstadter (Indiana University Press, Indiana; 1988)

——, *Hegel's Phenomenology of Spirit,* trans. Emad (Indiana University Press, Indianapolis; 1988)

——, *The Principle of Reason,* trans. Lilly (Indiana University Press, Indianapolis; 1991)

——, *Basic Questions of Philosophy,* trans. Rojcewicz (Indiana University Press, Indianapolis; 1992)

——, *History of the Concept of Time,* trans. Kisiel (Indiana University Press, Indianapolis; 1992)

——, *Heraclitus Seminar,* trans. Seibert (Northwestern University Press, Illinois; 1993)

——, *Being and Time,* trans. Macquarrie and Robinson (Blackwell, Oxford; 1995)

——, *Fundamental Concepts of Metaphysics,* trans. Walker (Indiana University Press, Indianapolis; 1995)

——, *Phenomenological Interpretation of Kant's Critique of Pure Reason,* trans. Emad and Maly (Indiana University Press, Indianapolis; 1997)

——, *Kant and the Problem of Metaphysics,* trans. Taft (Indiana University Press, Indianapolis; 1997)

——, *Pathmarks* (Cambridge University Press, Cambridge; 1998)

——, *Parmenides,* trans. Schuwer (Indiana University Press, Indianapolis; 1998)

——, *Contributions to Philosophy (From Enowning),* trans. Emad and Maly (Indiana University Press, Indianapolis; 1999)

——, *Elucidations of Holderlin's Poetry,* trans. Hoeller (Humanity Books, New York; 2000)

——, *Introduction to Metaphysics,* trans. Fried and Polt (Yale University Press, New Haven; 2000)

Humboldt, W.V., *On Language,* trans. Heath (Cambridge University Press, Cambridge; 1999)

Inwood, M., *Heidegger* (Oxford University Press, Oxford; 1997)

Kant, I. *Critique of Pure Reason,* trans. Kemp Smith (Macmillan, London; 1929)

——, *Critique of Judgement,* trans. Pluhar (Hackett, Indianapolis; 1987)

McDowell, J., *Mind and World* (Harvard University Press, Cambridge; 1998)

Malpas, J., (ed.), *Heidegger, Authenticity and Modernity* (MIT Press, Massachusetts; 2000)

Marion, J-L., *God Without Being,* trans. Carlson (University of Chicago Press, Chicago; 1995)

Meister Eckhart, *Selected Writings,* trans. Davies (Penguin, London; 1994)

——, *Selected German Sermons,* trans. Walshe (Watkins, London; 1979-81)

Milbank, J., 'Can a gift be given? Prolegomena to a future Trinitarian metaphysic', in *Modern Theology,* Jan. 1995 vol. 2 issue 1

——, *The Word Made Strange* (Blackwell, Oxford; 1997)

——, 'Sublimity: the modern transcendent', in ed. Blond *Post-secular philosophy: Between philosophy and theology* (Routledge, London; 1998)

——, 'The theological critique of philosophy' in *Radical Orthodoxy: a new theology* ed. Milbank (Routledge, London; 1998)

——, 'Truth and vision' in *Truth in Aquinas*, ed. Milbank (Routledge, London; 2001)

Mulhall, S., 'Re-monstrations: Heidegger, Derrida and Wittgenstein's Hand' in *Journal of the British Society for Phenomenology*, vol. 26 no. 1. Jan. 1995

——, *Heidegger and Being and Time* (Routledge, London; 1996)

Nietzsche, F., *The Will to Power*, trans. Hollingdale (Vintage, New York; 1968)

——, *The Gay Science*, trans. Kaufmann (Vintage books, New York; 1974)

——, *Ecce Homo*, trans. Hollingdale (Penguin, London; 1992)

Pattison, G., *The Later Heidegger* (Routledge, London; 2000)

Plato, *Complete Works*, ed. Cooper, J.M. (Hackett; Indianapolis, 1997)

Poggeler, O., *Martin Heidegger's Path of Thinking*, trans. Magurshak (Humanities Press, New Jersey; 1987)

Schelling, F.W.J., *Philosophy of Art*, ed. Stott (Minnesota University Press, Minneapolis; 1989)

The Wittgenstein Reader, ed. Kenny (Blackwell, Oxford; 1997)

Wittgenstein: A Critical Reader, ed. Glock (Blackwell, Oxford; 2001)

Wittgenstein, L., *Tractatus Logico-Philosophicus*, trans. Pears (Routledge, London; 1961)

——, *Blue and Brown Books* (Blackwell, Oxford; 1993)

——, *Culture and Value*, trans. Winch (Blackwell, Oxford; 1998)

——, *Philosophical Investigations*, trans. Anscombe (Blackwell, Oxford; 1998)

——, *Last Writings on the Philosophy of Psychology: the inner and the outer*, vol. 2, trans. Luckhardt (Blackwell, Oxford; 1999)

——, *On Certainty*, trans. Anscombe (Blackwell, Oxford; 1999)

Index